CONTEXTUAL BACH STUDIES

A series of monographs exploring the contexts of
Johann Sebastian Bach's life and music,
with a particular emphasis on theology and liturgy
Series Editor: Robin A. Leaver

Music has its own distinctive characteristics—melody, harmony, rhythm, form, and so forth—that have to be fully appreciated if it is to be effectively understood. But a detailed comprehension of all these musical elements cannot reveal the significance of all the compositional choices made by a composer. "What?" and "how?" questions need to be supplemented by appropriate "why?" and "when?" questions. Study of the original score and parts, as well as the different manifestations of a particular work, have to be undertaken. But if such study is regarded as an end rather than a beginning then the music itself will not necessarily be fully understood. One must go further. There are various contexts that impinge upon a composer's choices. Music is conditioned by time, place, and culture and therefore is influenced by particular historical, geographical, and social contexts; music written in fulfillment of a contractual agreement has an economic context; and so forth.

The music of Johann Sebastian Bach has been the object of intensive study and analysis, but in the past many of these studies have been somewhat narrow in focus. For example, the received view of Bach's music was to some degree incomplete because it was largely discussed on its own terms without being fully set within the contextual perspective of the music of his predecessors, contemporaries, and successors. It is only in fairly recent times that the music of these other composers has become accessible, allowing us to appreciate the nature and stature of their accomplishments, and at the same time giving us new perspectives from which to view a more rounded picture of Bach's genius.

The monographs in this series explore such contextual areas. Since much of Bach's music was composed for Lutheran worship, a primary concern of these monographs is the liturgical and theological contexts of this music. But Bach's music was not exclusively confined to these specific religious concerns. German culture of the time had more general religious dimensions that permeated "secular" society. Therefore, in addition to specific studies of the liturgical and theological contexts of Bach's music, this series also includes explorations of social, political, and cultural religious contexts in which his music was composed and first heard.

1. Cameron, Jasmin Melissa. *The Crucifixion in Music: An Analytical Survey of Settings of the* Crucifixus *between 1680 and 1800.* 2006.

The Crucifixion in Music

An Analytical Survey of Settings of the **Crucifixus** between 1680 and 1800

Jasmin Melissa Cameron

Contextual Bach Studies, No. 1

The Scarecrow Press, Inc.
Lanham, Maryland • Toronto • Oxford
2006

SCARECROW PRESS, INC.

Published in the United States of America
by Scarecrow Press, Inc.
A wholly owned subsidiary of
The Rowman & Littlefield Publishing Group, Inc.
4501 Forbes Boulevard, Suite 200, Lanham, Maryland 20706
www.scarecrowpress.com

PO Box 317
Oxford
OX2 9RU, UK

British Library Cataloguing in Publication Information Available

Library of Congress Cataloging-in-Publication Data

Cameron, Jasmin Melissa.
   The crucifixion in music : an analytical survey of settings of the crucifixus
between 1680 and 1800 / Jasmin Melissa Cameron.
      p.   cm.— (Contextual Bach studies ; no. 1)
   Includes bibliographical references and index.

   ISBN: 978-0-8108-5872-5

   1. Passion music—17th century—History and criticism.   2. Passion
music—18th century—History and criticism.   I. Title.   II. Series.

ML3260.C36   2006
782.32'32—dc22

                                                                    2005037859

For
Professor Michael Talbot
And also ILC

Contents

Figures and Tables

FIGURES

ix

TABLES

Reader's Note

Numbers following the names of composers and/or works refer to the index of *Crucifixus* settings and sources (appendix A).

Except where permission to reproduce a score is specifically acknowledged, the examples and *Crucifixus* settings are taken from my own editions. Primary and secondary sources are listed in appendix A or the bibliography.

The following should be noted in connection with the examples cited. Some minor changes have been made tacitly in the reproduction of musical examples and diagrams from published materials.

Bar numbers are usually counted from the beginning of the *Crucifixus*. The exceptions to this occur in appendixes I and J.

Editor's Foreword

The history of passion music is well documented, analyzed, categorized, and discussed. The monophonic quasi-plainsong German settings of Johann Walter and Schütz are differentiated from the earlier plainsong passions of the medieval Latin liturgy. The responsorial polyphonic settings of composers such as Vittoria and Lassus are distinguished from the through-composed settings of Byrd and Handl. Later concerted settings by Catholic composers such as Alessandro Scarlatti, Caldara, and Zelenka are contrasted with those by such Lutherans as Selle, Sebastiani, and Theile. Similarly, the larger-scale oratorio passions, from compositions by Telemann, Handel, and Mattheson to those of Randall Thompson, Penderecki, and Pärt, have been subjected to close scrutiny, with the two great passions of Johann Sebastian Bach occupying a central position, often being presented as the combined touchstone by which earlier and later settings of the passion are to be evaluated.

What these passions have in common is their subject matter. They are settings either of the text (or a paraphrase) of one of the four gospel narratives of the passion of Christ—Matthew, Mark, Luke, or John—or of a composite libretto drawn from all four accounts. But these are not the only ecclesiastical texts that deal with the passion of Christ. In the Nicene Creed, a confessional as well as a liturgical document, there is the fundamental statement concerning the passion: *Crucifixus etiam pro nobis sub Pontio Pilato, passus et sepultus est*—"Crucified for us under Pontius Pilate, he suffered and was buried." Thus, every composition of the complete Ordinary of the Mass must, of necessity, include "passion" (*passus*) music. But this credal passion music has not been the focus of attention and has received only incidental reference within the broader contexts of general and particular discussions of Mass settings. Of course, settings of the passion narratives are longer and independent works, whereas *Cruci-fixus* settings are usually briefer and dependent sections within compositions of the Creed as a whole, which are themselves but one part of settings of the Ordinary of the Mass. But the *Crucifixus* is a pivotal text for both Christian theology and liturgy, and therefore its various musical settings demand more than passing comment. It is this musicological lacuna, this other "passion music," that Dr. Jasmin Cameron explores in this timely, perceptive, and extremely effective study. Dr. Cameron's conclusions are particularly pertinent since they are based on investigations of a significant large number of *Crucifixus* settings composed within the time frame 1680–1800.

In the same way that Bach's passions are immediately called to mind when passion music is addressed, so reference to *Crucifixus* recalls Bach's superlative setting in the *B minor Mass*—and Dr. Cameron understandably makes references to Bach's *Crucifixus* throughout her book. However, Bach was neither the first nor the last to set this text. Therefore, this study focuses on the settings of this crucial text by composers before and after Bach, giving them the attention they deserve, analyzing them in detail and in reference to one another, and establishing their distinctive features and qualities. But at the same time, these discussions reveal how much Bach was—consciously or unconsciously—influenced by his predecessors, what is distinctive about his own setting, and how later composers approached the same text within different theological, liturgical, and musical environments. The by-product of this research therefore is the clearly delineated historical context for Bach's particular setting of the *Crucifixus* and as such is the most appropriate first volume in the Contextual Bach Studies series.

Robin A. Leaver
Series Editor

Preface

This book sets out to be a contribution to the study of the musical representation of words and also of the concepts and contexts to which words refer. Its chief aim is to examine the way in which the treatment of a literary text (namely, the *Crucifixus* from the *Credo*) coalesces into a recognizable tradition that individual composers follow, develop, modify, or ignore. An examination of what theorists of the time and also present-day theorists have written about the representation of text and musical rhetoric is included in this study. This is developed further to combine and reconcile the thoughts of past theorists (for example, Burmeister, Mattheson) with those of modern theorists (for example, Agawu, Tarasti, Rosen) in an attempt to discover common ground. A secondary aim is to provide a grounding and methodology for further studies in this field, and a variety of analytical techniques (both "transcendent" and "immanent," to use Kantian terminology) are critiqued, and their suitability for music of this genre and period is assessed. A series of case studies of noteworthy *Crucifixus* settings is presented together with a wider survey of settings of the same text. Patterns of influence are examined and possible methods of transmission discussed.

A combination of interests has prompted this research. First, an interest in the *Crucifixus*, as a section of the Mass in its own right: its codes, conventions, and symbolism as a religious text. Second, a fascination with various musical analytical techniques—and how to apply these to music from a period and of a genre where there are no ready-made systems of analysis available (and where there is a distinct lack of interest on the part of present-day analysts).[1] Third, a love of vocal music of this period, coupled with a curiosity to see for myself what exists in various research libraries. The research that has supported this study has been quite diverse: while much pertinent material exists, no single study (in either primary or secondary literature) has proved relevant in its totality. In other words, I have yet to discover any earlier work that shares quite the diversity in choice of analytical theory and method or that has opted to follow the setting of one text in quite so much detail through a period of musical history. In modern musical literature it is possible to find books, articles, and theses that devote themselves to music and rhetoric *or* musical semiotics or texted music (although this last category really has very little to offer) and so on, but none that offers a fusion of these different areas. The most valuable source of material and stimulation has been Irving Godt's "Music about Words," which is, at present, unpublished. Other works that have been important for me include Eero Tarasti's *A Theory of Musical Semiotics*, Kofi Agawu's *Playing with Signs*, and Mark Evan Bonds's *Wordless Rhetoric*. Dietrich Bartel's *Musica Poetica* has been, without doubt, the best-organized and best-researched reference work one could wish for when wading through the minefield that is musical-rhetorical terminology. The ever-widening interest in early musicology has made it relatively easy to gain access to the writings of such theorists as Burmeister and Mattheson. Their works have played a vital role in my research, too.

In a study of this type, so diverse in its scope, it is important to set the limits and respect practical constraints. Regarding limits, it was necessary at the outset to decide how many *Crucifixus* settings should be collected to form the basis for this research: the sample needed to be sufficiently large so that generalizations could be made and solid conclusions formed. As a consequence, the study encompassed a sample of just over a hundred settings of the *Crucifixus* drawn from the period 1680–1800 and embraced settings by (among others) Bach, Lotti, Caldara, Vivaldi, Mozart, and Haydn, concentrating on the Italian and German traditions. The French tradition was ignored on the grounds that it was stylistically rather separate from that of the Germans and Italians. The links between the latter two traditions were historically stronger, so it made sense to be realistic about the scope of the study and limit the survey in that way. The choice of time frame may at first seem strange since it encompasses two "distinct" musical periods. However, it is commonly recognized that

> Baroque and Classical Music were based upon the same criteria, a common set of premises, despite their obvious differences; they used one language, and their differences represented sublanguages of a universal eighteenth-century musical speech.[2]

The sample of *Crucifixus* settings that I collected was as broad as I could manage, but here practical factors (such as availability) were material in determining the assortment that resulted. Within the sample, there are settings that are "canonic" (in the sense of belonging to the standard repertory), such as Bach's setting from the *B Minor Mass* or Lotti's *Crucifixus a 10*, but also ones that are not available in any published or recorded form. The distribution of number and type of settings over this period varied greatly because of the intervention of these pragmatic factors, which included accessibility, cost, time, and the location of materials. This means that the sample cannot be used in a vigorously statistical manner. Likewise, the selection of analytical techniques had to be limited. It was equally important to choose modern methods of analysis that were familiar to me as a critic in addition to ones that were contemporary with the music of the period. Semiotic theory is closely akin to rhetoric and was therefore an obvious candidate for selection. Other techniques were deemed inappropriate for the study undertaken: the examination of a set of *topoi* that are word driven. For instance, Schenkerian analysis was not considered since it was marginal to the main interests of this study: it is not concerned with textual influence. As a result, it is referred to only tangentially and otherwise not utilized for this study.

Is this analysis viewed through a historical lens or history viewed through an analytical lens? In fact, it is both at the same time. The history of musical style cannot be unraveled except by analytical observation, and analysis is sterile unless applied to a historical context. By taking a tiny (though pregnant) fragment of liturgical text as the constant element, the workings of historical change and compositional choice become more transparent. Originality and tradition emerge as natural partners to one another since each, by its opposition, sets the other into relief and brings out its character.

NOTES

1. All analytical tools published in modern times are premised on instrumental theory and thus created to assist in the understanding of instrumental music.

2. Leonard G. Ratner, *Classic Music: Expression, Form and Style* (New York: Schirmer, 1980), xv–xvi.

Acknowledgments

First and foremost, I would like to express my gratitude to Professor Michael Talbot for his invaluable support, advice, and guidance throughout this research.

I must also thank the following:

Dr. Robin Leaver, for all his advice

Bruce Phillips, for patiently answering all my many questions during the conversion of the thesis into a book

Professor Irving Godt, for allowing me access to his unpublished work, and for all his advice and comments

Dr. Yo Tomita, for reading the chapter on Bach's *Crucifixus* setting and offering many useful comments and suggestions

Dr. Janice Stockigt and Dr. Brian Pritchard, for supplying me with reproductions of *Crucifixus* settings and relevant details concerning them

Dr. Dave Allen, for casting a critical eye over the manuscript in its final stages

The University of Liverpool

The Arts and Humanities Research Board, for funding the initial stages of this research

My thanks go also to the following:

Paul Drysdale, for the loan of a computer when hardware problems threatened to overwhelm me (and the thesis/book) and also for all his encouragement

Chris Ashley, for saving my editions of music from the jaws of "software death"

Ushir Patel, who helped with the typing of the original bibliography

Iain Greig, for moral support during the conversion process from thesis to book

My late grandmother in Germany, who helped me locate materials in the Bischöfliche Bibliothek in Münster

My mother, for helping me to sort out the necessary permissions during the process of turning the thesis into a book

My family for their continued support throughout this research and particularly that offered by my mother and my father

I would also like to thank the many publishing houses that have granted permission for the reproduction of various materials included in the original thesis. Individual acknowledgments are included in the passage of the text.

Finally, thank you to the many research libraries I accessed. I would particularly like to extend my gratitude to the many members of staff at these institutions whose help has been invaluable to me.

Part I

THE LITURGY AND ITS MUSICAL IMPLICATIONS

1

The *Crucifixus*: An Overview

Crucifixus etiam pro nobis sub Pontio Pilato, passus et sepultus est.

The *Crucifixus* is a short section of text contained within the *Credo* of the Roman Catholic Mass. It is commonly regarded as a climactic point within the *Credo*, showing a degree of musical intensity that often borders on the extreme. Christoph Wolff describes the *Crucifixus* as the "christological core of the liturgical *Credo*."[1] Many other commentators have also recognized the significance of this section of text.[2]

The expressive potential of the *Crucifixus* was recognized equally by eighteenth-century writers. This account by C. C. Rolle dates from 1794:

> The *Credo in unum Deum* . . . is intoned by the same cleric in front of high altar. As in the *Gloria*, the words of the collect are omitted from the composition. So the music usually follows on with the next words of the Creed, *Patrem omnipotentem coeli at terrae*. . . . It goes without saying that the *Crucifixus* . . . has to be properly elaborated with semitones [chromatic steps]. Since everything here is historical in content, the composer will try to help himself out with word-painting of a similar kind.[3]

This short clause offers a complete contrast to the rest of the *Credo*: it contains far greater potential for musical word painting and direct expression of the text. There is a strong contrast between the mood of this section and that of those that frame it: respectively, the mystery of *Et incarnatus* and the triumph of *Et resurrexit*. It is in essence a statement of negativity, expressing sadness, bitterness, and tragedy with an emphasis on the physical and mental suffering that Christ underwent on the cross. The significance of the Crucifixion is reflected in the paramount symbol of Christianity: the cross. This symbol is a constant reminder that Christ died to save mankind: God's sacrifice of His own Son. Perhaps another of the reasons that the *Crucifixus* is accorded such "exceptional" treatment within the context of the *Credo* is because the Mass itself surrounds a reenactment of the Last Supper (the Eucharist), which, of course, occurred not long before the Crucifixion. The main source for accounts of the Crucifixion is, naturally, the Bible. Table 1.1 is compiled from the four Gospels, detailing the parallels between the *Crucifixus* text of the Nicene Creed and those statements that, we may assume, were taken as its source.[4]

THE *CRUCIFIXUS* IN CONTEXT

The *Credo* is completely separate from the *Kyrie* and the *Gloria* and is placed in the ritual of the Mass at the end of the Liturgy of the Word. It stands isolated between the Gospel and Homily on one side and the Offertory on the other. The text is the longest by far of the six texts of the Ordinary, being a doctrinal text whose prime function is to affirm belief. The length of text has often prompted composers to condense the setting by telescoping the delivery of the text with resulting polytextuality (not always popular with the Church since this technique had the effect of masking the words). The length of the text also means that composers have not always been able to make the most of the word-painting opportunities available to them, although by the nature of its text there are fewer opportunities for word painting in the *Credo* than there are, for example, in the *Gloria*.[5] It was conceived principally as a narrative setting: for this reason, it has not invariably—or even usually—been set to music. When it is set to music, there is a tendency to subdivide the text into three sections. In musical settings of the period examined (1680–1800), the divisions usually fall as follows:

1. *Credo in unum Deum . . . et propter nostram salutem descendit de coelis.*
2. *Et incarnatus est . . . Crucifixus . . . et sepultus est.*
3. *Et resurrexit . . . Amen.*

Musically, these three divisions of the text can be articulated in a number of ways, notably, by change of meter, key, tempo, texture, or scoring (or any combination of these): a kind of tripartite structure. For most composers, the *Et incarnatus* becomes the central point in the *Credo*, depicting the mystery and miracle of Christ's conception and birth. This special character is usually brought out musically by one or more of the changes already mentioned. Frequently, the movement/section is tonally "open,"

Table 1.1. Identification of the Sources for the Text of the *Crucifixus* in the Nicene Creed

Nicene Creed	Gospel of St. Matthew	Gospel of St. Mark	Gospel of St. Luke	Gospel of St. John
Crucifixus	27:35 And they crucified him, and parted his garments, casting lots: that it might be fulfilled which was spoken by the Prophet, They parted my garments among them, and upon my vesture did they cast lots.	15:25 And it was the third hour, and they crucified him.	23:33 And when they were come to the place which is called Calvary, there they crucified him, and the malefactors, one on the right hand and the other on the left.	19:17 And he bearing his cross went forth to a place called the place of a skull, which is called in the Hebrew Golgotha. 18:28 Where they crucified him, and the two other with him, on either side one, and Jesus in the midst.
etiam pro nobis	26:28 For this is my blood of the new testament, which is shed for many of the remission of sins.	10:45 For even the Son of man came not to be ministered unto, but to minister, and to give his life a ransom for many. 14:24 And he said unto them, This is my blood of the new testament, which is shed for many.		6:51 I am the living bread which came down from heaven: if any man eat of this bread, he shall live forever: and the bread that I will give is my flesh, which I will give for the life of the world. 11:51 And this spake he not of himself [Caiaphas] but being high priest that year, he prophesied that Jesus should die for that nation.
sub Pontio Pilato,	27:27 Then released he Barabbas unto them: and when he had scourged Jesus, he delivered him to be crucified.	15:16 And so Pilate, willing to content the people, released Barabbas unto them, and delivered Jesus, when he had scourged him, to be crucified.	23:1 And the whole multitude of them arose, and led him to Pilate.	19:16 They delivered he [Pilate] him [Jesus] therefore unto him to be crucified. And they took Jesus and led him away.

Table 1.1. (Continued)

Nicene Creed	Gospel of St. Matthew	Gospel of St. Mark	Gospel of St. Luke	Gospel of St. John
passus	27:37 And set up over his head his accusation written, THIS IS JESUS THE KING OF THE JEWS. 27:45 Now from the sixth hour there was darkness over all the land unto the ninth hour. 27:46 And about the ninth hour Jesus cried with a loud voice saying, Eli, Eli, lama sabachthani? that is to say, My God, my God why hast thou forsaken me? 27:48 And straightaway one of them ran, and took a sponge, and filled it with vinegar, and put it on a reed and gave him to drink.	15:26 And the superscription of his accusation was written over, THE KING OF THE JEWS. 15:33 And when the sixth hour was come, there was a darkness over the whole land until the ninth hour. 15:34 And at the ninth hour Jesus cried with a loud voice saying Eloi, Eloi, lama sabachthani? which is, being interpreted, My God, my God, why hast thou forsaken me? 15:36 And one ran and filled a sponge full of vinegar, and put it on a reed, and gave him to drink saying, Let alone; let us see whether Elias will come to take him down.	23:35 And the people stood beholding. And the rulers also with them derided him, saying, He saved others; let him save himself, if he be Christ, the chosen of God. 23:36 And the soldiers also mocked him, coming to him and offering him vinegar. 23:37 And saying, if thou be the king of the Jews, save thyself. 23:44 And it was about the sixth hour, and there was a darkness over all the earth until the ninth hour.	19:19 And Pilate wrote a title, and put it on the cross. And the writing was, JESUS OF NAZARETH THE KING OF THE JEWS. 19:29 Now there was set a vessel of vinegar: and they filled a spunge with vinegar, and put it on hyssop and put it to his mouth.
et sepultus est.	27:59 And when Joseph [of Arimathaea] had taken the body, he wrapped it in a clean linen cloth and laid it in his own new tomb, which he had hewn out in the rock: and he rolled a great stone to the door of the sepulchre, and departed.	15:46 And he [Joseph of Arimathaea] brought fine linen, and took him down, and wrapped him in the linen, and laid him in a sepulchre which was hewn out of a rock and rolled a stone unto the door of the sepulchre.	23:53 And he [Joseph of Arimathaea] took it down, and wrapped it in linen and laid it in a sepulchre that was hewn in stone, wherein no man before was laid.	19:41 Now in the place where he was crucified there was a garden; and in the garden a new sepulchre, wherein was never man yet laid. 19:42 There laid they Jesus therefore because of the Jews' preparation day; for the sepulchre was nigh at hand.

and its tonality is in any case often unstable or ambiguous.[6] Block chords and frequent pauses are also highly characteristic of the *Et incarnatus*. The *Crucifixus*, which follows it, is quite often set as a completely separate section.

THE TEXT

"Crucifixus"

The *Credo* acquires the word "Crucifixus" from all four Gospels, all of which mention the Crucifixion. However, the version that appears in the *Credo* is a condensation of the verbal phrase from

They	crucified	him
subject	verb	object

to

He	was crucified
subject	verb

"etiam pro nobis"

This phrase is a neutral statement and one that not all New Testament writers include in their version of events (see table 1.1; the Gospel according to St. Luke does not express this). A possible reason for this may have been that there was no real need for a formulated declaration of belief to be established until later in the development of the early Church.[7] Indeed, the Nicene Creed was only fully established in the face of factional disputes within the early Church and was the latest of the six texts to be included as "standard" in the Mass. Thus, if an earlier creed (Apostles') is compared with the Nicene Creed, it can be seen that the former does not contain the statement "etiam pro nobis." This was clearly a statement that came to be included as the Nicene Creed evolved.[8]

"sub Pontio Pilato"

Again, this is a narrative section of text: informative but brief. It is merely factual. Pilate features in the account of the Crucifixion but is not central to the doctrine of belief. Why, then, was this short phrase included?

The character of Pilate is a shadowy one. "Under" is possibly interpreted as "under the governorship of Pontius Pilate"—or could it be "under the instructions of Pontius Pilate"? The word is perhaps subject to varying interpretation. From the accounts in the Gospels,

> [Pilate] seems so remarkably anxious to conciliate the Jews, and yet so unac-
> countably reluctant to concede to their wishes. He gives the impression of a
> man being tugged between two opposite and irreconcilable forces.
>
> Personally, I cannot escape the feeling that Pilate did not want to touch
> this. He had one idea paramount in his mind—*to get Christ acquitted*, some-
> how, and at all costs. We see this motif running through everything—the
> attempt to shift the matter to Herod, the thrice acclaimed innocence of the
> Prisoner, the washing of hands—the last desperate attempt to substitute Bar-
> abbas, as a sop to the insistence and clamour of the people. It was only when
> the sinister cry, "Thou art not Caesar's friend," began to make itself heard
> above the tumult that a new and greater fear triumphed over the one that
> had been gnawing at his mind.[9]

Despite his apparent reluctance to be involved with the conviction of Christ, Pilate is ultimately held responsible for His death. The decision he made on that fateful day has immortalized him not only in the testaments of the Bible but also in the *Credo* of the Mass on account of his special association with the Crucifixion and indeed with the symbol of Christianity itself: the cross.[10]

To return to the original question: why include this phrase in the *Credo*—why does it hold so much significance? A very likely explanation would be the following, proposed by Jungmann in connection with the Apostles' Creed (which also includes the same phrase): that the reference to "sub Pontio Pilato" (a reference to the "ruler" of the time) was in fact a standard method of dating events—thus it has been used to locate the Crucifixion in time. The second underlying aim of this statement is to emphasize that this was an "actual" event rather than some mystical story, and so it also serves the purpose of legitimizing the Crucifixion.[11]

"passus"

In table 1.1, I have tried to identify the various writings from the four Gospels that contribute collectively to the concept of "suffering." The cause of suffering can manifest itself in many forms: it need not necessarily be merely physical. Therefore, the taunts from the soldiers and people alike and also the title "King of the Jews" all formed part of the suffering that Christ had to endure, not just the events of physical agony like the Crucifixion itself or the sponge soaked in vinegar. Further, suffering is something that is by definition experienced over time (otherwise, we call it simply pain). We can deduce from the Bible that the duration of the Crucifixion was about six hours, so I have included the relevant references in table 1.1. This duration is mentioned by three of the four Gospels (Matthew, Mark, and Luke).

"et sepultus est"

The burial of Christ is significant because it is the event marking the end of his life on this Earth. The inclusion of this phrase in the *Credo* is important since one of the fundamental beliefs of the Christian faith revolves around the Resurrection: life after death. Including "et sepultus est" in the *Credo* emphasizes that Christ was indeed "dead and buried" (otherwise, *Et resurrexit* would have no force).

CONCLUSION

The *Crucifixus* is actually a largely factual statement amid the professions of belief in the *Credo*. To recite the *Credo*, a Christian has to believe in the statements he or she makes (*I believe in one God, the Father Almighty, maker of heaven and earth, of all things visible and invisible. And in one Lord Jesus Christ, the only-begotten Son of God, born of the Father before all ages. God of God, light of light, true God of true God. Begotten, not made, consubstantial with the Father, by whom all things were made*, etc.). The *Et Incarnatus* demands that same kind of belief (*And was incarnate by the Holy Ghost of the Virgin Mary; and was made man*), as does the *Et resurrexit* (*And on the third day he rose again, according to the Scriptures*). The *Crucifixus* stands out between these two sections as an account of an event, a statement of fact. It does not require the same kind of belief that the framing statements do. This exceptional objective quality may be another reason why the *Crucifixus* has so often been afforded special treatment in musical settings of the *Credo* to the extent whereby it has been accorded almost "individualistic" treatment in comparison to the remainder of the text.[12] A further reason for this is that the words of the *Crucifixus* seem to have provided composers with a number of key phrases that offer great potential for musical depiction.

The clearest opportunities for word painting are summarized in table 1.2:[13] a more detailed but still general discussion of these representations will form the basis of chapter 4. While the more obvious of these devices are used spontaneously by composers and are therefore almost "automatic" in their transmission, the less obvious need to be learned in order to be transmitted. The identity and transmission of these more unusual devices are crucial to this study since they form the backbone of its basic claim: that there was a shared *Crucifixus* tradition absorbed and transmitted by a long line of composers. If we were to examine only the more

Table 1.2. The Potential for Word Painting in the Text of the *Crucifixus*

Latin	English	Possible Musical Representation
Crucifixus	He was crucified	"Tortured" ("excruciating") intervals to express the agony of crucifixion (augmented seconds, diminished fourths, etc.), often creating a jagged vocal line. Notes arranged in the shape of a sign of the cross (i.e., in a zigzag sequence of pitches such as a'-g♯'-c"-b'). Use of sharps (in original notation taking the form of a cross); the German word for sharp is *Kreuz*, which also means "cross."
etiam pro nobis	also for us	Narrative setting, speechlike treatment.
sub Pontio Pilato,	under Pontius Pilate,	Narrative setting, speechlike treatment.
passus	suffered	Longer note values (relative to what has gone before), drawn-out vocal lines expressing suffering (since suffering is endured over time). "Tortured" intervals again, to express suffering. Melismatic lines.
et sepultus est.	and was buried.	"Directionality" of musical lines, in this case descending, to depict the lowering of the body into the grave.

obvious devices, it would be possible to argue that these were so spontaneous, even automatic, that they could have arisen even in the absence of such a coherent tradition.

NOTES

1. Christoph Wolff, "'Et incarnatus' and 'Crucifixus': The Earliest and Latest Settings of Bach's B-Minor Mass," in *Eighteenth-Century Music in Theory and Practice: Essays in Honor of Alfred Mann,* ed. Mary Anne Parker (New York: Pendragon Press, 1994), 3.

2. Bruce C. MacIntyre observes, "As it has been for centuries, the 'Et Incarnatus' is the true heart of the Credo—its twenty four words [these twenty-four words referred to here include the Crucifixus] describe the mystery, life, death and suffering of Christ." *The Viennese Concerted Mass of the Early Classic Period* (Ann Arbor, Mich.: UMI Research Press, 1986), 383.

3. C. C. Rolle, Neue Wahrnehmungen zur Aufnahme und weitern Ausbreitung der Musik (1794), quoted in Michael Talbot, *The Sacred Vocal Music of Antonio Vivaldi* (Florence: Olschki, 1995), 69.

4. *The Bible,* Authorized King James Version (Oxford: Oxford University

Press, 1998). Extracts from the Authorized Version of the Bible (The King James Bible), the rights in which are invested in the Crown, are reproduced by permission of the Crown's Patentee, Cambridge University Press.

5. Conversely, the text of the *Credo* is preeminently suited to an "objective" musical setting, as taken to its *ne plus ultra* by Arvo Pärt in his *Summa* (1978). For Pärt, the ritualistic dimensions are all important, the individual details insignificant.

6. "Tonally open" means that a *Credo* setting does not finish in the same key that it begins in—there is no tonal closure.

7. Kelly suggests that the Church was "from the start a believing, confessing, preaching Church" and points to "creed-like slogans and tags" that are present in the New Testament. To look for a more formulated Creed in the apostolic Church would, according to this view, be a mistake since solemn professions of faith certainly existed, particularly in a baptismal context, which is one place among several where such declarations would find a natural home. J. N. D. Kelly, *Early Christian Creeds* (London: Longman, 1972), 7, 13.

8. "Now when Christians recite the death of Jesus as an article of their belief, they add (if they are using the Nicene Creed) that it was 'for us' that he was crucified: *staurôthenta te huper hçmôn*. This interpretation of that death goes back at least as far as the middle of the first century A.D. Not all the New Testament writers express it [illustrated in table 1.1; the Gospel according to St. Luke does not express this]. Acts, on the whole, associates the death with the vindication of Christ and of God's design, rather than with the redemption of others. But St. Paul, reciting in I Cor. 15 information about Jesus which he received by tradition, adds that it was 'for our sins' that he died . . . ; and in other passages Paul says similar things, as do certain other New Testament writers, each in his own way." C. F. D. Moule, *The Origin of Christology* (Cambridge: Cambridge University Press, 1977), 117. The passage to which Moule refers in Corinthians is cited here:

1 Corinthians 15
15:1 Moreover, brethren, I declare unto you the gospel which I preached unto you, which also ye have received, and wherein ye stand;
15:2 By which also ye are saved, if ye keep in memory what I preached unto you, unless you have believed in vain.
15:3 For I delivered unto you first of all that which I also received, how that Christ died for our sins according to the scriptures. (In *The Bible*, Authorized King James Version)

9. Frank Morison, *Who Moved the Stone?* (London: Faber, 1958), 47.

10. "Augustine believed that the cross itself now proclaimed something new, and this too was the work of 'evil men' like Pilate, suddenly made good. The traverse beam now signified the breadth of love; the upright, perseverance towards the goal of heaven; even the depth of the cross on the ground symbolized 'the depths of the grace of God, which is beyond human understanding.' Not just the *titulus*, but the whole gibbet ordered by Pilate became a means to display the Glory of God. The pagan governor could not have done better if he tried." Ann Wroe, *Pilate: The Biography of an Invented Man* (London: Jonathan Cape, 1999), 281.

11. Josef Andreas Jungmann, *The Early Liturgy to the Time of Gregory the Great* (London: Darton, Longman and Todd, 1960), 92.

12. A few examples of *Mass* and *Credo* settings where the *Et incarnatus* and *Crucifixus* are treated in this individual manner are as follows: Vivaldi, *Credo* RV 591, where the bulk of the work is in a brisk $\frac{3}{4}$ time (Allegro). The *Et incarnatus* is, by contrast, marked "Adagio" and the ensuing *Crucifixus* "Largo." Musically, both movements are accorded highly differentiated treatment; A. Scarlatti, *St. Cecilia Mass* (1720), where the first section of the *Credo* text is treated as one movement, the *Et incarnatus* and *Crucifixus* each being set separately and the last section of text again being brought together as a single movement; Mozart, *Missa in C* ("Krönungs-Messe") KV 317 (1779)—the *Credo* here is in Rondo form with its most distinctive episode occurring at the *Et incarnatus* and *Crucifxus*; and Haydn, *Missa in Tempore Belli* Hob XXII:9 (1796); again, the *Et incarnatus* and *Crucifixus* make a contrast both to the outer sections and to each other.

13. Table 1.2: the reference to the notes arranged in the shape of the cross is taken from Talbot, *The Sacred Vocal Music of Antonio Vivaldi*, 321; Irving Godt has coined the term "directionality." He observes its occurrence in a Mass setting attributed to Benedetto Marcello: "The composer turned to conventions that had their roots in Renaissance word painting. . . . Commonplace directionality governs several melodic passages: a full octave descent of the tenor marching in whole notes represents 'descendit de coelis,' and a rapid ascent of seven steps in shorter notes depicts 'Et ascendit in caelum.'" "Italian Figurenlehre? Music and Rhetoric in a New York Source," in *Studies in the History of Music*, vol. 1, ed. Ronald Broude and Ellen Beebe (New York: Broude Brothers, 1983), 180.

Part II

INVESTIGATIVE APPROACHES

2

Music and Rhetoric: Representation of the Text as Conceived by Theorists of the Eighteenth Century

The aim of this chapter is to provide a background to the area of rhetoric in both linguistic and musical terms. While it is not intended to be exhaustive, it aims to place rhetoric in the context of this study. A further purpose is to underline the importance of rhetoric to musicians, composers, and theorists in the period 1680–1800 and so to show why a rhetorical analysis of music (which will be undertaken later in this study) from this time is appropriate and relevant.

THE RELEVANCE OF RHETORIC TO MUSICAL ANALYSIS

Although some modern commentators are skeptical about the links between rhetoric and music, it is important not to underestimate the role rhetoric played in Renaissance and baroque culture and the influence that it had on many of its "sister" arts.[1] Rhetoric was originally a linguistic "art": "the art of speaking or writing so as to persuade people."[2] It was a discipline that prescribed not only a structure but also a style for oratory in public life in the ancient civilizations of Greece and Rome. It is thought that the tradition of rhetoric was brought to Greece by the sophist Gorgias in about 428 B.C. The development of this art was a gradual process and was aided by the contributions of various philosophers, including Protagoras, Antiphon, Lysisas, Isocrates, and Plato.

The links between music and rhetoric have their roots in antiquity. Quintilian recognized the similarities:

> Music has two modes of expression in the voice and in the body (music includes dancing); for both voice and body require to be controlled by appropriate rules. . . . Now I ask you whether it is not absolutely necessary for the orator to be acquainted with all these methods of expression which are concerned firstly with gesture, secondly with the arrangements of words and thirdly with the inflexions of the voice, of which a great variety are required in pleading. . . . But eloquence does vary both tone and rhythm, expressing sublime thoughts with elevation, pleasing thoughts with sweetness, and ordinary with gentle utterance, and in every expression of its art is in sympathy with the emotions of which it is the mouth-piece. It is by the raising, lowering or inflexion of the voice that the orator stirs the emotions of his hearers, and the measure, if I may repeat the term, of voice and phrase differs according as we wish to rouse the indignation or the pity of the judge. For, as we know, different emotions are roused even by the various musical instruments, which are incapable of reproducing speech. . . . An orator will assuredly pay special attention to his voice, and what is so specially the concern of music as this?[3]

With the revival of interest in antiquity during the Renaissance and the rediscovery of the works of the classical writers, rhetoric became such a fundamental part of education and cultural life during the Renaissance and baroque that its influence permeated and consequently affected many areas. Rhetoric appears false and cumbersome to us, but it was so implicit in the seventeenth and eighteenth centuries that it was natural to embody it in all modes of life.[4] Musicians and composers steeped in this cultural tradition would embed rhetorical concepts as a matter of course in their music. But while rhetoric provided a ready vocabulary for the composer, learning (and using) merely by imitation must also have occurred. Composers instinctively used rhetorical devices: they would reproduce rhetorical effect without necessarily comprehending the potential of the tools they were using. Leopold Mozart comments on the instinctive use of rhetorical devices in his *Versuch einer gründlichen Violinschule*:

> The Appoggiature are little notes which stand between the ordinary notes and are not reckoned as part of the bar-time. They are demanded by Nature herself to bind the notes together, thereby making a melody more song-like. I say by Nature herself, for it is undeniable that even a peasant closes his peasant-song with grace notes. . . . Nature herself forces him to do this. In

the same way the simplest peasant often uses figures of speech and metaphors without knowing it.[5]

Vocal music, naturally, was a prime candidate for the application of rhetorical ideals and concepts. In its function as an oration, it enjoyed the additional dimension of music, which could serve to underline and comment on the words and further persuade the listener.

With a culture so steeped in rhetoric, it was natural to apply the principles of this discipline to the other arts. Therefore, rhetoric becomes an important issue to consider when analyzing music of this period. A musical-rhetorical analysis will ultimately help us understand further the composer's aims: which emotions was the composer trying to stimulate in the listener, and how did he go about it? From this, further issues arise: how aware was the listener of the musical-rhetorical structure and devices, and how exactly were these perceived and understood?

A second major influence on the thought process of musical theorists of the time (which had, in fact, a reinforcing effect on the use of rhetoric in music) was the work of the French mathematician and philosopher René Descartes (1596–1650):

> What characterizes the men of the generation of Descartes is above all the will to dominate, to control events, to eliminate chance and the irrational. This attitude was present in every field.[6]

This description mirrors the aims of musical rhetoric and the intentions of composers of the day: to control the feelings of their audience. Descartes is credited with founding rationalism (knowledge acquisition through reasoning or rationale). His philosophical theory is concerned with "dualism"; he defined the differences between *res extensa* and *res cogitans*—physical space, or "objects located outside the mind," and mental space, or "objects located within the mind."[7] One of his later works, *Passions de l'âme* (1646), attempts to explain some elements of human behavior within this framework of dualism; this work was to have a profound influence on baroque musical thought:

> The soul may have pleasures of its own, but as to those which are common to it, and the body, they depend entirely on the passions, so that the men whom they can most move are capable of partaking most of enjoyment in this life.[8]

Naturally, rhetoric was the ideal vehicle through which to rouse the "passions" and so "affect" the soul. Therefore, when rhetorical devices were employed for affect in music, the listener was involved in the act of perceiving these gestures. A double effect of "passions" occurs here, as "perception is also regarded as a 'passion' since 'it involves the soul's taking in or 'receiving' some representation.'"[9] Passions such as joy or sadness are invoked by musical affect in addition to perception, which Descartes classified as a passion in itself.

This climate of philosophical thought, coupled with the educational environment, explains in part why there is such a profusion of musical literature referring to "affect" in music. However, the effect of rhetorical devices would have been lost without an audience that had at least some understanding of such a system. As mentioned earlier, the listener needs to be able to perceive the meaning in order to have his or her emotions moved accordingly. There is, admittedly, a problem with carrying out rhetorical analysis on music from this period since it is never possible to state conclusively what the composer "meant" (it is impossible, in general, to state conclusively what a composer "meant" by analysis alone—but even less so in this case), each individual listener having a different understanding of what he or she is hearing.

In addition, in a culture so deeply permeated by rhetoric, a form of classical conditioning (or conditioned response) would have been in operation. Classical conditioning is a form of associative learning that suggests that a particular response to this type of music will occur: through education or training, the listener is conditioned to understand rhetorical gesture and respond to the gestures in a certain way.[10] So, to a certain degree, each baroque listener would have perceived rhetorical gestures in a similar vein. However, our modern understanding of music of the era is going to be very different from that of a contemporary listener because we are not conditioned to "respond" to the music in rhetorical terms. Even with a newfound awareness of rhetoric and its relation to music of the time, we must still be wary of our own rhetorical interpretation since our rhetorical "conditioning" will not be the same as that of a baroque listener.

RHETORIC AND MUSIC

So far, only the general connections between rhetoric and music have been examined, that is, the common aim of attempting to persuade the listener of the contents of the oration or music. However, the links go much deeper. Sixteenth- and seventeenth-century musical treatises attest to this: they show the musician absorbing and encompassing the theories of classical rhetoric to produce a musical theory derived from this ancient discipline. The art of rhetoric is an ancient tradition dating back beyond the fifth century B.C. and was associated with the judicial system. This system was concerned mainly with the presentation of an argument, that is, the persuasiveness of a speech. The art of rhetoric is still very much in evidence in our law courts today: the presentation of a case to gain the sympathy of the listener, in this case, the jury.

The Phases of Composition

Classical writers laid down a process for composing an oration. The stages were as follows:

inventio	invention
dispositio	arrangement
elocutio	expression
memoria	memory
pronuncio	delivery

Quintilian gives a clear account of these stages:

> The art of oratory, as taught by most authorities, and those the best, consists of five parts:—*invention, arrangement, expression, memory, and delivery or action* (the two latter terms being expressed synonymously). But all speech expressive of purpose involves also a *subject* and *words*. If such expression is brief and contained within the limits of one sentence, it may demand nothing more. For not only what we say and how we say it is of importance, but also the circumstances under which we say it. It is here that the need of arrangement comes in. But it will be impossible to say everything demanded by the subject, putting each thing in its proper place, without the aid of memory. It is for this reason that memory forms the fourth department. But a delivery, which is rendered unbecoming either by voice or gesture, spoils everything and almost entirely destroys the effect of what is said. Delivery therefore must be assigned the fifth place.[11]

This process of invention is referred to by music theorists of the Renaissance and baroque, illustrating the fact that musicians were profoundly influenced by rhetoric.

Lippius (1585–1612) was one theorist who commented on the many parallels between rhetoric and music in his treatises and who drew on rhetorical theory to support and construct his musical premises.[12] Discussion of compositional process also features in Mattheson's *Der vollkommene Kapellmeister* (1739). What is interesting to note is that Mattheson is in fact selective about the phases that correspond musically. *Memoria* carries no great significance in the musical oration (at least when it is not improvised), so it is not discussed.

Structure

In classical rhetoric, an oration was organized according to a structure (the *dispositio* phase of composition) that prescribed a pattern for presenting a case. An outline of classical oratorical structure is given in table 2.1.[13] Again, for the musician, with his inbred rhetorical training, it was a natural and logical progression to translate this structure into an "organised compositional plan based on rhetorical theory."[14]

Music theorists of the period based their recommended methods of organizing a composition around rhetorical theory. Joachim Burmeister, in his *Musica Poetica* of 1606, refers to a compositional plan that is clearly derived from the structure of the oration:

> Sectioning the piece into affections means its division into periods for the purpose of studying its artfulness and using it as a model for imitation. A piece has three parts: (1) the exordium, (2) the body of the piece, (3) the ending.
>
> The *exordium* is the first period or affection of the piece. It is often adorned by fugue, so that the ears and mind of the listener are rendered attentive to the song, and his good will is won over. The exordium extends up to the point where the fugal subject ends with the introduction of a true cadence. This is seen to happen where a new subject definitely different from the fugal subject is introduced. However, examples do not confirm that all musical pieces should always begin with the ornament of fugue. . . .
>
> The body of the musical piece is a series of affections or periods between the exordium and the ending. In this section, textual passages similar to the various arguments of the confirmation in rhetoric are instilled in the listener's mind in order that the proposition [*sententia*] be more clearly grasped and considered.

Table 2.1.   The Structure of a Classical Oration

Element	Description
exordium	An introduction where the speaker may attempt to ingratiate him- or herself with the audience: "The rhetorical manoeuvres this involved are still recognisable by connoisseurs of the after-dinner speech: flattering allusion to the eminence of the auditors ('this distinguished company'), the speaker's confession of his own inadequacy ('ill qualified as I am'), the appeal for goodwill and a fair hearing ('if I may ask you to bear with me') . . ."
narratio	Where the speaker generalizes about the case and provides an outline and perhaps background information
confirmatio	Supporting arguments are introduced, together with evidence
confutatio	The speaker takes this opportunity to anticipate any arguments against his case, thus further persuading his audience that he has a solid grasp of the case he is handling.
peroratio	Conclusion, summing up

The body should not be protracted too much, lest that which is overextended arouse the listener's displeasure. For everything that is excessive is odious and usually turns into a vice.

The ending is the principal cadence where either or all the musical movement [*modulatio*] ceases or where one or two voices stop while others continue with a brief passage called *supplementum*. By means of this, the forthcoming close in the music is more clearly impressed on the listener's awareness.[15]

Mattheson, similarly, has clear ideas about the structure of a composition:

Our musical disposition is different from the theoretical arrangement of a mere speech only in theme, subject or object: hence it observes those six parts which are prescribed to an orator, namely the introduction, report, discourse, corroboration, confutation and conclusion. *Exordium, Narratio, Propositio, Confirmatio, Confutatio, and Peroratio.* . . .

The *Exordium* is the introduction and beginning of a melody, wherein the goal and the entire purpose must be revealed, so that the listeners are prepared and stimulated to attentiveness. . . .

The *Narratio* is so to speak a report, a narration, through which the meaning and character of the herein-contained discourse is pointed out. It occurs with the entrance or beginning of the vocal part or the most significant concerted part, and relates to the *Exordium*, which has preceded, by means of a skilled connection.

The *Propositio* or the actual discourse contains briefly the content or goal of the musical oration, and is of two sorts: simple or compound, wherein also belongs the varied or embellished *Propositio* in music, of which nothing is mentioned in rhetoric. . . .

The *Confirmatio* is an artistic corroboration of the discourse and in melodies is commonly found in the well conceived repetitions which are used beyond expectations. . . .

The *Confutatio* is a dissolution of the exceptions and may be expressed in melody either through combining, or even through quotation and refutation of foreign appearing ideas: For through just such antitheses, if they are well stressed, the hearing is strengthened in its joy, and everything which might run against it in dissonances and syncopations is smoothed and resolved. Meanwhile one does not find this aspect of disposition in melodies as much as in other things: yet it is truly one of the most beautiful.

The *Peroratio* finally is the end or conclusion of our musical oration, which must produce an especially emphatic impression, more so than all other parts. And this occurs not only in the course or progress of the melody, but especially in the epilogue, be it in thorough bass or in a stronger accompaniment; whether or not one has heard this ritornello previously. Custom has established that in arias we close with almost the very same passages and sounds with which we have begun: consistent with which then our peroration is replaced by our *Exordium*.[16]

So, as in an oration, the theorists' ideas concerned the presentation and development of an idea—in this case a musical idea. Sonata "form" reflects this layout.[17]

Figures

The area of rhetoric adopted by music that has been the subject of the closest appraisal is that of musical figures (*Figurenlehre*, literally "Doctrine of Figures," is the name German scholars of the early 1900s gave to the general corpus of prescriptive and interpretative statements about musical figures found in theoretical sources of the seventeenth and eighteenth centuries). The problematic nature of *Figurenlehre* is examined later in this chapter. Such musical figures were based on the concept of the "figures of speech" used by the orators. The development and importance of these figures of speech can be traced back as far as Aristotle. Both Quintilian and Cicero refer to them, emphasizing their use as *decorati*, as this extract from Quintilian's *De Institutione Oratoria* demonstrates:

> What the Greeks call φράσιν, we in Latin call *elocutio* or style. Style is revealed both in individual words and in groups of words. As regards the former, we must see that they are Latin, clear, elegant and well-adapted to produce the desired effect. As regards the latter, they must be correct, aptly placed and adorned with suitable figures.[18]

The anonymous work *Rhetorica ad Herennium* (which is thought to be contemporary with Cicero's work) lists forty-five such figures.[19] These figures of speech were used for the embellishment of an oration, to "decorate" the ideas and so further persuade and move the emotions of the listener. Ten of these were categorized as "special figures of speech" (for example, *nominatio* [onomatopoeia] and *translatio* [metaphor]), later to become known as "tropes." What sets them apart from the other figures of speech (such as *articulus* [phrase] and *interrogatio* [interrogation]) is the fact that the language "departs from the ordinary meaning of words and is with certain grace applied in another sense."[20]

The following quotation gives definitions (classical) and examples (sixteenth century) of a specimen figure of speech and a specimen trope:

> *Gradatio* (climax): [figure]
>   Quintilian: Schema: A more obvious and less natural application of art [than *acervatio*] and should therefore be more sparingly employed. It . . . repeats what has been already said and, before passing to a new point, dwells on those which precede.
>
>   Puttenham: Peace makes plenty, plenty makes pride,
> Pride breeds quarrel, and quarrel brings war.

Nominatio (onomatopoeia)

Quintilian: Trope: The creation of a word . . . scarcely permissible to a Roman. It is true that many words were created this way by the original founders of the language who adapted them to suit the sensation which they expressed.

Peacham: 1. A hurliburly, creaking.
            2. The roaring of lions, the bellowing of bulls.
            3. Luds-town of Lud, now London.
            4. Scholarlike, thickskin, pinchpenny, bellygod (glutton),
               pickthank (flatterer).[21]

By the Renaissance, writers on rhetoric were admitting a further proliferation of figures.[22] The emphasis had shifted from form to style, hence the greater importance of figures within rhetoric.[23]

There was now a bewildering array of figures, writers defining each term as they wished. With our fondness for classification and grouping, this has proved a problem for modern writers on the subject. Figure 2.1 shows a selection of figures, together with definitions and the similarities between each term.[24]

Renaissance music (sacred and secular) abounds in musical decoration whose aim is to illustrate the text: a musical figure of speech. Sometimes referred to generically by the modern phrase "word painting," these are recognized as part of the family of musical-rhetorical devices. Burmeister, in his *Musica Poetica* of 1606, was the first theorist to include a detailed account of musical figures. He refers to these figures in rhetorical terms, using their Greek and Latin names, which can be misleading; often, one receives the distinct impression that Burmeister is hard-pressed to find an exact musical parallel to a figure of speech bearing the same name.[25] This certainly seems to have set a precedent for future theorists (for example, Scheibe, Lippius, Nucius, Walther, Bernhard, and Kircher), all of whom used the same Greek and Latin terminology in profusion but to mean or represent quite different figures (see figure 2.2; compare figures 2.1 and 2.2 for parallels between linguistic and musical figures).[26]

With Burmeister, there is an emphasis on structural musical-rhetorical devices (most notably fugal), which, according to Gregory G. Butler, was a legacy of the relationship between language and music:

Music came to be viewed more and more as a highly effective form of artful expression imbued with all the learned artifice and persuasive qualities of its sister art, poetry. . . . In the late sixteenth century . . . the trend toward the application of rhetorical precept to music manifests itself in a particular predilection on the part of theorists to refer to certain musical structures and compositional techniques in terms of specific musical figures. From the very

Figure 2.1. Figures of Speech

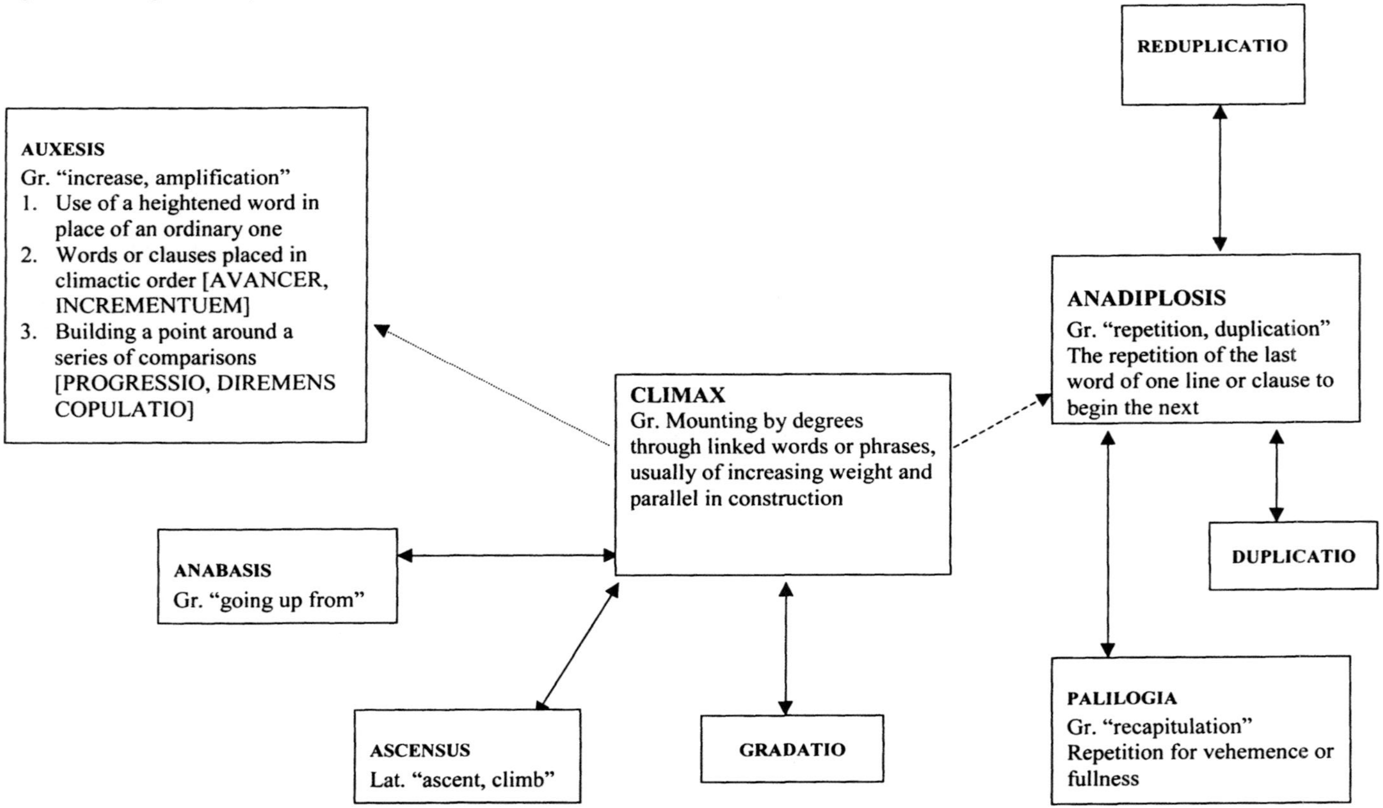

REDUPLICATIO

ANADIPLOSIS
Gr. "repetition, duplication"
The repetition of the last
word of one line or clause to
begin the next

DUPLICATIO

PALILOGIA
Gr. "recapitulation"
Repetition for vehemence or
fullness

CLIMAX
Gr. Mounting by degrees
through linked words or phrases,
usually of increasing weight and
parallel in construction

GRADATIO

ASCENSUS
Lat. "ascent, climb"

ANABASIS
Gr. "going up from"

AUXESIS
Gr. "increase, amplification"
1. Use of a heightened word in
   place of an ordinary one
2. Words or clauses placed in
   climactic order [AVANCER,
   INCREMENTUEM]
3. Building a point around a
   series of comparisons
   [PROGRESSIO, DIREMENS
   COPULATIO]

Figure 2.2. Musical Figures of Repetition

AUXESIS

(Bartel): Successive repetitions of a musical passage which rise by step.

Burmeister: The *auxesis* occurs when the harmonia grows and increases with a single twofold, threefold, or further repetition only of combined consonances [*noema*] using one and the same text.

Walther: The *auxesis* occurs when a passage or melody is repeated twice or three times while at the same time, however, always rising higher.

ANABASIS, ASCENSUS

(Bartel): An ascending musical passage which expresses ascending or exalted images or affections.

Kircher: The *anabasis* or *ascensio* is a musical passage through which we express exalted, rising, or elevated and eminent thoughts, exemplified in Marole's *Ascendens Christus in altum*.

Spiess: *Anabasis* or *ascensus* or ascent occurs when the voice also rises as directed by the text, for example, He ascended into heaven.

CLIMAX, GRADATIO

(Bartel): 1) A sequence of notes in one voice repeated either at higher or lower pitch, 2) two voices moving in ascending or descending parallel motion, 3) a gradual increase or rise in sound and pitch, creating a growth in intensity.

Burmeister: The *climax* repeats on similar notes but on pitches one step apart [...].

Nucius: It occurs when two voices progress upward or downward in parallel motion, for example, when the soprano and bass proceed in parallel tenths or the bass and tenor in parallel thirds. The use of this figure is most frequent at the end of a composition, to which we strive to engage the listener who eagerly awaits the conclusion.

Walther: The *climax* or *gradatio* is 1) a word figure, for example, when the words are set as follows: rejoice and sing, sing and glorify, glorify and praise; 2) a musical figure which occurs when two voices progress upwards and downwards by step in parallel thirds; 3) when a passage with or without a cadence is immediately repeated several times at progressively higher pitches; 4) this term can also be given to a four-part canon in which, as the first two voices reenter, each time one note higher, the other two voices remain in the previous key and yet still harmonize.

ANADIPLOSIS

(Bartel): 1) A repetition of a mimesis; 2) a repetition of the ending of one phrase at the beginning of the following one.

Burmeister: An embellishment of the *harmonia* constructed out of a double *mimesis*. This ornament is similar to the mimesis, for it repeats that which was first introduced through a *mimesis*.

Vogt: The *anadiplosis* occurs when we form a beginning out of the preceding ending.

Mattheson: The *epanalepsis, epistrophe, anadiplosis, paronomasia, polyptoton, antanaclasis, ploce,* etc. assume such natural positions that it almost seems as if the Greek orators borrowed these figures from the art of musical composition. For they are purely *repetitiones vocum,* repetitions of words, which are applied to music in various different ways.

PALILOGIA

(Bartel): A repetition of a theme either at different pitches in various voices or on the same pitch in the same voice.

Burmeister: The *palilogia* is a repetition of either the entire or only the beginning of the structure of the *melos* or theme on the same pitch in the same voice, occurring with or without intervening rests in all events in one voice.

Walther: The *palilogia* refers to an all-too-frequent repetition of the same words.

beginning of this movement, fugue is conspicuous as the most frequently
mentioned of these techniques. . . .

This whole movement was largely highly learned and intellectual, even
academic, in nature, and of course *fuga* was looked upon as a highly learned
element of composition. Secondly, the *fuga* was a structure of great artifice
and at the same time a highly expressive and affective musical force, and
therefore highly valued as a powerful musical-rhetorical device. Thirdly,
poetry deals largely with verbal imagery, and there is growing evidence that
the *fuga* was thought of in terms of a highly artificial image, and was therefore a prime ingredient of *musica poetica*.[27]

However, Brian Vickers suggests that this attention to structural devices
occurred because Burmeister was still working with the rhetorical system
of the Middle Ages, where

questions of content were treated as questions of form, and where figures
and tropes were mere verbal devices, unconnected with the feelings and passions. In [the] Renaissance rhetoric[al] form and feeling cohere again.[28]

Specific references to fugue tend to occur in the earlier treatises, but even
with the demise of *fuga*, musical rhetoric still relied on structural devices,
as well as textual imagery, for effect. Later in this book, I will argue that
the underlying structure of the *Crucifixus* is inseparable from the surface
effects and that structural devices therefore form an intrinsic part of
"effect."

It is interesting to note that, almost without exception, the treatises on
musical rhetoric from this time are of German origin. The Italian tradition
of musical rhetoric (whose existence is evident from Italian music) is
largely undocumented.

Dietrich Bartel suggests that

the Italian rejection of music's numerological and cosmological significance
in favor of its direct affective and aesthetic effect led to a form of musical
expression which focussed on a modern aesthetic principle of expressing
and stirring the affections rather than explaining the text. Although the text
was central to musical composition, it became the springboard for musical
expression rather than the object of the composition. The expressive musical
devices which characterize the Italian *nuove musiche* were developed with an
aesthetic rather than exegetic principle in mind. Instead of introducing an
intermediate level of linguistic and theological significance to the musical
phenomena as was done in Lutheran Germany, the Italians sought to speak
directly and immediately to the senses.[29]

Again, this comment indicates a culture steeped in rhetoric, the goal
being to move the listener; however, judging by this comment and the

lack of documented evidence, the Italians seem to have taken a more "direct" approach to the expression of the text. With the modern revival of interest in this area of music, attempts were made by theorists such as Brandes (1935), Unger (1941), and Schmitz (1950) to set up a "standardized" Doctrine of the Affections—which had never been in historical existence.[30] While this has been identified by modern commentators as a problem, miscategorization and misrepresentation of musical figures are still problems that persist to the present.[31] Therefore, if an analysis of music from this period is carried out, while it is important to consider the role of *Figurenlehre*, the whole area must be approached with a degree of caution. To achieve this, some background knowledge is needed. The extent to which composers recognized and used these figures in their music generally must first be established. Some knowledge of the treatises in circulation at the same time must also be gathered.

Modern views of rhetoric are often distorted: there seems to be a divide between modern historians specializing in baroque and classical music, respectively. While many writings on classical music are admirably comprehensive and acknowledge its connections with rhetoric, they fail to grasp the true meaning of the discipline or to explain exactly what its relationship was to musical form and textual expression. Naturally, one would not expect a clear break between baroque and classical practice in respect of their dependence or nondependence on rhetorical models and concepts. Music was—and is—a constantly evolving process; as with anything that evolves, elements of old and new are fused together. The present study, one aim of which is to examine a set of transmitted *topoi*, will support this view.[32]

In addition, while there are similarities between language and music, there are also differences that cannot be ignored. Music will never be able to express an "idea" since it does not employ words as a vehicle: a musical "idea" is going to be a very different concept from a linguistic idea—music cannot communicate a concrete statement in the same way that language can. Notes cannot be strung together to create the equivalent of words. A musical sentence will not be understood as a linguistic sentence is, where the words have a natural hierarchy, are both referent and logical, and ultimately have concrete meaning. While both are temporal arts (that is, they exist in time), music is in effect two-dimensional when compared with language. It depends on a different set of criteria to create its meaning.[33] While some figures of speech will never be able to be translated literally in musical terms, others may express certain concepts in musical terms perhaps better than in linguistic ones. So, again, an element of caution must be exercised when undertaking analysis in rhetorical terms, especially with regard to the parallels that exist between language and music.

THE RELEVANCE OF RHETORIC TO THIS STUDY

The subject of word painting, which is examined here in connection with settings of the *Crucifixus*, can be considered a part of the musical-rhetorical language of the time. Word painting was a more literal representation of the content of the text, another strategy for "persuading" the listener. The fact that rhetoric was so widely accepted and used supports the case for the present study: that it is valid to look for links between rhetorical/word painting devices used in the *Crucifixus* settings—common gestures used to portray the words of a widely used text—and so to establish that a possible tradition, or set of *topoi*, existed and was handed down from composer to composer. It must be reemphasized, however, that I shall be treating rhetoric of the baroque age not as a complete, self-sufficient explanatory system but only as one means among many of exploring what composers may have intended to say, how their contemporaries received it, and how we can receive it today. Chapter 9 presents a more detailed discussion of musical-rhetoric in connection with a case study, with examples of rhetorical "figures" that could be used for the expression of the *Crucifixus* text, while a more general account of my findings is documented in chapter 13.

NOTES

1. Brian Vickers is one such example: "How far can the terms of rhetoric be applied directly to music? How far can one aesthetic system, a linguistic one, be adapted to another, non-linguistic?" "Figures of Rhetoric/Figures of Music?," *Rhetorica* 2, no. 1 (1984): 2.

2. Paul Procter, ed., *Longman New Generation Dictionary* (Harlow, U.K.: Longman, 1981), 586.

3. Quintilian, *De Institutione Oratoria*, trans. H. E. Butler (London: Heinemann, 1921), I. x. 22–7: ed. cit., I, 171–73.

4. George J. Buelow comments, "The humanistic basis of education aspiring to teach every student the art of rhetorical eloquence permeated musical thought for centuries. As early as the first decades of the sixteenth century Italian musicians sought a closer tie between rhetoric and music." "The *Loci Topici* and Affect in Late Baroque Music: Heinichen's Practical Demonstration," *Music Review* 27 (1966): 161.

5. Leopold Mozart, *Versuch einer gründlichen Violinschule*, trans. Editha Knocker (London: Oxford University Press, 1945), 166, quoted in Elaine R. Sisman, *Haydn and the Classical Variation* (Cambridge, Mass.: Harvard University Press, 1993), 20.

6. F. E. Sutcliffe, introduction to *Discourse on Method and the Meditations*, by René Descartes, trans. F. E. Sutcliffe (London: Penguin Classics, 1968), 21.

7. Thomas B. Sheridan, "Descartes, Heidegger, Gibson, and God: Toward an Eclectic Ontology of Presence," *Presence: Teleoperators and Virtual Environments 8*, no. 5 (1999): 552.

8. René Descartes, *Passions de l'âme*, in *The Philosophical Works*, vol. 1, trans. Elizabeth S. Haldane and G. R. T. Ross (London: Cambridge University Press, 1968), III. ccxii. 427.

9. John Cottingham, *Descartes* (Oxford: Blackwell, 1986), 153.

10. Rita L. Atkinson, Richard C. Atkinson, Edward E. Smith, and Daryl J. Bem, *Introduction to Psychology* (Fort Worth, Tex.: Harcourt Brace Jovanovich, 1993), 254–55. What psychologists refer to as classical conditioning relates to the philosophers' rationalism: associative learning.

11. Quintilian, *De Institutione Oratoria*, iii. 1–3: ed. cit., I, 383–85.

12. A detailed discussion of Lippius's rhetorical and musical ideas is found in Benito V. Rivera, *German Music in the Early Seventeenth Century: The Treatises of Johannes Lippius* (Ann Arbor, Mich.: UMI Research Press, 1974), 167–85.

13. The number of sections in an oration varies, depending on which treatise is being referred to. For example, *Rhetorica ad Herennium* cites six parts—*divisio* being included between *narratio* and *confirmatio*. The quotation in table 2.1 referring to "connoisseurs of the after-dinner speech" is taken from Walter Nash, *Rhetoric: The Wit of Persuasion* (Oxford: Blackwell, 1989), 9.

14. Peter Seymour, "Oratory and Performance," in *Companion to Contemporary Musical Thought*, vol. 2, ed. John Paynter, Tim Howell, Richard Orton, and Peter Seymour (London: Routledge, 1992), 916.

15. Joachim Burmeister, *Musical Poetics*, trans. Benito V. Rivera (New Haven, Conn.: Yale University Press, 1993), 203–5.

16. Ernest C. Harriss, *Johann Mattheson's Der vollkommene Capellmeister* (Ann Arbor, Mich.: UMI Research Publications, 1981), 470–72.

17. One can easily see how such a layout transfers to sonata form with the *exordium*, *narratio*, and (perhaps) *propositio* becoming the exposition of the latter form, the *confirmatio* (and possibly the *confutatio*) the development, and the *confutatio* and *peroratio* the recapitulation. Seymour, "Oratory and Performance."

18. Quintilian, *De Institutione Oratoria*, VIII. i. 1: ed. cit., III, 194–95.

19. *Rhetorica ad Herennium*, Book 4, quoted in James Jerome Murphy, *Rhetoric in the Middle Ages: A History of the Rhetorical Theory from St. Augustine to the Renaissance* (Berkeley: University of California Press, 1974), 21.

20. "Ab usitata verborum potestate recedatur atque in aliam rationem cum quadem venustate oratio conferatur," *ad Herennium*, IV. xxxi. 42., quoted in Murphy, *Rhetoric in the Middle Ages*, 20.

21. Lee A. Sonnino, *A Handbook to Sixteenth-Century Rhetoric* (London: Routledge and Kegan Paul, 1968): *Gradatio*, quoted at 101–2, *Nominatio*, quoted at 132–33.

22. For example, Susenbrotus, *Epitome Troporum ac Schematum* (1541); J. C. Scaliger, *Poetices Libri Septum* (1561); and Vives, *De Ratione Dicendi* (1533), to name only a few.

23. "The accretion of schemes was such as to suggest a trivial ingenuity, and indeed led to numerous overlaps not convincingly explained away; in many cases

the distinctive value of the figure might elude all but the most exacting analyst. It was not simply that the emphasis in rhetorical studies had shifted from structure to style, or had relegated *taxis* to the domain of logic, in order to concentrate on *lexis*. That certainly happened; but what also followed was of consequence, observable in fields, of developing a meta-language—a terminology—in excess of practical functions, so that the terminology itself displaces the proper concerns of the subject." Nash, *Rhetoric*, 14.

24. Definitions taken from Richard A. Lanham, *A Handlist of Rhetorical Terms* (Berkeley: University of California Press, 1991).

25. Burmeister's definitions of terms such as *anadiplosis* bear scant resemblance to the original linguistic figures (compare the definitions in figures 2.1 and 2.2). Dietrich Bartel suggests that Burmeister's intent was to establish a rhetorical-musical system of terminology based on linguistic terminology rather than proposing musical figures that were exact musical replicas of linguistic figures. Dietrich Bartel, *Musica Poetica: Musical-Rhetorical Figures in German Baroque Music* (Lincoln: University of Nebraska Press, 1997), 180–81. Brian Vickers also suggests that "the formation of musical rhetoric takes the form of a theorist looking at a rhetorical textbook in order to find a figure in rhetoric that applied to, or could be adapted to, a musical effect or structure." "Figures of Rhetoric/Figures of Music?" 2.

26. Definitions taken from Bartel, *Musica Poetica*.

27. Gregory G. Butler, "Fugue and Rhetoric," *Journal of Music Theory* 21, no. 1 (1977): 49–50.

28. Vickers, "Figures of Rhetoric/Figures of Music?" 38.

29. Bartel, *Musica Poetica*, 59.

30. "Problems arise only when the theorists from Burmeister onwards are scanned today in order to erect a system of *Affekten*, a rhetoric supposedly followed by important composers of that period." Peter Williams, "The Snares and Delusions of Musical Rhetoric: Some Examples from Recent Writings on J. S. Bach," in *Alte Musik: Praxis und Reflektion*, ed. Peter Reidemeister and Veronika Gutmann (Winterthur, Switzerland: Amadeus Verlag, 1983), 231. "Attempts by writers such as Brandes, Unger and Schmitz to organize the multitude of musical figures into a few categories have not proved successful." George J. Buelow, "Rhetoric and Music," in *The New Grove Dictionary of Music and Musicians*, vol. 15, ed. Stanley Sadie (London: Macmillan, 1980), 795. The works referred to are Heinrich Brandes, *Studien zur musikalischen Figurenlehre im 16. Jahrhundert* (Berlin: Triltsch und Huther, 1935); Hans-Heinrich Unger, *Die Beziehungen zwischen Musik und Rhetorik im 16.–18. Jahrhundert* (Würzburg, Germany: Triltsch, 1941); Arnold Schmitz, *Die Bildlichkeit in der wortgebundenen Musik J. S. Bachs* (Mainz, Germany: Schott, 1950).

31. Leonard G. Ratner is one such author, Leonard G. Ratner, *Classic Music: Expression, Form, and Style* (New York: Schirmer, 1980), and such problems are still evident in the latest edition of the *New Grove Dictionary of Music and Musicians*: George J. Buelow, Peter A. Hoyt, and Blake Wilson, "Rhetoric and Music," in *The New Grove Dictionary of Music and Musicians*, 2nd ed., vol. 21, ed. Stanley Sadie (London: Macmillan, 2001), 260–75.

32. For an in-depth discussion on the merits and drawbacks of modern writings on rhetoric, see Jasmin Melissa Cameron, "Rhetoric and Music: The Influence of a Linguistic Art," in *Music and Words*, Liverpool Symposium III (Liverpool: Liverpool University Press, 2005), 28–72.

33. "The meaning of music can be specified—in a crude over-simplification that neglects the emotional characteristics—as inner coherence of the relations among the tones constituting a work. . . . Musical meaning is intentional; it exists only in so far as a listener grasps it." Carl Dahlhaus, *The Esthetics of Music*, trans. William Austin (Cambridge: Cambridge University Press, 1982), 12.

3

Modern Analytical Views Relevant to the Subject and Their Relationship to Rhetoric

A musical analysis which succeeds in discovering and describing interesting relations in music, in whatever terms, has essentially a semiotic character.[1]

As a consequence of our modern interest in musical analysis, many different analytical systems and techniques have been invented and developed during the course of the twentieth century. One of the concerns surrounding these analytical techniques is their ultimate purpose. All too often, musical analysis seems to be carried out for the sake of analysis itself rather than aiming, for instance, to support a historical theory or perhaps explain why or how a composer achieved a musical style or effect. What is interesting about most of these analytical techniques is that they take the classical era as their starting point, largely ignoring the vast body of music that existed before 1750. Further, there is a distinct bias toward the analysis of instrumental rather than vocal music.[2]

Of the many analytical techniques that have been developed, it is the practice of musical semiosis that holds most significance for the present study. This is because of its many similarities of conception and approach to the eighteenth-century (and earlier) view of music and rhetoric. There are even aspects of semiosis that build directly on the classical rhetorical approach. This chapter explores the similarities between musical rhetoric and musical semiotics before proceeding to discuss which semiotic techniques will benefit the analyses that follow and how they will be applied.

I also examine the work of theorists who seek to explore the issues surrounding textual representation or attempt to draw parallels between music and linguistic theory and models and then attempt to relate these issues to my current study.

MUSICAL SEMIOTICS AND ITS RELATIONSHIP TO RHETORIC

The area of musical semiotics is concerned with

> musical meaning drawing on some aspects of the study of "signs": such study may be called either "semiotics" (the discipline associated with twentieth-century trends in American philosophy and communications theory) or "semiology" (the discipline associated with French linguistics and literary criticism), the historical distinction having played no great part in musical adaptations of these ideas.[3]

Immediately, one can see parallels with the relationship between rhetoric and semiotics. Both of these systems that have had so much impact on the understanding of music come from outside the musical domain itself, originating in the linguistic tradition. Both are about communication: rhetoric concerns itself with how to persuade the listener, semiotics with how signs are used to communicate meaning:

> There is a signification system (and therefore a code) when there is the socially conventionalized possibility of generating sign functions, whether the functives of such functions are discrete units called signs or vast portions of discourse, provided that the correlation has been previously posited by a social convention.[4]

The basis of modern-day semiotic theory was developed simultaneously but independently by two scholars: Ferdinand de Saussure (1857–1913), based in Switzerland, and Charles Sanders Peirce (1839–1914), an American philosopher.

Whereas Peirce views the "system" of signs as tripartite, Saussure sees signs as bipartite, consisting of the signifier and the signified, that is, the object and the symbol/sign or word (being largely concerned with linguistics) that represents it. While Saussure's representation was significant, Peirce's definition is possibly the more important since he recognizes the separate role of the interpretant in the object-sign relationship. It is the interpretant who creates the meaning of the sign. Therefore, according to Robert Samuels, "meaning is created by the receiver of the message rather than being self evident."[5] Again, the similarities to rhetoric are clear. The listener is the interpreter of a series of signs (conventions). Samuels goes on to discuss the application of semiotic concepts to music:

> If musical signs can be identified, and their signifying structures brought to light, then the concern for a correct reading of structure which is so much a feature of Anglo-American analysis can be replaced by a more open-ended inquiry into the possible multiple meanings which the musical text can carry.[6]

It is most revealing that Umberto Eco, a well-established scholar in the field of semiotics, actually includes rhetoric in his definition of the field of semiotics.[7]

MUSICAL RHETORIC, SEMIOTICS, AND NARRATIVITY

We have established that semiotics is about communication: hence, musical semiotics is about musical communication. While semiotics per se is a relatively new field, to assume that the nature of communication was never considered prior to the emergence of semiotics as a distinct field would be quite wrong. Kofi Agawu highlights the existence of the "prehistory" of semiotics, beginning with the work of seventeenth- and eighteenth-century theorists.[8] The critical writings of musical theorists from the period are of course concerned with the transmission of music so as to "persuade" the listener most successfully—the concern for effective communication is very evident. Agawu describes this interest in communication as a "semiotic awareness," and my understanding of the similarities between the two areas conforms to this general approach. Raymond Monelle expresses the point thus:

> Eighteenth-century views of musical meaning are, in fact, much nearer to semiotic theory than the Romantic views that succeeded them. The sign that signifies by resembling its object (the imitative view), and the sign that is in natural contiguity with its object (the expressive view), are classes recognised by the semiotic theory of Peirce. . . . The eighteenth century was mainly concerned with the setting of words to music; writers sometimes affirmed that music without words "signifies nothing" (Rousseau on "Sonata" in the *Encyclopédie*) or is "only noise" (D'Alembert in the *Discours Préliminaire* to the same work). They were therefore chiefly interested in the specific emotional expression and content of music, so that it could be aptly fitted to its text.[9]

Peirce's three components of semiosis (a sign, its object, and its interpretant) are reflected by Jean-Jacques Nattiez's thinking on musical semiotics (composer, piece, performance, or analysis—both performance and analysis requiring an interpretant). Both of these formulations obviously demonstrate the basis of communication: communication demands both a transmitter and a receiver. Here, the interpretant is the listener or receiver of the music, and the meaning of the music is dependent, to a certain extent, on the listener's interpretation. As I have already argued in chapter 2 with reference to the field of rhetoric, if there is a cultural convention, the music/sign will be interpreted in a conventionalized style.[10]

In chapter 2, I also suggested that since we have not experienced the specific musical training and conditioning of that age, we listen to music of the seventeenth and eighteenth centuries in a different way from a contemporary listener; therefore, the "signs" given out by the music can be understood to have changed in the course of its "reception history":

> The iconic cuckoo in Beethoven's "Pastoral Symphony" is as legitimate a musical sign as the indexical phrase repetition that constitutes much of the musical argument in the first movement. Since it is possible in general to make interesting statements relating musical and natural events, notes taken to be in an iconic relationship to the song of a cuckoo may justifiably be viewed as having a sign function. But it may also be that the notes A, B-flat, D, C at the beginning of the same symphony are the iconic sign of a type of bird song that none of us has ever encountered; and that someone might one day, on discovering such a bird, come to understand the opening of the "Pastoral" in the same way that we understand the cuckoo figure. This example alone makes it absurd to think that the sign character of a work has any permanence.[11]

Stopford also points out that the listener will contextualize what he or she hears in terms of his or her own experience and knowledge (that is, knowledge acquisition). So again we have an overlap between many different fields that convey the same essential idea (rhetoric, semiotics, psychology).

The most obvious application of semiotic theory to seventeenth- and eighteenth-century music is in aid of a rhetorical analysis. Each musical-rhetorical figure can be seen as a "sign" in its own right, and the paradigmatic analysis system devised by Nattiez and Nicolas Ruwet can be used to dissect the music for motivic similarity. The question that interests us would then be, How does the motivity of a *Crucifixus* setting relate to the words? A point that has to made immediately is that there is no hard-and-fast rule stipulating that each textual idea must necessarily be musically expressed in the same way each time (this question is discussed later in this chapter with reference to Irving Godt's "Music about Words"); therefore, any motivic analysis of the music has to be approached with a high degree of caution.

Eero Tarasti discusses narrative program structure and proposes that two types of program should be recognized: surface structure (structures of communication) and deep structure (structures of signification):

> The rhetorical figures of the Baroque period were narrative techniques situated in the structures of communication (or perhaps elements of technique, since by narrativity one has to understand only the syntagm, the temporally ordered continuum consisting of these elements). The narrativity of the deep level "grasps" passages having a ready-made signification and weaves a narrative texture using them as material.[12]

Musical semiotics analyzes music in order to identify musical actors and the relationships between them. This procedure is akin to carrying out an analysis for rhetorical figures but with an added dimension since, in semiotic terms, the precise functionality of these actors can be examined in musical terms.

Tarasti refers to modalities as "general attitudes by which a subject evaluates and humanizes an object." He lists the following levels:

being	*être*	state of rest, stability
doing	*faire*	musical action, event dynamism, dissonance
becoming	*devenir*	"normal" temporal process of music
kinetic energy	*vouloir*	the tendency to move towards something—musical direction
know	*savoir*	musical information, cognitive moment of music
can	*pouvoir*	power/efficiency of music, technical resources, particularly in performance (performance techniques, idiomatic writing, etc.)
must	*devoir*	aspects of genre and formal type
believe	*croire*	epistemic values of music, its persuasiveness in reception, etc.

Tarasti then refers to modalities in the terms of passions:

> We meet the level of modalities ("will," "know," "can," "must"), which combine into different passions. By "passion" we mean a certain constellation of modalities, their articulation, and the resulting virtual-actual state, which accordingly, is already determined by the modalities it consists of, and can be conceived as a distinct emotion.[13]

Tarasti draws an analogy between this and the way in which Descartes derived various passions from six basic passions in his *Passions de l'âme*:

> But the number [of passions] which are simple and primitive is not very large. For, in making a review of all those which I have enumerated, we may easily notice that there are but six [of this category], i.e., wonder, love, hatred, desire, joy, and sadness; and that all the others are composed of some of these six, or are species of them. That is why, in order that their multitude may not embarrass my readers, I shall here treat the six primitive passions separately; and afterwards I shall show in what way all the others derive from them their origin.[14]

It is most revealing that modern theorists continue to draw on treatises and philosophies of the era under examination in this study. Agawu's comments also support this observation.[15] This analogy further underlines the presence of links between the domains of rhetoric and semiology.

Rhetorical figures of the early eighteenth century and their descendants, which are often referred to as topics (or *topoi*), are recognized in semiotic terms as musical signs by Agawu:

> Each sign, following Saussure, is the indissoluble union of a signifier and a signified. The signifier of a topic is itself comprised of a set of signifiers, the action of various parameters. The musical signifier therefore embodies, even at this primitive level, a dynamic relation. The signified is more elusive. As Nattiez puts it, "Insofar as the only way to find out how the semantic content of music is perceived is to proceed with verbalization, the musical signified, as such, can never be pinpointed accurately." In any case, what is signified by a given topic remains implicit in the historically appropriate level invoked—singing style, *Sturm und Drang*, learned style and so on. Furthermore, just as low-level signs can combine to form higher level ones, so topics in a particular local function can combine to form topics on a higher-level. And so, we have—theoretically, at least—a process of infinite semiotic linkage with regard to topic, reaching beyond the individual phrase, section or movement to the work as a whole, and beyond.[16]

Agawu refers to the analysis of classical music for these topics as "extroversive semiosis" (musical discourse). A topic is a musical sign that is made up of a signifier and a signified. In general terms, the signifier refers to the "expression," while the signified refers to the "content": this means that in musical terms, the signifiers are concerned with the "building blocks" of the sign—melody, harmony, rhythm, and so on—while the signified refers to these units as a sign within the context of eighteenth-century culture. Agawu goes on to suggest that the number of topics in a work can be limited by style and such practicalities as length and complexity of musical organization. He confirms my experience of rhetorical devices—that they overlap and can also combine. He also considers whether there is a hierarchical ordering of topics but concludes that if there is, it would need to be related to the harmonic framework of a piece.

The rhetorical organization of a musical piece can be related to semiotic theory in this way—it is akin to the deep-level narrative structure discussed by Tarasti: "All semiotics can be treated either as system or process, and hence the narrative structures can be defined as constituents of the deep level of the semiotical process."[17] This brings us back to the issue of rhetorical structure as was discussed in chapter 2 and more specifically again to the question, How, exactly, does rhetorical organization translate to music?

Before I attempt to answer this question, I think that it is necessary to mention the link between the two structural levels that Tarasti identifies. These structural levels (surface and deep) are comparable with Agawu's extroversive and introversive semiology. However, it is impossible to detach one level from the other. Ultimately, the surface structure has a dependence on the deep structure. The deep-level structure is inevitably going to affect the surface. While it is possible to conduct analysis at two different levels, these levels need always to be related to each other.[18]

To return to the last question: How, exactly, does rhetorical organization translate to music? If we attempt to transfer the oratorical model to music, the peripheral parts of the oration become the most important, that is, the introduction and conclusion. It becomes possible to discern a relationship: the "introduction" and "conclusion" are reflected in the key structure of a piece of music because tonally (and maybe thematically) the "conclusion" relates to the "introduction" (as happens in an oration—where the conclusion relates to the material of the introduction as a form of summing up):

> Narrativity can be understood in the very common sense as a general category of the human mind, a competency that involves putting temporal events in a certain order, a syntagmatic continuum. The continuum has a beginning, development and end; and the order created in this way is called, under given circumstances, a narration. With this view, the logic of narration appears to be very abstract and of a fairly general level. It turns out to be a certain tension between the beginning and the end, a sort of arch progression.[19]

Narrativity in music is the subject of much discussion in Tarasti's book. However, since Tarasti examines mainly instrumental music, one can see why his argument for the existence of narrativity can prove such a problematic point. In the case of the *Crucifixus* settings, we are already provided with a text and therefore with a narrative—as already mentioned in chapter 2. A kind of "double narrativity" exists by virtue of both the text's and the music's expression of the same text. Although the *Crucifixus* is not necessarily a stand-alone movement (some composers did in fact set the *Crucifixus* on its own, but these were in the minority), within this short section of text it is possible to see the potential for the "arch effect" that Tarasti describes. The words of the *Crucifixus* form a narrative, describing the events of the Crucifixion and its outcome: the death of Christ. The words contain a sequential structure that is tripartite and reflects the narrative structure (and hence the oratorical structure mentioned earlier) of beginning–middle–end:

Crucifixus	=	action
etiam pro nobis/sub Pontio Pilato	=	contextualization
passus et sepultus est	=	action

This simple layout also demonstrates a second "arch-like" structure in terms of the action of the text. This further supports the view that the conclusion usually refers to the opening in some way in order to create some semblance of coherence. As already mentioned, in musical terms coherence is created by tonal closure and unifying thematic devices. Tarasti regards this organization as an "arch." It is also possible to perceive it as a circular layout: throughout the history of music, circularity has played an important role. Sonata "form" can be viewed as a circular organization, as can the cyclicity of many nineteenth-century works. Tarasti uses the terms "embrayage" and "débrayage" (engagement and disengagement) to describe narrativity in music; these two terms demonstrate once again a circular organization:

In Greimasian semiotics, the concept of *débrayage/embrayage* points out movement from (*débrayage*) and return to (*embrayage*) a center. . . .
    Narrativity in music is realized precisely as a deliberate disengagement/ engagement of the enunciator (composer), by which he or she diverts the primal energy of movement from its "normal" course, manipulates phases of the melodic line and harmonic tension, and guides their resolution. Such a shifting or disengaging activity is possible only when realized against this innate kinetic quality of music.[20]

For example, sonata "form" becomes engagement–disengagement– reengagement (reflected musically by tonic–excursion–tonic)—essentially a tripartite structure. The tonal organization of sonata "form" reflects this harmonic tension and release. The most recent writings on sonata form tend to dismiss the established (and arguably rather simplistic view) of a three-part form in favor of a bipartite structure (reflecting the tonal structure); Mark Evan Bonds is a representative scholar. Theorists in general are so dogmatic about sonata "form"—for them it must be either bi- or tripartite—that no one appears to have considered the possibility that elements of bi- and tripartite organization were occurring simultaneously in separate domains. However, tripartite organisation would appear to reflect the beginning–middle–end paradigm.

This emphasis on and interest in tonality and harmony reflects Schenkerian methods—and Schenkerian analysis is something that has been identified as introversive semiosis (where introversive semiosis is defined as dealing with "pure" musical signs) in Agawu's book on semiotic analysis in music. Agawu suggests that Schenker's *Ursatz* is in fact the beginning–middle–end narrative paradigm at its lowest common denominator.[21] Tarasti likewise recognizes this:

> [While] Schenkerian analysis is concerned with musical space and not with temporal organisation . . . his model could easily be developed into a method of narrative analysis of music. Its basic premise—that a musical work is a totality created by a structure wherein all events relate to a basic model and the tension it provides—corresponds well to the syntagmatic demand of narrativity.[22]

Similarly, Richard Littlefield and David Neumeyer see the relation between narrative and Schenkerian theory:

> No matter what it recounts, any account—whether factual, scientific, or hermeneutical—remains an account: report, story, narrative. Heinrich Schenker labels his music-syntactical narratives "representations" (*Darstellungen*), which we may take as plots, accounts, or stories.[23]

So how justified are we in applying Schenkerian analysis to music of the preclassical era and looking for an *Ursatz*? Most analytical writers have a tendency to begin with the classical era. Charles Rosen states,

> The greatest change in eighteenth century tonality, partly influenced by the establishment of equal temperament, is a new emphatic polarity between tonic and dominant, previously much weaker. . . . It is not until the eighteenth century, with the full establishment of equal temperament, that the possibilities of modulation could be completely articulated, and the consequences of this articulation were only realized in the latter half of the century.[24]

> The movement to the dominant was part of musical grammar, not an element of form. Almost all music in the eighteenth century went to the dominant: before 1750 it was not something to be emphasized; afterward, it was something that the composer could take advantage of. This means that every

eighteenth-century listener expected the movement to the dominant in the sense that he would have been puzzled if he did not get it; it was a necessary condition of intelligibility.[25]

Schenker does in fact apply his analytical techniques to Bach, but for composers before Bach, caution needs to be exercised when examining the "deep" structural level.[26]

Table 3.1 attempts to draw together all the different terminologies and technicalities discussed previously.

Semiotic analysis, on the evidence gathered to support this chapter, can be understood as an umbrella term used to cover a variety of techniques. As we have seen, even Schenkerian analysis, while not designed specifically as a semiotic analytical tool, can be used for this purpose. Agawu certainly views it as such. This is consistent with John Stopford's view, quoted at the outset of this chapter.

The whole argument for and against narrativity in music is rendered somewhat simpler when texted music is considered. Texted music has an imposed sequentiality, governed by the words, and although one might argue that music can negate or contradict the words and indeed even the beginning–middle–end construct of the textual passage, the narrativity of the text is most often reflected in the music.

With the *Crucifixus*, if we are going to look at the beginning–middle–end paradigm, it will be important to examine it in the context of the whole setting: does the *Crucifixus* appear within a larger *Credo*, or does it stand alone? Is there a clear deep structure echoed within the *Crucifixus*? (That is, I, V, I in the local key, reflected at a global level by the same construct—in the entire *Credo*, for example?) We find echoes of Tarasti's theory in more specific studies on the *Credo*:

A kind of "arch structure" results, the center being the "Et Incarnatus"—the spiritual core of the Credo where one of Christianity's greatest mysteries is described.[27]

Table 3.1. "Deep" Structural Level and Its Equivalence

Narrativity	Beginning	Middle	End
Tarasti	*embrayage*	*débrayage*	*embrayage*
Schenker (*Ursatz*)	I	V	(V)-I
Crucifixus	action	contextual	action
Rhetoric	exordium	narratio/confirmatio, etc.	*peroratio*
Stability	stable	unstable	stable
Sonata form	exposition	development	recapitulation

John Stopford states,

> A musical analysis which succeeds in discovering and describing interesting
> relations in music, in whatever terms, has essentially a semiotic character.[28]

He goes on to say,

> On the other hand, to identify semiotics with any one relational way of
> seeing music goes too far—the fact that something is informative does not
> mean that it is the case.[29]

This is the one of the problems with musical analysis and certainly a difficulty to be overcome in this study. In the pure sciences, a complete consistency benefits the collation of data and is indeed vital to the correct
reading of an analysis; therefore, the same principle has to be applied to
all samples. A comparable "one-relational" way of seeing music would
not benefit this study at all. Rather, the aim will be to draw on a number
of analytical systems using whatever system is considered appropriate to
uncover matters of interest about the music. I will sometimes apply analytical techniques to areas of music where these working methods are not
usually employed. If Stopford's initial comment is upheld in the context
of this study, then the analytical approaches used in this book *are* all ultimately semiotic in nature. Even a rhetorical analysis fits the description.
This observation lends further support to my view, shared by many semi-
oticians, that rhetoric and semiotics are extremely similar.

TEXTUAL REPRESENTATION

One of the present-day writings that has proved most useful for this
study has been Irving Godt's unpublished book "Music about Words."
The reason that this work is so relevant to this study is that its focus is on
the relation between text and music. Godt's observation of the instrumental bias that affects our perspectives of vocal music has been mentioned
earlier (see note 2):

> We live now at the end of an era (beginning around the age of Beethoven) in
> which composers who sought to achieve the sublime did so chiefly in the
> major instrumental genres: the symphony, quartet, sonata. Accordingly, our
> training biases us in favor of abstract, non-verbal, non-interpretive—that is
> instrumental—schemes of analysis. There is nothing inherently wrong with
> those analytical systems, but rather with the way they are applied to vocal
> music. . . . They can serve vocal music usefully only when built upon a foun-
> dation of text studies; that is, as secondary descriptions. No system of analy-

sis can claim to deal comprehensively with vocal music unless it makes text-influence the cornerstone of its description.[30]

Bonds represents the more prevalent view when he comments,

> The demonstrable and important connections between vocal and instrumental forms deserve serious consideration, but the issues of text setting raise a variety of problems that go well beyond the concept of form in its more abstract sense, independent of textual dictates and restraints.[31]

While Godt's work takes in elements of rhetoric, this is not his prime focus: the musical representation of text is. While Godt uses madrigals and indeed madrigalisms as supporting evidence (for the view that text was the starting point and prime focus for vocal works), his study goes far beyond the dimension of mere word painting. It examines the many ways in which a text can have a formative influence in shaping the music.[32] If a composer is composing music for a text, then that text is what he begins with: it is the "starting point," and from this the composer will create the "musical content, surface, and structure."

Feeling that "nonverbal" schemes of analysis are unsatisfactory for vocal music, Godt proposes a system of analysis specific to vocal music—a new system that is a first attempt at a more appropriate approach. Some elements of it will be used to support my study of textual representation of the *Crucifixus*.

Godt categorizes textual influences as shown in figure 3.1.[33] He suggests that a text influences the music largely through its structural or acoustical characteristics and calls these the linguistic influences—these are the properties that a composer has least influence over (that is, is unable to change). The composer has most direct control over the semantic properties: those effects in music that are created via the direct influence of the meaning of the text.

Godt proposes a system of analysis for vocal music that attempts to establish a rational approach to textual influences. There are some fundamental problems with the analysis of textual influences:

1. Inconsistency: This is where the composer does not use the same musical figure or unit for the recurrence of a word; that is, the musical representation of a single word may be different each time it (the word) appears; because of its context within the setting, it may not be possible to present the word in the same way as before. Inconsistency may likewise be demonstrated by pieces from the same composer; again, there is no obligation to use the same device or approach to set a similar or even identical text (for example, there can be great inconsistencies between a single composer's different settings of the Mass).[34]

Figure 3.1. Textual Influences

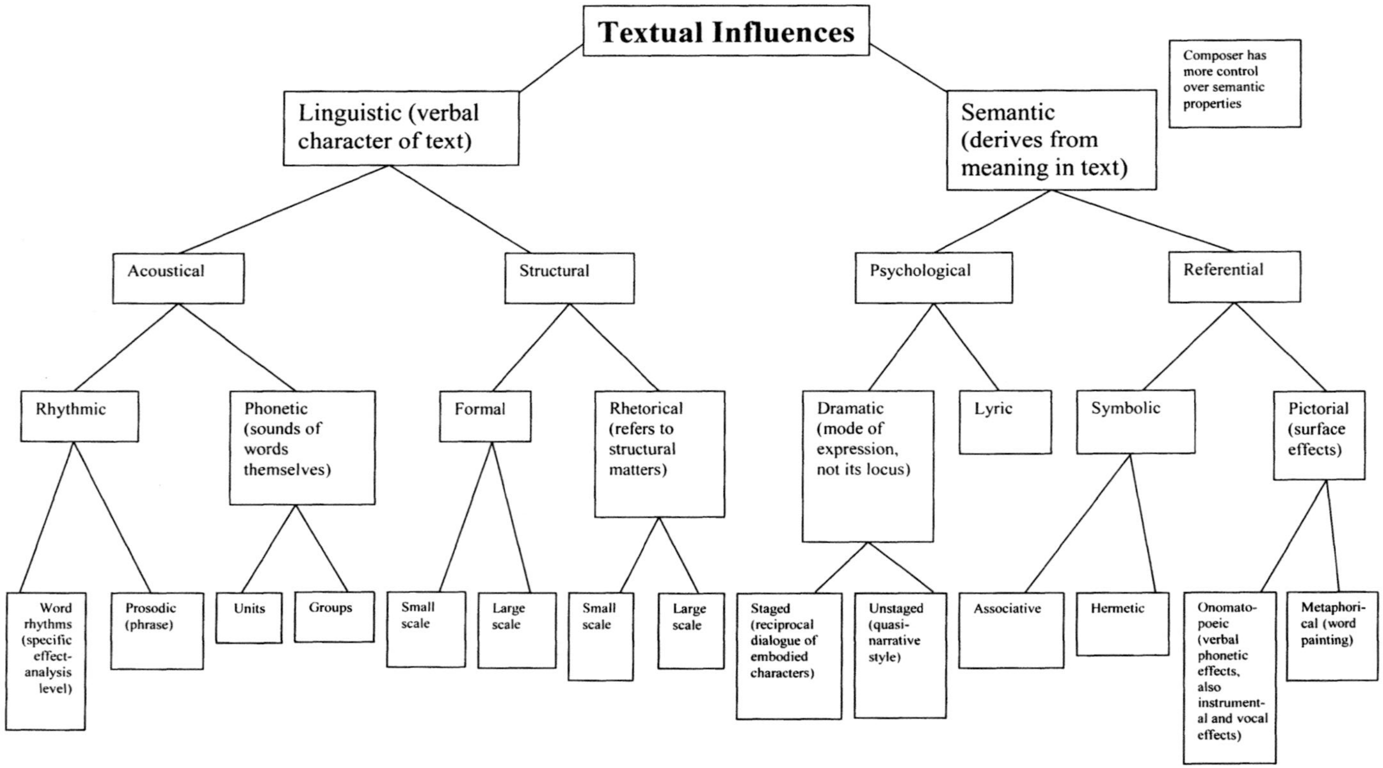

2. Interference: This is where the composer may not necessarily seek to depict the text—he "blocks the semantic response to the text."[35] Godt makes the point that this also occurs where a contrafactum is used (an interesting case in point here is J. S. Bach's setting of the *Crucifixus* in the B Minor Mass, which is a parody of one section of an earlier cantata movement [see chapter 6]); the use of preexisting material imposes severe constraints and so causes "interference" to textual influences. Interference may be caused by the text itself: an inconvenient layout of words—for example, "significant words clump[ed] together"—may inhibit the use of word painting and/or other devices.[36]

3. Musical Law: The rules of composition themselves may not permit textual expression. Some styles may allow more textual expression than others. Godt takes the example of traditional counterpoint:

> When all parts move homorhythmically, at least one voice must normally move in a direction contrary to others, even if that waywardness should seems to contradict the symbolism of the other voices. In such passages, we must weigh the relative prominence of the two directions in order to make a judgement. Further, we may expect that if two or more moving parts coincide on a word, one voice may occupy the symbolic foreground, while the others merely accompany. . . . The presence of a symbolic element in one voice alone may serve to identify it as a leading voice—a useful performance indication.[37]

4. Formality: The structure of a piece can affect the textual expression. The obvious example here is the strophic song, where repeated sections of music set to different words each time may not allow for the expression of the text.

Godt proposes a system of classifying textual influences (see figure 3.2) together with a way of working out word-painting density—expressed as a ratio (the number of incidences of word painting over the number of words in the text) (see figure 3.3) and levels of word painting (Godt lists six levels: see figure 3.4).[38] The aim of working out the ratio of word-painting density is to

> allow us to weigh the significance of semantic influence in a composition and permit us to compare that estimate with other pieces by the composer and with pieces by other composers. They could provide a very coarse numerical scale for analysis.[39]

In the absence of any other proposed model for the analysis of textual influences, elements of Godt's system are certainly very appropriate for this study. Some of the elements bear similarity to other analytical systems or draw on preexisting systems of analysis. There are similarities

Figure 3.2. A Systematic Classification of Semantic Textual Influences

Sound (S)

1. SILENCE (Rests, Interruptio): silence, breathlessness, sighs, breathing, death, cutting, breaking, pause, amazement, absence
2. ONOMATOPOEIC CONVENTIONS: conventional imitations of animal cries, natural sounds, musical instruments; voice timbres (young/old; shrill/sweet; masculine/feminine)
3. RANGE CONVENTIONS: high/low = small/large, activity/response, feminine/masculine, young/old, loud/soft, distant/close, life/death
4. NUMERICAL CONVENTIONS: solo = alone, one, duet = binary concepts, coupling of lovers, few/many = increase/decrease; *tutti* = totality, unanimity, multitude, large ensembles = multitude
5. TEXTURE CONVENTIONS: imitation = following, sequence, directional motion, order; polyphony = congeries (plenitude), disorder, difference, conflict; high/low = feminine, youth, positive/masculine, age, negative; congruence = all (totality), sameness, unity, simplicity, purity, beauty; parallelism = unanimity, "fauxbourdon" = lamentation 1 + 3 (+ 4 etc.) = conflict (but also sameness, unanimity)
6. DYNAMICS: loud vs. soft = large/small, strong/weak, male/female, strength/weakness, authority/subjection, young/old, (or, depending on context, old/young)
7. VOCAL REGISTRATION (Vocal Orchestration): treble/bass = old/young, feminine/masculine, light/dark, height/depth, life/death, heaven/earth

Harmony (H)

1. HARMONIC TENSION: poetic or emotional tension
2. HARMONIC INACTIVITY: poetic or emotional stasis, great size, Earth, affirmation, delay, void, direct address
3. ABRUPT CHANGE: changing context, emphasis, negation
4. FLAT MOVEMENTS: sweetness, softness, lamentation
5. SHARP MOVEMENTS: harshness, bitterness
6. TONAL AMBIGUITY: poetic or emotional instability or uncertainty, chaos, negation
7. MODULATION: change, disorder, uncertainty, negation
8. DISSONANCE: unpleasant, painful or unstable ideas
9. CHROMATICISM: pain, effort, strangeness, grief
10. KEY CONVENTIONS: major/minor = cheerful, sad
11. KEY CONTRAST: difference, distance, displacement
12. CHANGE TO MONOPHONY: dearth, rhetorical emphasis by contrast (*noema*)
13. RETURN TO HARMONY: abundance, congeries, rhetorical emphasis by contrast
14. SUSPENSION: delay, yearning
15. CADENCE: completion, fullness

Melody (M)

1. ALTITUDE CONVENTIONS: high = heaven, lightness, flying, light, greatness, triumph, (activity?), happiness (despair?); low = Earth, grave, rest, darkness, sorrow, defeat
2. DIRECTIONAL CONVENTIONS: upward = height, climbing, flying, resurrection, hope, affirmation, joy, growth, triumph; downward = fall, sadness, despair, negation, death, burial, defeat, diminution

Figure 3.2.   (Continued)

3. MAGNITUDE CONVENTIONS (Interval Size with Image Size): semitones = smallness, gentleness, sympathy, humility, hesitance, timidity, weakness, proximity; large skips = great size, amplitude, distance, effort, power, assurance, boldness
4. MELISMATIC CONVENTIONS: fluid elements (fire, air, water), motion, animate creatures, spatial extension, emphasis
5. CONJUNCT MOTION: tranquil, pleasant, or simple ideas
6. IRREGULAR DISJUNCT MOTION: restlessness, uncertainty, tension
7. CIRCULATIO: round objects, circular motion, perfection
8. TRIADIC MOTION: trumpets, valour, authority, empire, joy
9. SEQUENCE: repetition, *cumulatio, congeries*
10. INVERSION: reversal, antithesis, negation
11. CHROMATICISM: pain, effort, lament, strangeness, mystery
12. UNCONVENTIONAL INTERVALS: effort, error, strangeness
13. MONOTONE: physical or emotional inactivity, Earth, emptiness, permanence, insistence
14. RETURNING PITCH: insistence, persistence, stability, return
15. OSCILLATIONS: trembling, sinuous movement, sensuality
16. REPETITIVE FIGURES: repetitive actions (cradle rocking etc.)
17. NONPICTORIAL MELISMAS: melismatic emphasis

Rhythm (R)

1. TEMPO CONVENTIONS: speed = brevity, impermanence, haste, fear, flight, merriment, lightness, light, vitality; slowness = slow, delay, rest, permanence, tranquillity, weight, heaviness of spirit, darkness, death
2. DURATIONAL CONVENTIONS: short notes = smallness, rapidity, brevity, jollity, fear, light, lightness; long notes = massiveness, slowness, tranquillity, weight, heaviness of spirit, darkness
3. RESTS: see Sound (1)
4. REGULARITY: continuity, movement toward or away, flow, flying, tranquillity, affirmation
5. IRREGULARITY: restlessness, jollity, intermittence, interruption, gesture (?), negation, uncertainty, confusion
6. REPETITION: *repetitio, cumulatio* (small dimension), nonpictorial emphasis or intensification, affirmation
7. TRIPLE METER CONTRAST: dance, cheerfulness, joy, eroticism
8. METER CHANGE: change of topic or mood, new emphasis, fickleness, uncertainty
9. RHYTHMIC CONFLICTS: poetic conflict, or opposition, confusion
10. RHYTHMIC DENSENESS: confusion, conflict, enthusiasm
11. LONG-SHORT FIGURES: slow = stretching, leaning, yearning; fast = hopping, leaping, jollity
12. REVERSE DOTTING: negation, hopping, leaping, limping, awkwardness, shaking, wilfulness
13. DOT LENGTHENING: stretch, flow, delay, yearning

Growth (G)

1. RETURN OR REPETITION: return, repetition, affirmation, increase (also: text repetition)

Figure 3.2.   (Continued)

2. CONTRAST: contrast, conflict, antithesis, denial
3. VARIATION TECHNIQUE: sameness or change (variability)
4. ADDITIVE STRUCTURES: enlargement, increase, *cumulatio*
5. OSTINATO: permanence, repetition, law, eternity, but also restlessness, tragedy

Indirect Applications (IA)
1. PREEXISTENT MUSICAL EMBLEMS (such as the *crux*; ostinato and descending fourth = lament, etc.)
2. THEMATIC ASSOCIATIONS (Similar to *Leitmotiv*): symbolic or dramatic identifications, for example, *Dies Irae* with death; also fanfares, national tunes and commercial jingles
3. HEXACHORD CONVENTIONS: traditional associations with hardness and softness (ideas, emotions, objects)
4. NUMBER SYMBOLISM: number of voices, entries, motives, etc., may have conventional associations (for example, triple time may symbolize the Trinity or perfection)
5. SOGGETTO CAVATO DALLE VOCALI
6. AUGENMUSIK
7. COMPOSER-DEFINED MEANINGS: Don't we wish that Beethoven hadn't made that remark about Fate knocking at the door!

Figure 3.3.   Densities of Word Painting

$$\text{Textual Density} = \frac{\text{Word Painting (in lines, words, or syllables)}}{\text{Total (lines, words, or syllables)}}$$

Where: the total number of madrigalisms in a piece is represented by word painting. Textual Density is therefore the "ratio between the observed instances of word painting measured in words, or syllables and the total number of words or syllables in a text."

$$\text{Durational Density} = \frac{\text{Word Painting (in beats or tactus)}}{\text{Duration of a piece (in beats or tactus)}}$$

The durational density of a piece is important as one long word-painting effect in a short piece will affect the "character of a work as a whole more decisively than a few passing incidents in a very long composition"—for example, a long melismatic effect will affect the length of the piece.

$$\text{Image Density} = \frac{\text{Word Painting (number of instances)}}{\text{Total number of opportunities}}$$

This is because the text may only have an optimum possible number of word-painting opportunities—effectively this ratio expresses what the instances of word painting are compared with the actual number of opportunities available.

Figure 3.4.   Levels of Word Painting

LEVEL 1: MOMENTARY INCIDENTS USUALLY ONLY LASTING A BEAT OR TWO

"Melody, harmony or rhythm (or some combination of them) will normally express a single word or idea which coincides with them or lies sufficiently close to them to leave no reasonable doubt about the composer's intentions" (for example, an isolated high note to express the concept of "sky" or "heaven").

LEVEL 2: MOMENTARY INCIDENTS POLYPHONICALLY OR LINEARLY EXTENDED

"Devices barely larger than and not necessarily different from those of the first level prolong their influence through contrapuntal elaboration, repetition, or durational exaggeration."

LEVEL 3: EXTENDED INCIDENTS

"Devices of this order, by their nature, take more time for completion" (such as an ascending scalic figure to express, for example, the word "ascendit" will naturally be a more drawn-out textual expression).

LEVEL 4: COMPOUND EFFECTS

"Applications which may be longer than those of level 3, and which usually involve all the sounding parts, and often through more than a single element (S, H, M, R, G [see Figure 2.2])." Godt cites the following example: "The conclusion of the *Absalon, fili mi* attributed to Josquin, with its text, *sed descendam in infernum plorans* (but go down into Hell, weeping), involves medium-range downward triadic figures that fall with the text. . . . It makes a wholesale slide into the musica ficta inferno of G-flat, combining expressively falling melodic figures with falling harmonies."

LEVEL 5: GROSS EFFECTS

"The overall disposition of musical materials so as to imbue a whole piece (or section of a piece) with a text-associated meaning. The texts of such applications may be fairly brief, but operative passages may dominate the total text. Most of the examples that spring to mind at this level come from Baroque music. . . . Many of the practices covered by the modern German term *Affektenlehre*—which applies specifically to Baroque style—fall into this category."

LEVEL 6: SURFACE EFFECTS

"The control of musical materials in the largest dimension to create a textually appropriate atmosphere, expressive in general rather than in detail. A composer may create an appropriate musical surface either with or without the locally descriptive details of lower levels. At this highest level, the setting responds—in a way familiar from Romantic music—to the text as a whole rather than to its parts. Our response to a vocal work usually depends first upon our perception of this level. . . . Control at Level 6 represents the most natural approach to strophic composition. When setting a strophic text with excessive contrasts, a composer usually avoided conflicts by adopting a somewhat neutral style that devoted more attention to fundamental musical values: attractiveness of melody, harmony and rhythm. This invites performers to act out what music fails to express."

with semiosis, for example, and these links have already been hinted at in the first part of this chapter.

Some of the semantic textual influences described in figure 3.2 are obviously akin to a number of rhetorical figures described in eighteenth-century treatises. For example, directional conventions are analogous with *catabasis* (downward directional convention) and *anabasis* (upward directional convention). The meaning of *catabasis* is summarized thus:

> The *catabasis* is used to depict musically either a descending or lowly image supplied by the text, thereby creating the implied affection.[40]

> *Catabasis sive descensus periodus harmonica est, qua oppositos priori affectus pronounciamus servitutis, humilitatis, depressionis affectibus, atque infirmis rebus exprimendes, ut illud Massaini: Ego autem humilitatis sum nimis, & illud Massentii: descenderunt in infernum viventes.*

> [The *catabasis* or *descensus* is a musical passage through which we express affections opposite to those of the *anabasis*, such as servitude or humility, as well as lowly and base affections, as in: "I am, however, greatly humbled" (Massainus), or in "The living have descended into hell"(Massentius).[41]]

The emphasis on the role of rhetoric in instrumental music has already been discussed. One musicologist who has examined the role of textual representation and also rhetorical figures in text is Frits Noske, who has explored Latin dialogues in the seventeenth century.[42] Noske recognizes that rhetorical figures were used to support the representation of the text:

> Dialogues abound with rhetorical figures, illustrating the words and their emotional background. Among the most frequently applied are the *climax* or *auxesis* (the repetition of a melodic entity a second or third higher), the *exclamatio* (the upward leap of a minor sixth), the *pathopoeia* (a chromatic passage), the *saltus duriusculus* (a dissonant leap, often clashing with harmony), various types of *hypotyposis* (word painting), the *faux-bourdon* (homophonically descending sixth chords denoting sadness), and the *aposiopesis* (a general pause, mostly connected with death or eternity). The use of these figures reminds us of the dialogue's true character, which is that of a rhetorical, rather than a lyrical, composition. It is also for this reason that for a long time its melodic style resisted the growing tendency, apparent in other genres, to employ mechanical rhythms. When, eventually, rhetoric became subordinated to abstract melodic patterns, the dialogue faded from the musical scene.[43]

While an "immanent" critique (in Kantian terms, a critique conducted within a system recognized by the creator of the object studied) is always valuable, it is vital that it should maintain its integrity. There is always a lurking danger of incoherence and confusion wherever old (in many versions), semimodernized, and modern concepts and terms are allowed to mingle promiscuously without careful distinction.[44] Far clearer is Godt's approach, which, while it generally runs parallel with the older, rhetorical theory and shows awareness of it, uses its own terminology for its own ends, thus offering a "transcendent" critique (that is, one conducted within a system not recognized by the creator of the object studied).

NOTES

1. John Stopford, "Structuralism, Semiotics and Musicology," *Journal of the British Society of Aesthetics* 24, no. 1 (1983): 133–34.

2. Irving Godt, "Music about Words: Madrigalisms and Other Text Influences in Music" (unpublished manuscript, 1990), 19. See quote associated with note 30.

3. Jonathan Dunsby and Arnold Whittall, *Music Analysis in Theory and Practice* (London: Faber, 1988), 211.

4. Umberto Eco, *A Theory of Semiotics* (Bloomington: Indiana University Press, 1976), 4.

5. Robert Samuels, *Mahler's Sixth Symphony: A Study in Musical Semiotics* (Cambridge: Cambridge University Press, 1995), 3.

6. Samuels, *Mahler's Sixth Symphony*, 5.

7. "*Rhetoric*: the revival in studies of rhetoric is currently converging on the study of mass communication (and therefore communication with the intention of persuasion). A rereading of traditional studies in the light of semiotics produces a great many new suggestions. From Aristotle to Quintilian, through medieval and renaissance theoreticians up to Perelman, rhetoric appears as a second chapter in the general study of semiotics (following linguistics) elaborated centuries ago, and now providing tools for a discipline which encompasses it. Therefore a bibliography of the semiotic aspects of rhetoric seems identical with a bibliography of rhetoric." Eco, *A Theory of Semiotics*, 13–14.

8. V. Kofi Agawu, *Playing with Signs: A Semiotic Interpretation of Classical Music* (Princeton, N.J.: Princeton University Press, 1991), 11.

9. Raymond Monelle, *Linguistics and Semiotics in Music* (Chur, Switzerland: Harwood Academic Press, 1992), 5.

10. "Eco's *Theory of Semiotics* (1977) is one of the most sustaining expositions of a general theory of signs. Central to his thought is the concept of 'code.' In earlier theory, the code is the body of knowledge that a receiver of a semiotic message must possess in order to be a competent user of the system." Samuels, *Mahler's Sixth Symphony*, 6.

11. Stopford, "Structuralism, Semiotics and Musicology," 132–33. Samuels also comments on this: "A semiotic analysis is interested in the signifying potential of the text, which does of course change in the course of its reception history." *Mahler's Sixth Symphony*, 6.

12. Eero Tarasti, *A Theory of Musical Semiotics* (Bloomington: Indiana University Press, 1994), 26.

13. Tarasti, *A Theory of Musical Semiotics*, 72.

14. Descartes, *Passions de l'âme*, in *The Philosophical Works*, II. lxix. 362.

15. Agawu refers to "structural rhythm" as a "discourse . . . moving in and out of topics" and in a footnote states that "something of that larger rhythmic motion may be traced back to seventeenth and eighteenth century discussions of the affections and passions." Agawu refers specifically to Marmontel in this case. Agawu, *Playing with Signs*, 39.

16. Agawu, *Playing with Signs*, 39. The quotation from Nattiez is taken from "The Contribution of Musical Semiotics to the Semiotic Discussion in General," in *A Perfusion of Signs*, ed. Thomas A. Sebeok (Bloomington: Indiana University Press, 1977), 124.

17. Tarasti, *A Theory of Musical Semiotics*, 27.

18. "In order to hear Classic Music in a rewarding way, then, one needs to apprehend the continuing dialectic between a referential surface loaded with signification and the inevitable contrapuntal background without which that surface cannot exist." Agawu, *Playing with Signs*, 79.

19. Tarasti, *A Theory of Musical Semiotics*, 24.

20. Tarasti, *A Theory of Musical Semiotics*, 79, 100. Algirdas Julien Greimas was a semiotician who was concerned primarily with "structural semantics."

21. Agawu, *Playing with Signs*, 51–53. Agawu also assimilates Mattheson's references to rhetorical organization to Schenker's theories: "It is Mattheson's belief that rhetorical strength of a composer's musical ideas be given in a particular order, the strongest arguments at the beginning, the weaker ones in the middle, and stronger ones at the end. What is of interest here is not merely the rhetorical ploy, but the implicit recognition of a whole structure shaped by three constituent parts. . . . The same concern for the piece of music as a dynamic tonality is at the heart of Schenker's theory—but where Mattheson offers only a schematic outline, Schenker details the actual musical elements that are embodied in that outline. There is, to be sure, no explicit concern with beginning–middle–end paradigm in Schenkerian theory (some intriguing remarks about endings in *Der freie Satz* notwithstanding [Heinrich Schenker, *Free Composition* (New York: Schirmer, 1979), 129]) but various voice leading procedures strongly suggest such an orientation."

22. Tarasti, *A Theory of Musical Semiotics*, 24.

23. Richard Littlefield and David Neumeyer, "Rewriting Schenker: Narrative–History–Ideology," *Music Theory Spectrum* 14, no. 1 (1992): 65.

24. Charles Rosen, *The Classical Style* (London: Faber, 1972), 26.

25. Rosen, *The Classical Style*, 33.

26. Heinrich Schenker, *Five Graphic Music Analyses* (New York: Dover Publications, 1969), 31–37.

27. Bruce C. MacIntyre, *The Viennese Concerted Mass of the Early Classic Period* (Ann Arbor, Mich.: UMI Research Press, 1986), 319.

28. Stopford, "Structuralism, Semiotics and Musicology," 133–34.

29. Stopford, "Structuralism, Semiotics and Musicology," 134.

30. Godt, "Music about Words," 19.

31. Mark Evan Bonds, *Wordless Rhetoric: Musical Form and the Metaphor of the Oration* (Cambridge, Mass.: Harvard University Press, 1991), 10.

32. "Where music is wedded to words an awareness of text influences is vital to the fullest understanding of that marriage." Godt, "Music about Words," 16.

33. Figure 3.1 is taken from Irving Godt, "A Clean Canvas for Word Painting," in *Yearbook of Interdisciplinary Studies in the Fine Arts*, vol. 1, ed. Matthew Cannon Brennan (Lewiston, N.Y.: Edwin Mellen Press, 1989), 113, and "An Essay on Word Painting," *College Music Symposium* 24, no. 2 (1984): 120.

34. A detailed discussion of these points occurs in Godt, "Music about Words," chapter 14.

35. Godt, "Music about Words," 323.

36. Godt, "Music about Words," 325.

37. Godt, "Music about Words," 328.

38. Figure 3.2 is from Godt, "Music about Words," 514. The Sound, Harmony, Melody, Rhythm, and Growth outline of this figure is based on Jan LaRue's *Guidelines for Style Analysis* (New York: W. W. Norton, 1970). Figure 3.3 is work in progress and appears in Godt, "Music about Words," 520–22. Figure 3.4 appears in Irving Godt, *Guillaume Costeley (1531–1606): Life and Works* (New York: New York University Press, 1969), 172–85.

39. Godt, "Music about Words," 523.

40. Dietrich Bartel, *Musica Poetica: Musical-Rhetorical Figures in German Baroque Music* (Lincoln: University of Nebraska Press, 1997), 214.

41. This citation is taken from Kircher, *Musurgia Universalis sive ars magna consoni e dissoni* (Rome, 1650); the Latin is taken from Dietrich Bartel, *Handbuch der musikalischen Figurenlehre* (Laaber: Laaber-Verlag, 1985), 112, and the translation from Bartel, *Musica Poetica*, 215. The original is taken from *Musurgia* L, VIII, 145. Massainus and Massentius are in fact the same composer: Tiburzio Massaino (ca. 1550–ca. 1608).

42. Noske describes Latin musical dialogue as "sung conversation on a sacred subject involving two or more characters, each of whom is represented by a single voice." *Saints and Sinners: The Latin Musical Dialogue in the Seventeenth Century* (Oxford: Clarendon Press, 1992), 3.

43. Noske, *Saints and Sinners*, 22–23.

44. See chapter 2, notes 31 and 32.

Part III

ANALYSIS

4

A Musical Overview

The aim here is to provide a framework for the following chapters by offering a general overview of the *Crucifixus* settings that have been examined. The succeeding chapters will be more specific, dealing with case studies and presenting analyses in greater detail.

THE TEXT: "CRUCIFIXUS"

The opening word of this short section of the *Credo* translates as "He was crucified." It is a compound word with several implications in a musical and symbolic context. First, it refers to the cross itself. The cross is recognized as a distinct shape, this shape being the accepted symbol for the Christian faith. This concept of shape can be expressed musically as a zig-zag arrangement of notes. Irving Godt lists a number of commonly recognised cross arrangements in music (see figure 4.1) and refers to two examples of music that explicitly use the musical sign of the cross: Lud-

Figure 4.1.   Commonly Recognized "Cross" Arrangements in Music

wig Senfl's *Missa super signum crucis* and the tenth of Biber's *Mystery So-natas* for violin and continuo, where a musical sign of the cross is even included as part of the title page.[1] Of course, the organization of music into a zigzag shape would be something slightly more subtle: it would take a trained ear, a knowledge of musical notation, and a sense for "wordplay" to "hear" the zigzag arrangement and then interpret it. This type of visual (rather than aural) reference is known as *Augenmusik*, literally "eye-music." Fortuitously, the polysyllabic structure of the word "Crucifixus" enabled it to employ four notes placed like the points of a cross. A more obvious example of *Augenmusik* in the same context is the inclusion of sharps in the musical line. In manuscripts and prints of the time, a sharp usually has a much more clearly "crosslike" form than in modern notation, where it is more elongated.

A further feature of the word "Crucifixus" is its direct reference to pain and suffering, which offers great potential to the composer. Again, the fact that this is a polysyllabic word gives added opportunity for extreme expression of its sense via chromaticism and altered intervals. This "cruel and unusual" punishment can be expressed by anguished, excruciating intervals or by semitonal movement (as will be shown later). The intervals that best convey pain are those that "grate" on the ear; these are listed in table 4.1. As a result, the music will be harmonically tense but will not necessarily be chromatic; for example, the interval between F and B, while certainly a tritone, is not chromatic within C major and A minor. The sound of the word "Crucifixus" itself affects the musical delivery. It is a high-energy word, the opening "Cr" itself seeming expressive of pain and calling for a strong attack. The word gives scope for the creation of a four-note motive that can be treated repetitively in imitation. Figure 4.2 quotes a passage of music containing several of these features. The setting by G. A. Perti (1661–1756) comes from his *Messa Canone a 3* (87). In this excerpt, the musical sign of the cross is evident: a'-g♯'-c''-b'. Within the motive there appears a "tortured" interval (the diminished fourth g♯-c), which creates a jagged vocal line. The motive is imitated by each voice in turn. The opening motive also introduces a sharp (again symbolizing the cross). Another interesting point is that there is a zigzag forma-

Table 4.1.   Intervals Suitable for the Expression of Pain

Interval	Inversion
diminished third	augmented sixth
diminished fourth	augmented fifth
diminished fifth	augmented fourth
diminished seventh	augmented second

Figure 4.2. "Crucifixus"

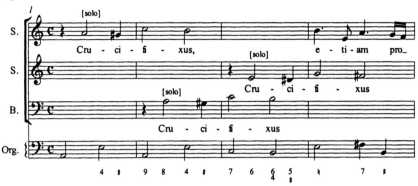

G. A. Perti (87): Messa Canone a 3 (ca. 1700–1720)

tion for the vocal entries (S1, B, S2); this, too, may possibly allude to the cross.

THE TEXT: "ETIAM PRO NOBIS" AND "SUB PONTIO PILATO"

The following sections of text, "etiam pro nobis" and "sub Pontio Pilato," form a narrative, their main purpose being to divulge information. "Etiam pro nobis" translates as "also for us," while "sub Pontio Pilato" means "under Pontius Pilate." Both are neutral phrases, holding no great emotive significance in this section of the Liturgy when placed in relation to more intense phrases such as "Crucifixus" and "passus." The doctrinal importance of these phrases for the *Credo* has been discussed in chapter 1. However, their neutral character meant that these phrases did not receive any overtly "special" treatment when composers set the *Crucifixus*. Nor did they offer any obvious potential for musical pictorialism.

The two phrases offer a direct contrast to the word "Crucifixus," with its direct reference to pain and suffering. They provide relief after the "agony" of crucifixion by their matter-of-factness. In order to express the reversion to a more normal state they may, for example, be kept diatonic in contrast to the chromaticism of the opening subject. Paradoxically, they become expressive by abandoning expression. A common way of highlighting the difference between the two emotional states is to set a chromatic subject ("Crucifixus") against a diatonic countersubject ("etiam pro nobis"). The settings can also mirror the natural rhythm of the words in the music, suggesting objectivity by their conformity to the rhythms of

ordinary speech. The phrases are frequently set to dactylic rhythmic patterns that reflect speech almost naturalistically. Both phrases carry
unstressed vowels, which are easily accommodated within dactylic patterns. Examples of dactylic rhythms that might be expected to occur in
the settings of these phrases (on the words "etiam" and "Pontio") are
shown in figure 4.3.

Another way of imitating speech in music is to set the words virtually
as a monotone. Syllabic delivery on a monotone is a traditional musical
"mode of narration" (as when the text of letters is read out in baroque
operas). An example of the device is shown in figure 4.4, where Zelenka
uses speechlike rhythm (the dactylic rhythm discussed previously) to
set this section of text. The accompanying harmony here uses diminished sevenths and suspensions to represent the underlying agony of
crucifixion.

Figure 4.3.   Dactylic Rhythmic Patterns

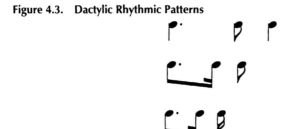

Figure 4.4.   "etiam pro nobis," "sub Pontio Pilato"

J. D. Zelenka (98): Missa Circumcisionis (1724)

THE TEXT: "PASSUS ET SEPULTUS EST"

"Passus" means "he suffered." The word makes a contrast with the immediately preceding section of text, although it recaptures the sense and mood of the first word ("Crucifixus"), of which it is a near synonym. The word contains two long syllables, which, fortuitously, lend themselves well to the idea of prolongation. As was pointed out, suffering is a prolonged process, to be endured over a period of time. When Jesus was nailed to the cross, his was certainly a long-drawn-out period of suffering, and it is this dimension, rather than simple pain as such, that composers seek to illustrate. In other words, the connotations of "passus" that are not shared by "Crucifixus" take priority. The two most obvious means of musical prolongation are melisma and syncopation, in addition to the use of longer note values relative to the ones that have appeared previously, whether directly before (in "sub Pontio Pilato" and "etiam pro nobis") or at the start. Suffering is brought about by pain; therefore, to make the underlying harmony expressive of pain by employing dissonance and chromaticism remains desirable. Figure 4.5, taken from Draghi's *Missa a 9*, illustrates this move to relatively long note values. Syncopation occurs in the second soprano line, creating the impression of added prolongation, while the tenor has one long-drawn-out statement of "passus," set melismatically.[2]

"Et sepultus est" ("he was buried") is a low-energy phrase. The most obvious word-painting device that it suggests is a descending line to depict the lowering of the body into the grave. The "u" of "sepultus" is a highly appropriate sound, almost sepulchral and therefore extremely effective in low tessituras. "He was buried" implies a gradual, reverent

Figure 4.5. "passus"

A. Draghi (19): Missa a 9 (1684)

lowering of the body into the ground. One might accordingly expect solemn, slow, regular downward movement, preferably stepwise. Figure 4.6 shows Haydn's adherence to this line of thought. The vocal lines descend to convey the act of burial, sopranos and tenors forced down to the lowest extremes of their range. The instrumental lines also descend, most notably in the postlude. Note here the timpani accompaniment, which contributes to the sombre, ceremonial atmosphere of the setting.[3]

VOCAL SCORING OF THE TEXT

Since about 1600, composers have enjoyed a choice when writing vocal music: whether to set for one voice or for several. Where a genuine choice exists (that is, where it is not determined in advance by custom or available resources), the decision depends on who is being identified "poetically." In our case, the *Crucifixus* is a doctrinal statement: an account that is not very appropriate for solo setting. This portion of text contains the phrase "etiam pro nobis" (also for us), which refers explicitly to the collective of the Christian community. Therefore, the natural expectation of a *Crucifixus* setting is that the composer will use the choir throughout as a surrogate for the collective. When speaking of a "choir," I mean a polyphonic ensemble—not necessarily one with more than one singer per part. A solo setting of a section of the Mass equates with an individual utterance styled as a prayer. This is conventionally the case (after ca. 1700) in settings of the *Christe eleison*, although part of the reason for the preference here for a solo setting must be purely musical: the desire to offer contrast to the framing *Kyrie eleison*. Solo settings of the *Crucifixus* do nevertheless very occasionally occur; see chapter 13, which discusses a solo setting by Cimarosa, a rare example of its type.

LAYOUT AND ORGANIZATION OF THE TEXT

The layout of any text naturally has structural implications for a musical setting. In the case of texted music, it must be remembered that music has traditionally taken its lead from the words, even though purely musical structural criteria are liable to be superimposed, once the demands of the words have been met. In the case of the *Crucifixus*, there are three key phrases: "Crucifixus"; "passus"; "et sepultus est." There are also two connecting phrases: "etiam pro nobis" and "sub Pontio Pilato." Here, the "key phrases" are so termed because they play a crucial part in expressing events. They can be regarded as the "action" of the text. The very fact that there is a contrast between "active" and "neutral" phrases sets up an

Figure 4.6. "et sepultus est"

F. J. Haydn (42): Theresienmesse (1799)

equilibrium that can be very useful for the composer. This "equilibrium" gives him a textual justification for musical contrasts (between the "expressive" and "neutral," for instance) that he would have wished to introduce at all events.

The danger with key phrases is that they very often become oversaturated with meaning. If there are too many (so-called) key phrases, the music easily becomes incoherent or monotonous: there is an insufficient sense of stability. Neutral words, with no pressure on the composer to depict musically what is occurring, therefore perform a vital function. Key phrases in fact acquire significance and depth when set against a neutral background, whether this is achieved "horizontally" through the succession of contrasted sections or "vertically" though contrapuntal combination (as when a chromatic "Crucifixus" subject is set against a diatonic, neutral "etiam pro nobis" subject).

With the risk of saturation so evident, a composer is justified if he rations pictorialism in the music he composes. The rationing will depend on a number of factors, such as the intended length of the movement. If a composer is limited by the number of bars at his disposal, he will recognize a practical limit to the number of pictorial events that can be included without weakening the musical solidity of the piece. To adduce a culinary metaphor, the smaller the fruitcake, the fewer the cherries. This factor is what Irving Godt terms the "density of word painting" (see figure 3.3).

CONTEXT OF THE CRUCIFIXUS

The position of the *Crucifixus* within the *Credo* has already been discussed briefly in chapter 1. It was mentioned that the most common division of the *Credo* text for musical purposes between 1680 and 1800 places the *Et incarnatus* and *Crucifixus* in a separate musical section. However, this was not a compulsory division, and there are many instances where the *Crucifixus* can stand alone as a self-contained movement. One familiar example is J. S. Bach's setting of the *Crucifixus* (see chapter 6). The type of Mass under consideration (for example, *Missa brevis*) will affect the degree of compression of the movements.[4] This will in turn determine whether the *Crucifixus* is a brief incident or whether it is a truly separate movement. If it is indeed a separate movement or definable section, what are the signs of its demarcation? For example, as early as Palestrina, the *Crucifixus*, while not a separate movement, is nevertheless distinct from its surroundings. How does Palestrina achieve this? Can the roots of this "singling out" be traced back further than this period? And a further point: if the *Crucifixus* is regarded as a separate movement rather then a section or episode, what exactly do we mean by this in view of the fact that the term "movement" has existed only in its modern sense since about 1800? If a *Credo* is subdivided, should we think of it in terms of a single composite movement or of a cycle of movements?

The *Crucifixus* is framed on either side by the *Et incarnatus* and the *Et resurrexit* (table 4.2).[5] In musical terms, the *Et incarnatus* will, by the beginning of the eighteenth century, attempt to convey the mystery of the spirit becoming flesh by shifting tonal center frequently. This section tends also to be tonally open; the ambiguity again acts as an expression of the mystery. The *Et resurrexit* is the perfect negation of the *Crucifixus*, demanding an energetic, joyful setting. Usually it will be set in the major mode, whereas the obvious choice for the *Crucifixus* is the minor mode.

TRADITION ACCORDING TO LOCATION

The present survey considers a range of settings of the *Crucifixus* from Italy, Austria, and southern Germany. When collating the analytical data and examining it in a search for patterns, I needed to assess how relevant geographical location was. Was there any good reason to differentiate between the Italian and southern German traditions? The danger with regionalization in a study of this kind is that it can so easily create an artificial and inexact picture. As explained in the preface, a practical limit to the collection of *Crucifixus* settings for analysis had to be drawn. If the geographical aspect were to be examined, it might mean that one region, city, or musical establishment would be represented by just one *Crucifixus* setting. It would obviously be wrong to attempt to make a judgment or generalization about one area on the basis of just one work. In addition, the background research for this study established that there was a healthy interchange of Italian and German musicians and composers in

Table 4.2. *Et incarnatus*, *Crucifixus*, and *Et resurrexit*: Texts and Translations

Latin	Translation
Et incarnatus est de Spiritu Sancto ex Maria Virginie; et homo factus est.	And he was made incarnate by the Holy Ghost of the Virgin Mary; and was made man.
Crucifixus etiam pro nobis sub Pontio Pilato, passus et sepultus est.	He was crucified also for us under Pontius Pilate, suffered and was buried.
Et resurrexit tertia die, secundum Scripturas. Et ascendit in coelum, sedet ad dexteram Dei Patris.	And on the third day he rose again, according to the Scriptures. And ascended into heaven, and sitteth at the right hand of God the Father.

the courts and musical establishments in these areas. As the musical style
of most composers tended to be influenced by what they were exposed to
musically, it is possible to conclude that the musical style was pretty
much an "international" one—at least in the matter under consideration.[6]
In Vienna, for example, during the baroque there was a tendency to
employ Italian composers and musicians, together with a great interest in
Italian music. Monteverdi's operas were performed there. Orazio Benevoli (1605–1672) served at the court of Archduke Leopold Wilhelm
between 1643 and 1645 before moving on to the Vatican (1645–1672) to
become *maestro di cappella*. Antonio Draghi was in service at the Viennese
court from 1658. Caldara was another Italian who worked in Vienna.
Meanwhile, in Dresden, Lotti (1667–1740), Ristori (1692–1753), and also
Zelenka (1679–1745) were employed in important roles. The following
quotation gives an idea of the role of the Church in Dresden and the musical styles and influences from different musical centers in Europe that
were prevalent in the high baroque:

> From at least 1730 music in the church culminated in the annual perform-
> ance of an Easter Oratorio, but was rather less in the public eye, as Saxony,
> the home of the Reformation only tolerated its princes' conversion [Friedrich
> August I converted to Catholicism in order to strengthen his claim to the Pol-
> ish throne] and failed to grant the Catholic Church any significant status.
> Moreover, the electors, doubtless in imitation of the papal chapel, strove to
> give their church music an air of mystery and exclusiveness; the copying and
> circulation of Zelenka's sacred works was forbidden. . . . Dresden followed
> Venice and Rome in opera and looked to Vienna for church music (Electress
> Maria Josepha was Austrian by birth and Zelenka had links with the Vienna
> school of composers centred on Fux and Reutter).[7]

The movement between Italy and Germany was by no means a one-way
traffic. Hasse was employed at the *Ospedale degli Incurabili* in Venice and
also studied with Porpora and Scarlatti in Naples. Handel visited both
Venice and Rome. His opera *Aggripina* was written for Venice (1709). Figure 4.7 attempts to illustrate how the musical education of composers of
this time was inextricably linked.

THE DEVELOPMENT OF CHURCH MUSIC

The liturgical changes introduced by the Reformation and subsequent
Counter-Reformation had an impact on the musical settings of the Mass
in a variety of ways. The Counter-Reformation and the forum for its
implementation, the Council of Trent, introduced many new changes to
the Mass, many inspired (albeit tacitly) by the Reformation itself. The

Figure 4.7. Examples of Composer-Pupil Relationships

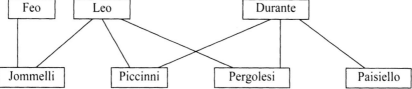

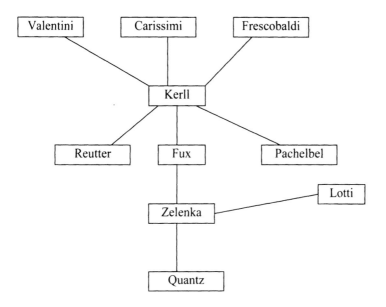

Church had to rethink the expression of its fundamental beliefs. Many medieval features and techniques, such as tropes, were banished: the purpose was to make the texts more transparent to the congregation (an echo of the Reformation). The unification of the liturgy throughout the Church resulted in the loss of many distinctive regional features. The style of music written for Masses henceforth had to embody the qualities of "purity" and restraint. Palestrina's contrapuntal style and clear gestures toward syllabic word setting came to represent, for subsequent generations of composers, the ideal for Catholic Church music:

> Composers of liturgical music in the first decades of the seventeenth century had two methods of composition: the *stile antico* and the *stile moderno*. The *stile antico* resulted from the attempts of conservative Roman composers to

maintain the tradition of Palestrina (already revered as the supreme master of Catholic church music) on the grounds that it was the most suitable for worship.[8]

This association of the *stile antico* with sacred music is one that persisted until well into the classical era and beyond, sustained by a perception of what Church music—or, at least, *some* Church music—should be like.[9]

Rosen comments on the fact that even so late a composer as Mozart was able to compose movements in a genuine *stile antico* language:

> Mozart's mastery of the older style is unquestionable. It would take a sharp ear and a considerable amount of hindsight to distinguish stylistically between the great double fugue in the Requiem and one of Handel's, and if the chromaticism is not Handelian, it was not beyond the reach of Bach.[10]

Naturally, musical developments in secular music affected the domain of Church music, although such influences were usually slow to make themselves felt. This "delay" was again due to the constraints placed on the composition of sacred music by the Church and by adherents of conservative taste. By the late baroque, the Catholic Church felt more secure; as a consequence, secular influences began gradually to permeate sacred compositions of the whole period. Here we see a trend toward the universality of language that characterizes the musical thought of the period. It we examine settings of the *Crucifixus* composed between 1680 and 1750, we note a growing fondness for *Affekt* in music. The use of rhetorical devices to support the expression of the text increases. In addition, elements of the more "modern" orchestration and musical structure were absorbed into the genre. Opera was equally a formative influence on Church music, although the inclusion of operatic features was usually approached in a cautious manner by composers since opera was commonly frowned on by the Church authorities. The Classical influence itself is fully established only toward the end of the period 1680–1800, although the style had more or less consolidated itself in all other genres by about 1770.

Harmonic factors also played a role in the development of Church music. For example, while the tritone played a small role in the harmonic language of the Renaissance, by the mid-baroque it became strongly exploited as both a harmonic and a melodic device. In addition, a wide palette of augmented and diminished intervals became available for the production of special effects. In general, composers of the baroque were far more adventurous with their harmonic language and were more prepared to use chromaticism, venturing into the extreme region.[11] This new-found resource offered wonderful opportunities for word painting.

The sense of a beginning, middle, and end is already conveyed by the text of the *Crucifixus* in its account of a series of events. It is the three key phrases within this section of text that present the sequence of events. When setting this text to music, a composer was confronted by a dilemma. How could the sequentiality be preserved despite the combinatorial polyphonic practices of the time? Portions of text can obviously be superimposed when a setting is written for several voices. So composers had to decide whether to allow the logical sequence of the text rigorously to dominate the structure of the *Crucifixus* setting or to concede some deviation from strict sequentiality in the interest of musical development and expression.

If the length of the setting permitted, there might be scope for repeating the text in its entirety. If the composer went a second time through the text, what would happen? Would he bring back all the original motives? How mandatory was the fixed correspondence of a word to a given musical phrase? With respect to the three key phrases, how were the links between them to be established? Were there to be clean breaks or dovetailed overlaps? The following chapters attempt to answer some of these questions.

NOTES

1. Irving Godt, "Italian Figurenlehre?" Music and Rhetoric in a New York Source," in *Studies in the History of Music*, vol. 1, ed. Ronald Broude and Ellen Beebe (New York: Broude Brothers, 1983), 186. Figure 4.1 is reproduced by arrangement with Broude Brothers Limited.

2. Why syncopation should convey a sense of prolongation or delay greater than that of the same values presented without syncopation may be hard to establish in a rigorous, scientific sense—but it certainly does have this empirical effect. The French term *retard* (retardation), commonly used for suspensions, builds the effect into musical terminology. Figure 4.5 is reproduced by permission of Akademische Druck und Verlagsanstalt: Antonio Draghi, *Missa a 9*, in *Kirchenwerke*, Denkmäler der Tonkunst in Österreich 46, ed. Guido Adler (1916; reprint, Graz, Austria: Akademische Druck und Verlagsanstalt, 1960).

3. Figure 4.6 is used by permission of G. Henle Verlag, München: F. J. Haydn, *Theresienmesse*, in *The Complete Works*, ser. XIII, vol. III, ed. Günter Thomas (München-Duisberg, Germany: G. Henle Verlag, 1965).

4. Regional practices dictated the organization and length of the Mass. In Dresden, the royal court favored a lengthy setting of the Mass (which the Church accepted), while the Italian Mass tended to adopt an abbreviated form: a *Kyrie* and *Gloria*, supplemented, sometimes, by the *Credo* (the *missa tota* did exist in Italian Church music of the late baroque—Alessandro Scarlatti's *St. Cecilia Mass* is a notable example—but they are greatly outnumbered). Very often, the special requirements of the establishment for which a composer worked had to be accommodated in a Mass setting. For example, by 1722, "Hieronymus, Count Colloredo

had become Archbishop of Salzburg. When a young Mozart returned from his third visit to Italy, he had, in his official capacity as *konzert-meister* to the archiepiscopal court, to adjust his music to the demands of his patron. The Prince insisted, for example, on brief compositions for the masses he celebrated. The sacred works Mozart wrote for the new ruler were not only shorter, but also simpler in character." Karl Geiringer, "The Church Music," in *The Mozart Companion*, ed. H. C. Robbins Landon and Donald Mitchell (London: Faber, 1986), 365.

5. The text and translations are taken from J. S. Bach, *Mass in B Minor* BWV 232, ed. Julius Rietz (Leipzig: Bach-Gesellschaft, 1856; reprint, New York: Dover Publications, 1989), viii.

6. France, however, was a different case. National peculiarities of musical style inform French sacred music all through the seventeenth and eighteenth centuries, and it was thought wisest to exclude it in its entirety from the investigation, even though many parallels would doubtless have emerged.

7. Ortrun Landmann and Wolfram Steude, "Dresden," in *The New Grove Dictionary of Music and Musicians*, vol. 5, ed. Stanley Sadie (London: Macmillan, 1980), 619.

8. Alec Harman and Anthony Milner, *Late Renaissance and Baroque Music*, vol. 2 of *Man and His Music* (London: Barrie and Jenkins, 1988), 502–3.

9. See Bruce C. MacIntyre, *The Viennese Concerted Mass of the Early Classic Period* (Ann Arbor, Mich.: UMI Research Press, 1986), 50–51, for descriptions of an ideal "church style" by various writers of the period.

10. Charles Rosen, *The Classical Style* (London: Faber, 1972), 368.

11. In fact, the cultivation of the bizarre found many adherents right up to the end of the baroque, although its heyday had passed by 1650.

5

Analytical Results

Chapter 4 provides a general overview of *Crucifixus* settings, discussing the reasons why the *Crucifixus* might be treated in a distinctive manner, and how this distinctiveness might possibly manifest itself. This chapter aims to be more specific, giving an account of the results from the analysis of the sample of *Crucifixus* settings collected. For the purposes of this study, a summary of these settings, with their known or approximate dates (it was difficult to date accurately some of the manuscript sources), is given as appendix A. Each setting has been given a separate identification number, and the settings have been arranged in alphabetical order according to composer. The 102 settings were collected from various printed and manuscript sources and date from between 1680 and 1800. These settings belong primarily to the Italian and German traditions.

THE CONTEXT OF THE *CRUCIFIXUS*

Type of Work

I have already suggested that the *Crucifixus* might be regarded as a movement in its own right or that, at the very least, it might exist as a distinct section within the *Credo*. The survey of *Crucifixus* settings certainly supports this view. The distinct quality of many settings occurring within a Mass is often striking. The majority of settings in the sample were indeed taken from "complete" Mass settings ("complete" Mass meaning either the inclusion of the five texts of the Ordinary or the Italianate shortened form of *Kyrie–Gloria–Credo*); however, notably fewer came from separate *Credo* settings (only six of the 102 settings), while those movements that appeared to be totally independent *Crucifixus* settings certainly formed a

71

small minority. They totaled only four, and I suspect that some of them have survived only as extracts, divorced from their original larger context. This tendency to copy (and thus to transmit) the *Crucifixus* as an individual movement (or quasi-movement) separately from its parent work suggests a desire to appreciate these "exceptional" musical settings separately and therefore lends further support to my theory of the special appeal of the *Crucifixus* text to composers.

Length

The length of these settings varied enormously. While, naturally, the words of the *Crucifixus* held a definite dramatic attraction and offered a high potential for word painting, the composer still had to consider the overall proportions of his work. It must be remembered that the length of the Mass setting as a whole has a direct effect on that of the setting of the *Crucifixus*. More compact Mass settings require the text of the whole *Credo* to be set as a single movement. Despite this limitation, composers are still likely to view certain passages of text within the *Credo* as having distinct characteristics and to attempt to include at least some acknowledgment of their distinctiveness in their musical setting. The three central portions are those that are most often given exceptional treatment, perhaps also because this group of statements is so central to the Christian faith.

At the other extreme, the "cantata" style of Mass setting allows more space all round and therefore more scope for diversification and expression in the setting of the *Credo* and its components. Under these circumstances, the *Credo* may be divided into several, sometimes as many as eleven, distinct sections or movements. I have already cited J. S. Bach's setting of the *Crucifixus* as one example of a "separate-movement" *Crucifixus*: this high degree of separateness and formal elaboration was possible only because of the vast scale of the *Credo*, as of the entire *B Minor Mass* BWV 232 (chapter 6 examines this *Crucifixus* setting in more detail). Most other *Crucifixus* settings display far less autonomy because of the smaller scale of the parent Mass setting.

The length of a Mass was laid down locally by the Church authorities and varied from area to area. However, the evidence presented in this study suggests that a basic minimum of textual expression relating specifically to the *Crucifixus* was achieved by composers almost regardless of how compressed the movement or section had to be within the framework of the *Credo*. In Dresden, the royal court, defiant in its Catholicism (since most of its subjects were Lutheran), prescribed a lengthy, concerted Mass setting (Zelenka composed many of his Masses for the royal court at Dresden, and this preference for a lengthy Mass in "cantata" style is certainly evident in his music). Table 5.1 shows that one of the longest

Table 5.1. Length of *Crucifixus* Settings

Length in Bars	Composers and Setting Reference Numbers
5–9	J. D. Heinichen (50), J. D. Zelenka (102), G. Reutter (90), F. J. Haydn (33), L. Hofmann (51), W. A. Mozart (75, 76, 77, 78, 81, 83, 84), J. M. Haydn (46, 47)
10–19	J. C. Kerll (54), A. Scarlatti (92, 93), G. Perti (87), J. J. Fux (23, 24, 25, 26), A. Lotti (62, 63, 64, 67), A. Caldara (11, 12, 13, 14), J. D. Zelenka (98, 101), J. D. Heinichen (49), F. Durante (21), G. B. Pergolesi (attrib.) (86), A. Carl (15), F. Schmidt (94), J. C. Bach (3), J. A. Hasse (32), F. J. Haydn (34, 36, 37, 38, 43), W. A. Mozart (70, 71, 72, 73, 74, 79, 82, 85), K. D. von Dittersdorf (18), F. L. Gassmann (30), L. Hofmann (51, 52), J. M. Haydn (45, 48), A. Salieri (91), D. Cimarosa (16)
20–29	Colonna (17), A. Draghi (19, 20), G. Legrenzi (56), J. J. Fux (22), J. C. Kerll (55), H. I. von Biber (6), G. Perti (88), A. Lotti (61, 65, 66), J. D. Zelenka (99), L. Leo (57), G. Abos (1), N. Jommelli (53), F. G. Bertoni (5), L. Mozart (69), F. J. Haydn (35, 39, 41, 42, 43), W. A. Mozart (80)
30–39	F. Gasparini (29), A. Vivaldi (95), A. Caldara (9, 10), A. Biffi (7), G. Giorgi (31), J. D. Zelenka (96), B. Marcello (attrib.) (68), N. Porpora (89), F. J. Haydn (40)
40–49	L. Leo (58), J. D. Zelenka (100), A. Lotti (59, 60), J. G. Albrechtsberger (2)
50–59	A. Caldara (8), J. S. Bach (4)
60 +	J. D. Zelenka (97), B. Galuppi (27)

Crucifixus settings (sixty-three bars) is by Zelenka, in his *Missa Votiva* of 1739. In contrast, a so-called Italian Mass might be pared down to just a *Kyrie* and *Gloria* (for example, Zelenka's *Missa Divina* and also Bach's short Masses), which would naturally result in the absence of a *Crucifixus* setting. Of course, the prescription for the length of a Mass could not but affect the style of its *Crucifixus* setting at a more detailed level. The longer the setting of the *Crucifixus*, the more space was available for tonal and harmonic events, for the employment of imitation to intensify expression, for repetition, and for word painting.[1] The shortest settings reach no more than four to six bars in length (J. M. Haydn and W. A. Mozart), while the longest attain around sixty bars in total (Caldara, Zelenka, and Galuppi). An objection could be raised with this method of determining the length of a setting on the grounds that a "bar" is not a meaningful common unit in terms of length of duration or in terms of the number of musical notes or "events" it contains. While there are several considerations here, it must be remembered that ultimately the words exercise the greatest control over the length of the music. In addition, the majority of these settings are in slow tempo, so there is no question of having to identify longer but faster settings and attempting to match these against shorter but slower settings. There was a general trend toward lengthy settings around the middle of the eighteenth century (that is, at the height of the baroque period). Added to this are regional factors dependent on the liturgical practice in a specific locality.

Figure 5.1 is one example of a compact setting by W. A. Mozart (78) that attempts to express the text despite the severe limitations of musical space. This *Crucifixus* follows on directly from the *Et incarnatus*, which finishes in B-flat major. Mozart switches to the tonic minor almost directly on the "-fi-" of "Crucifixus" and on the next chord introduces a grating augmented fourth between the bass and alto lines, in keeping with the well-established tradition of describing the agony of crucifixion by means of chromatic intervals. The phrases "etiam pro nobis" and "sub Pontio Pilato" are both set to speechlike rhythms: note the use of dactylic patterns here. The brevity of this setting does not allow much spinning out of the word "passus," but there is at least some contrast between the soprano line and the bisyllabic setting of this word in the three lower parts. There is a descent in the soprano line for "et sepultus est." Other details within this short setting add to the overall atmosphere, such as the soprano's movement through the highly emblematic progression of a chromatic fourth (from the opening of this example up to bar 3). The orchestration of this setting demonstrates further traditions. Throughout this example, there is an underlying rhythmic pulse (*organo*, bar 4^3 on), initially given to the strings (Vln I and II) as triple-stopped chords, then to the *organo* line. The semiquaver motion in the organ line is transferred to the strings in bar 4^3. Trombones, too, are used to accompany this section (introduced only here—not used in the *Et incarnatus*), mainly doubling the vocal lines.

Segregation of Movements

The *Crucifixus* very often appears as a distinct unit within the Mass/*Credo*. The whole issue of the term "movement" needs to be addressed here. Remarkably, the term "movement" was introduced under its modern meaning into musical vocabulary only relatively recently. Originally, the word was used to refer to the characteristic tempo and meter of any given passage of music:

> The primary and original meaning, synonymous with "motion," refers to the rhythmic character of the music in its totality as it results from a combination of metre, tempo prescription, and chosen note values. . . . The *Vocabolario dell'Accademia della Crusca* published in Florence in 1733 has no musical meanings listed in its entries for "moto" and "movimento," but the defini-

Figure 5.1. **Example of a Short *Crucifixus* Setting**

W. A. Mozart (78): Missa in C KV 220 (1775/1776)

tion of "tempo" as applied to music—". . . si dice la Misura del moto delle voci, e de' suoni per lunghi, o brevi intervalli, per moderare il ritmo, secondar la battuta, e regolar la velocita, le tardanze, e le pause" uses "moto" in exactly the same sense. We may add that in French and Italian this primary sense has never disappeared, as such instructions as "reprenez le mouvement" and "il doppio movimento" remind us.[2]

It is important to establish in this context whether the *Crucifixus* should be regarded, in general, as a "movement" or a "section"—and here I am using modern terminology. The term "movement" began to be used in its present sense only toward the end of the eighteenth century. The difficulty occurs in trying to define exactly what a movement is—what properties define movement? In music of the chosen period, to base this definition on the use of thin-thick double bar lines is pointless since the convention now in use was established as late as the nineteenth century. Michael Talbot cites John Daverio's definition: a unit "capable of functioning as a complete musical discourse when removed from its original surroundings."[3]

I think that the test is to examine the setting within the context of the work. If the *Crucifixus* can be taken out of context from its surroundings, then it can be regarded as a distinct movement. Those settings copied from a Mass as separate movements provide examples—they function as a "whole," complete in themselves. Many of the manuscript settings were copied as single movements, extracted from the respective composer's Mass. (For example, setting 88 exists in a volume owned by the Royal College of Music, 661/27. The following is inscribed at the head of the piece: *Crucifixus levato d'una Messa di Giacomo Perti canone a 3.*) If, on the other hand, the *Crucifixus* is dependent on the movements on either side of it, to such an extent that an incomplete picture is gained by viewing it alone, it should preferably be thought of as a "section." On the whole, the tendency is for these three middle movements of the *Credo* to be separated, the separation marked by some clear form of indication such as a double bar line or else a change of meter, key, or tempo. In three of the Lotti (63, 64, 67) *a cappella* settings, the three movements are continuous, but this case constitutes an exception. If units are linked at all, this generally occurs between the *Et incarnatus* and the *Crucifixus*. Scarlatti's *Missa Clementina* (93) features this linkage. It is noteworthy that the interconnection of these two movements is particularly prevalent in the Viennese tradition, beginning with Fux and moving through to Haydn. Other examples include settings by Hasse (32), Dittersdorf (18), and Gassmann (30). This is further supported by evidence presented in Bruce C. MacIntyre's study *The Viennese Concerted Mass:*

With only a few exceptions all Credos—including those in both long and short Masses—are designed around a tripartite division of the text: (1) "Credo/Patrem," (2) "Et incarnatus est," (3) "Et resurrexit." . . . Some 43 of the 71 Credos under study (60.6%) consist of exactly these three movements.[4]

My thoughts on the distinction between a section and a movement conform to Michael Talbot's ideas. He lists general criteria for the "definition" of a section and a "movement":[5]

Sections	Movements
Tonally open or closed	Tonally closed
Connected to surrounding material	Disconnected from surrounding material
Monothematic	Polythematic
Progressive or rounded form	Rounded form

The concept of a "rounded form," of course, is connected with the idea of the beginning–middle–end paradigm discussed in chapter 3; this paradigm will be explored further in both this and subsequent chapters.

Among the *Crucifixus* settings studied, there was a high proportion of tonally open movements. In fact, the number of tonally closed movements was only marginally higher, giving a nearly fifty-fifty split. However, when the same feature was examined in settings that were linked in some way to the preceding *Et incarnatus* (that is, where the two sections could be regarded as comprising one "movement"), twice as many, proportionately speaking, were tonally open.

Tempo

Among *Crucifixus* settings bearing a tempo indication, only one was marked in a quick tempo (from the *Missa Superba* by Kerll [55] [1690], marked as *Allegro*). The majority were cast in some form of slow tempo, generally *Largo* or *Adagio*. The other settings possessing some form of tempo indication belonged to an "intermediate" category: *Andante* or *Andantino*.

Out of the 102 settings analyzed, forty-eight had a slow tempo marking, thirteen an intermediate marking, and one a fast marking, while the rest had no specific indication. This seems to suggest that composers responded to the gravity of the text by selecting a slow tempo for the music. More often than not, this slow tempo was reserved for the *Et incarnatus* and *Crucifixus*, the rest of the *Credo* being faster (very often, also for practical reasons, in order to accommodate the exceptionally long text of the *Credo*). As a general rule, the *Et incarnatus* was likewise set to an intermediate or slow tempo, while composers tended to opt for a quick tempo for *the Et resurrexit* (more often than not, an *Allegro* of some description).

Scoring: Vocal

As already mentioned, the *Crucifixus* is a textual phrase whose sense demands a collective commentary. Most composers indeed set the *Crucifixus* for SATB choir; solo settings are distinctly in the minority. The exceptions are the following:

A. Caldara (12)	1 solo bass
A. Carl (15)	1 solo soprano
L. Hofmann (51)	1 solo bass
L. Hofmann (52)	1 solo bass
F. Schmidt (94)	1 solo tenor

A number of settings are scored for solo voices in combination; these are listed in table 5.2. Although solo voices are used in these settings, they nevertheless amount to a collective comment on the Crucifixion.

A number of settings include elements of responsorial treatment; these

Table 5.2.   Combinations of Solo Voices Used in *Crucifixus* Settings

Crucifixus *Setting*	*Composer*	*Vocal Scoring*
9	A. Caldara	Solo B_1B_2
16	D. Cimarosa	Solo S, *tutti* SATB
17	G. P. Colonna	Solo SAT
19	A. Draghi	Solo S_1S_2TB
20	A. Draghi	Solo S_1S_2T
35	F. J. Haydn	Solo AB
36	F. J. Haydn	Solo SATB
40	F. J. Haydn	Solo TB_1B_2 / *tutti* SATB
41	F. J. Haydn	Solo SATB / *tutti* SATB
42	F. J. Haydn	Solo SATB
43	F. J. Haydn	Solo B, *tutti* SATB
44	F. J. Haydn	Solo S, *tutti* SATB
45	J. M. Haydn	Solo SATB
53	N. Jommelli	Solo T, solo A, SATB
54	J. C. Kerll	Solo SATB
55	J. C. Kerll	Solo $S_1A_1T_1B_1S_2$
57	L. Leo	Solo SA
69	L. Mozart	Solo SAB
81	W. A. Mozart	Solo SATB and *tutti* B, then *tutti* SATB
92	A. Scarlatti	Solo S_1S_2ATB

are shown in table 5.3. This "call-and-response" (responsorial) technique reproduces the procedure within the tradition of ecclesiastical chant where the priest intones a phrase to which the congregation responds. Again, this treatment is most appropriate for a section of prose that is clearly in the collective, not the singular, domain. The following examples illustrate "responsorial imitation" where this "one-versus-many" opposition is employed but the two elements are knit together in imitation. Figure 5.2 is taken from Albrechtsberger's *Missa Annuntiationis* of 1763 (2).[6] The soprano line is given the "call" ("etiam pro nobis") in a decorative manner, and the lower three voices "respond" at the end of this phrase. Note here the chordal setting, together with the typical narrative rhythms. In bar 6, the soprano begins a chromatically ascending phrase, punctuated again by chordal responses from the alto, tenor, and bass. Albrechtsberger here mixes the portions of text, the soprano moving ahead to "sub Pontio," while the other voices comment with "etiam." The repetition of "etiam" lends an emphasis to this word; the phrase is completed in bars 10 to 11—a strong reminder that "Christ died for us." Figure 5.3, from Hasse's *Mass in D Minor* (1751) (32), demonstrates a much more compact treatment, the soprano line beginning one beat before the other voices. The lower three voices have once again a chordal setting in which speech-like rhythms are applied to this neutral phrase.

Scoring: Orchestral

In general, if a Mass or *Credo* setting was scored for full orchestra, the *Et incarnatus* and *Crucifixus* needed to have some form of reduced scoring. Very often, the *Et incarnatus* was greatly reduced, the *Crucifixus* having slightly fuller scoring and the *Et resurrexit* returning to full scoring in order to highlight the joyfulness and triumph of the resurrection. The nar-

Table 5.3. *Crucifixus* Settings Including Elements of Responsorial Technique

Crucifixus *Setting*	*Composer*
2	J. G. Albrechtsberger
3	J. C. Bach
16	D. Cimarosa
25, 26	J. J. Fux
32	J. A. Hasse
39	F. J. Haydn
49	J. D. Heinichen
77, 81, 83	W. A. Mozart
86	G. B. Pergolesi (attrib.)
90	G. Reutter

Figure 5.2. Responsorial Technique

J. G. Albrechtsberger (2): Missa Annuntiationis *(1763)*

rowing down of the number of instruments for the *Crucifixus* serves to underline the tragedy of these few words.

The present study is revealing in that to a certain extent it encompasses the development of orchestral practice during this time. At the earlier end of this survey (late seventeenth century/early eighteenth century), the "old-fashioned" scoring practices are in evidence: instruments have little independence but are used mainly to double vocal lines. The older mode of scoring with two or sometimes more violas is often adopted. Biber's *Missa St. Henrici* (6) (1701) exemplifies both practices: three violas are used to double the soprano, alto, and tenor, respectively, with reinforcement from two trombones, used to double the lower two voices. The practice of doubling the voices in fact persists throughout this period (1680–1800). Hasse (32) employs the same technique in his *Mass in D Minor*, and both Mozart and Haydn make the instruments double the voices, although by this stage doubling creates a desired timbral effect rather than having the main purpose of bolstering vocal parts. Trombones appear in some of these earlier settings, and these instruments are used throughout the period under examination. Table 5.4 gives a summary of settings employing trombones. Mozart introduces the instrument in a number of his Masses. This conforms to Salzburg tradition, which used

Figure 5.3.   Responsorial Technique

J. A. Hasse (32): Mass in D Minor *(1751)*

"trombones to reinforce alto, tenor and bass voices of the chorus and a string orchestra without the violas."[7]

It is interesting to note that while the trombone held no place in the classical symphony until Beethoven, it retained its position in Church music during the classical era. Ratner comments on this:

> Trombones, traditional in church music to double voices, also were heard in ceremonial brass music and upon solemn occasions, as in the Handel commemoration of 1784. Mozart used them in the Magic Flute, 1791, to signify the serious aspects of this opera. Marsh says that they were the most powerful instruments of the orchestra. Possibly for this reason, they could not be assimilated into the chamber-style symphony and the elegant accompaniments in opera . . . their heavier, less mellow tone befits the mood of tragedy with which the opera Alceste [Gluck] begins.[8]

Table 5.4. *Crucifixus* Settings with Trombone(s)

Crucifixus *Setting*	*Composer*	*Approximate Date*
6	F. I. von Biber	1701
9	A. Caldara	ca.1710–1720
25	J. J. Fux	ca.1730
51	L. Hofmann	1760
71	W. A. Mozart	1768/1769
72	W. A. Mozart	1769
73	W. A. Mozart	1769
76	W. A. Mozart	1774
77	W. A. Mozart	1774
78	W. A. Mozart	1775
79	W. A. Mozart	1776
80	W. A. Mozart	1777
81	W. A. Mozart	1777
82	W. A. Mozart	1777
83	W. A. Mozart	1777
84	W. A. Mozart	1779
91	A. Salieri	1788

Gordon Jacob comments on the tone of the trombone in his well-known primer of orchestration:

It is a mistake to imagine that the sole function of the trombones is to make an overwhelming noise. This is, admittedly, one of their important duties, but their capacity for pianissimo delivery is very great, and the essential nobility of the trombone tone remains unchanged at all dynamic degrees.[9]

The addition of trombones to the score adds a certain ambience that appealed to composers: the use of the instrument lends a certain darkness to the texture. In the German tradition, the "last trump" of Judgment Day is in fact a trombone (*die letzte Posaune*). Trombones therefore symbolize the "gravity" of Church music. Biber, Mozart, and Salieri use trombones to double the vocal lines. In Salieri's setting (91), trombones double the alto and tenor lines during only the first half of the movement. This makes a great contrast with the remainder of the *Crucifixus* (*Mass in D*, 1788). Caldara employs trombones to double the strings, which have a fragmented, pulsing line, characteristic of many *Crucifixus* settings, while Hofmann (51) uses a similar idea, except that the strings alternate with the trombones and continuo, creating a even pulsation (see figures 5.4 and 5.5).[10]

A number of factors affected the orchestration of liturgical music: first, as we have already seen, the restrictions imposed by the Church on the

Figure 5.4.   Use of Trombones

The inscription at the beginning of this section reads:

Con viole e Tromboni Che suonano li V.V. ancor le [parti] de le Viole a due Bassi soli.

[With the violas [or possibly viols] and trombones, with the violins playing as well as the parts for viola [or viol], for two solo basses.]

A. Caldara (9): Mass for 4 Voices (ca. 1720)

Figure 5.5.   Use of Trombones

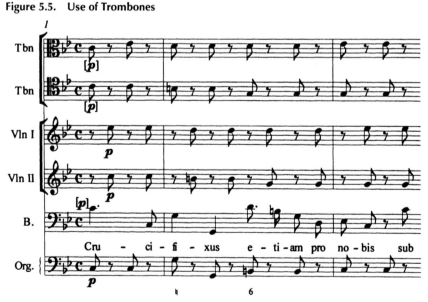

L. Hofmann (51): Missa in Honorem Sanctae Theresiae in C (before 1760)

use of instruments in musical settings for sacred purposes, and, second, the influence of orchestration practices from genres outside Church music that sooner or later became absorbed into its style.

The introduction of the *basso continuo* in the seventeenth century had several implications for Church music. Since the chords were now being filled out by the continuo player, a thinning out of the texture in the obbligato parts was made possible. This permitted a more imaginative and flexible approach to the setting of liturgical texts. It made interchange between one or two voices and a combination of several voices possible. The possibility also arose of introducing instrumental introductions, interludes, or postludes (often described as ritornellos or sinfonias) with all voices silent. The importance of this musical development should not be underestimated:

> Under the influence of the new continuo harmony the old technique [that is, *stile antico*] was misunderstood: it is significant that arrangements of Palestrina's works were published which provided a continuo bass.[11]

Before the introduction of the *basso continuo*, the vocal parts themselves were responsible for ensuring that the harmony was sufficiently full; this gave little opportunity for reducing the number of voices for the sake of contrast.[12] Because of this "harmony by necessity," Renaissance music did not allow any horizontal "space" within the setting: as a consequence, musical phrases needed to dovetail into one another, even if dialogue was being expressed. The addition of continuo—and of instruments in general—enabled the creation of *horizontal* space in the vocal parts (instruments now supplying the continuity) and made sectional overlaps optional rather than essential.

Nearly all settings (with the exception of the rare "pure" *a cappella* setting) include a continuo line, normally played by the organ. The issue of doubling instruments needs to be addressed in this connection. It should not be assumed unthinkingly that the continuo line is always to be doubled in baroque music:

> The automatic inclusion of bass line instruments in seventeenth-century music is based on the flimsiest evidence, and their use in the eighteenth century may have been more limited than one is led to believe.[13]

However, in the case of baroque Church music, the writer (Borgir) does concede that the inclusion of a bass line instrument as part of the continuo line was necessary in order to maintain a balance in performing ensembles of this size. Evidence exists to prove that this practice occurred in sacred vocal music in the form of separate continuo parts for the bass player. This is evident in some music published after 1680. It is evident also in some of the manuscript settings of the *Crucifixus* that I have edited, with clear indications for performers of melody instruments to double the *organo* line. However, in the case of *a cappella* SATB/organ settings, there is justification for using organ alone. If, as Borgir claims, the inclusion of a bass instrument depended on the size of ensemble, then perhaps, in the case of an otherwise purely vocal setting, only the organ was required for accompaniment.

Toward the end of this period, there is far more flexibility of orchestration. There are some examples of "unusual" scorings; for example, Haydn (34) uses two *cors anglais* to double the upper voices in his *Missa in Honorem Beatissimae Virginis Mariae* (1766). The classical style also witnesses the addition of timpani to the orchestra, in both Leopold Mozart's (69) setting from his *Mass in C* (ca. 1764) and many of W. A. Mozart's settings. Haydn similarly uses timpani to good effect (see figure 4.6). Galuppi, too, employs them in his *Credo Papal*. Used in the right places, these instruments can underline and comment on the text effectively. These settings also adhere to the common orchestral usage of the day whereby doubling of lines (by strings or woodwind) is practiced to heighten or underline a phrase.

Quite apart from the practical questions surrounding the increased use of instruments during the classical period, there was an aesthetic, even religious, factor to consider. This is noted by Charles Rosen:

> The classical style is at its most problematic in religious music. This was a genre beset with difficulties that could not trouble the secular field.[14]

Rosen goes on to comment,

> The hostility of the Catholic Church to instrumental music throughout the eighteenth century was a factor in these difficulties. The use of instruments in church was even restricted by order of the Austrian Government during the 1780s, a time of great creative activity for both Haydn and Mozart. In most periods the Church had not encouraged stylistic innovation: it disliked the heavily chromatic music of many Renaissance composers just as it had refused to accept the centralized church preferred by most Renaissance architects. There are many works even of Palestrina that would not pass the church's test for orthodoxy in music style. A conservative taste is not illogical in an institution that relies so fundamentally on continuity of tradition. Nevertheless, the dislike of instrumental music is more deeply motivated: vocal music has always been considered more apt for a religious service, and the reputation for purity that is attached to *a cap[p]ella* writing has symbolic value. At least with purely vocal music the words of the service make their presence felt. The classical style, however, was in all essentials an instrumental one.[15]

Throughout the periods in which the settings under consideration were produced, strings were frequently used. These instruments are often retained in the *Crucifixus* despite the preference for a reduction in scoring there. Toward the end of the baroque, the strings gain far greater independence and are often used to set up some kind of accompanimental pattern that creates an appropriate background for the text.

Upper strings are often given arpeggiated accompaniment patterns. "Sighs" are commonly represented by rests in the instrumental lines or by appogiaturas. Figure 5.6 shows Biffi initiating in the first few bars a string accompaniment pattern that persists throughout his setting. The bass line keeps a steady four crotchet beats to the bar for the duration of this movement, another common feature of *Crucifixus* settings.[16]

Form and Style

With a representative sample of over one hundred settings, there will obviously exist a wide range of musical forms and styles. The two elements are interdependent: the form of a movement or section may be often be a result of the style employed and vice versa.

Figure 5.6. Use of Strings

A. Biffi (7): Credo in D Minor *(ca. 1730)*

The form and style of the *Crucifixus* settings seem to be influenced to a high degree by the words. As we already know, the *Crucifixus* is a very short section of text that demands a through-composed approach by its very nature. It recounts a sequence of events: "Crucifixus etiam pro nobis sub Pontio Pilato, passus et sepultus est." Logically, when these words are expressed musically, "Crucifixus" must come first: "passus" and "et sepultus est" are dependent on this first event, as are the narrative phrases of "etiam pro nobis" and "sub Pontio Pilato." While "Crucifixus" and "passus" share a potential for word painting, the text will not accommodate easily a rondo-like structure with a regular refrain. A further reason why composers adopt a through-composed approach is the context of this movement. This section of the *Credo* (from the *Et incarnatus* on) describes, in brief, the life of Christ. Again, it is a sequence of events—there is a "direction" to the text: from birth to death to resurrection. This again suggests through-composition, passing from one event to the next: the unfolding of a continuous narrative. In the settings that I have examined, there is a logical "encasement" of word setting. Without fail, whatever words or sections of text are repeated or, indeed, "jumbled" in the middle of the setting, the settings invariably begin with "Crucifixus" and end with "et sepultus est." There is an indestructible sense of beginning and end.

Many settings are written in the *stile antico*. The *stile antico* of around 1700 was not by any means a strict copy of Palestrina's style—it was more of a compromise between this and current practices. By this time, the *stile antico* was characterized by the following features:

1. *A cappella* writing (unaccompanied voices or voices doubled by instruments in a strict manner).
2. Regulated treatment of dissonance according to the norms existing around 1600. Tonality was used rather than modality, phrasing and rhythmic structure becoming more foursquare (that is, quadratic phrase structure is not avoided), and some inclusion of linear chromaticism had become acceptable.

A number of *a cappella* settings are included in the sample of *Crucifixus* settings. These come mostly from the earlier end of the sample. Draghi, Kerll, Legrenzi, and especially Fux contribute some of the earliest specimens of *stile antico* settings to the sample. Many of Lotti's Mass settings are cast in the *stile antico*; the sample contains similar settings by Leo and Durante. Some of the most impressive *stile antico* settings are those by Caldara (*Crucifixus* for sixteen voices) and Lotti (*Crucifixus* settings for six, eight, and ten voices).[17]

Some settings adopt a fugal style. In many of the cases, a more accurate description would be "imitation based" since the subject is frequently too short—and, as a result, the entries are too closely packed—to produce the required tonal opposition between subject and answer. (The expression "fugal style" is used here in preference to "fugal form" since fugal technique does not prescribe any detailed plan of organization, as would be implied by the term "form.") Often, the sequence of words "Crucifixus etiam pro nobis" is treated as the basis for a fugal subject since the word "Crucifixus" would by itself be too short for the purpose. Examples of such fugal treatment occur in the following:

5	F. Bertoni
7	A. Biffi
10	A. Caldara (see figure 5.7)
17	G. P. Colonna
27	B. Galuppi
56	G. Legrenzi
79	W. A. Mozart
87	G. A. Perti
96	J. D. Zelenka

Many settings use shorter motives that allow "Crucifixus" and "etiam pro nobis" to have separate thematic identities. These motives are discussed in greater detail in the next section. Many settings are frankly chordal rather than imitative. Those that are chordal tend, predictably, to be the shorter settings (imitative settings by their very nature have the effect of drawing out the text).

EXPRESSION OF THE TEXT

In chapter 4, I discussed in general terms the possibilities for apt expression of the *Crucifixus* text. Here, I focus more closely on how the results from the sample support or contradict these generalizations.

"Crucifixus"

Of all the expectations and potential devices for word painting that I had considered beforehand as applicable to the setting of the *Crucifixus* text, it was the setting of the word "Crucifxus" that proved the most surprising in terms of its nonconformity. The devices that I thought would be used in profusion, while certainly in evidence, did not occur to the extent that I expected. This immediately prompts the question "why not?" and causes one to reexamine the settings to see what composers did instead—

Figure 5.7. "Crucifixus etiam pro nobis" Used as a Subject

and to discover whether there was another established tradition not pre-viously considered.

One of the devices that I thought might be widely used was the musical sign for the cross. There are a few settings that contain this motive—figure 4.2 by Perti offers one such example. There is a second setting by the same composer, again containing a similar zigzag arrangement of notes. While some settings do not have the actual musical "cross" figures exemplified by figure 4.1, they nevertheless display a clear zigzag organi-zation of notes. Table 5.5 provides a summary of these findings. Figure 5.8 gives examples of these, except where otherwise indicated.[18]

A. Caldara (9): Crucifixus *from Mass for 4 Voices (ca. 1720)*

The other prediction made for the depiction of the Crucifixion was the use of chromatic intervals to express the agony and torture of this punishment. While this was evident in approximately a third of the settings analyzed, I had expected a much higher proportion of settings to display the trait. Intervals that appear in conjunction with the word "Crucifixus" were mainly diminished and augmented fourths and fifths, and these in a variety of guises. Some of these "tortured" intervals were "horizontal," that is, a melodic or linear interval within one vocal part; others were "vertical," that is, a harmonic interval. The extra category I employed here was "diagonal," where an interval is perceived by a combination of verti-

Table 5.5.   Musical Sign of the Cross and Other Closely Related Figures

Crucifixus *Setting*	*Composer*	*Comments*
19	A. Draghi	Sign of the cross used in imitation. Second entry is amended to accommodate this imitation.
87	G. A. Perti	Clear sign of the cross (see figure 4.2).
88	G. A. Perti	Zigzag arrangement. Does not return to opening note but still recognizable as the "cross."
8	A. Caldara	Musical sign of the cross.
9	A. Caldara	Clear zigzag arrangement of notes (see figure 5.4).
12	A. Caldara	Motive spans an octave, with the inclusion of a lower auxiliary note.
97	J. D. Zelenka	Zigzag organization—five- rather than four-note motive.
70	W. A. Mozart	Zigzag pattern of notes, but one has the impression that this musical line arises from the underlying harmony.

Figure 5.8.   Musical Sign of the Cross and Other Related Figures

A. Draghi (19): Missa a 9 (1684)

G. A. Perti (88): Kyrie, Gloria and Credo (ca. 1700–1720)

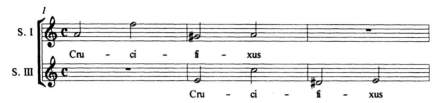

A. Caldara (8): Crucifixus a 16 Voci *(ca. 1730)*

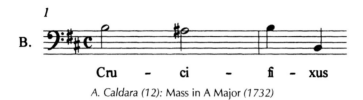

A. Caldara (12): Mass in A Major *(1732)*

J. D. Zelenka (97): Missa Votiva ZWV 18 *(1739)*

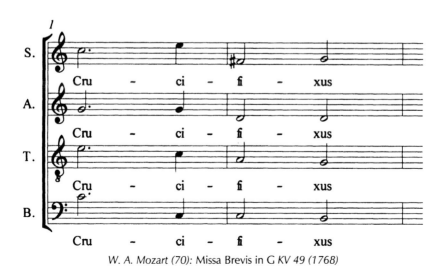

W. A. Mozart (70): Missa Brevis in G KV 49 *(1768)*

cal and horizontal association. Here, the sound of a particular note on an initial beat (or subbeat) is still so strong in the listener's consciousness that it is "heard" as the first note of an interval when a note in another part is sounded on the following metrical unit. An example of a grating "diagonal" interval occurs in the *Crucifixus* setting by Heinichen (see figure 5.9) between the d in the bass and the a♯′ in the soprano on the first beat of the following bar.

Table 5.6 gives details of composers who seem to be attempting to depict the Crucifixion through the use of chromatic intervals. Figure 5.9 adds some further examples to those already given. The leap of an augmented or diminished interval in the vocal line (or indeed instrumental), described here as a melodic or harmonic "tortured" gesture, was known by the rhetorical term of *saltus duriusculus*.

The number of settings that had a "Crucifixus" motive with a sharp in the line was again limited (the "visual" sign of the cross). Many of these were the settings with the musical sign of the cross, which are also included in table 5.6; usually the introduction of a sharp has the concomitant effect of creating an augmented or diminished interval of some description. Again, the total was about a third of the number of pieces analyzed. More of the early settings contain a sharp somewhere in the depiction of the word "Crucifixus," which reflects the practice of notating a sharp by using a cross in earlier music. Sharps were notated mostly in a modern, less crosslike form by Mozart's time. For German composers, there existed the additional association of the word *Kreuz* (German for "sharp"), which means "cross" in German. So with both the use of chromatic intervals and the use of the sharp to allude to the words "cross/crucifixion," there is definite evidence of a tradition. A third of the sample analyzed is enough to constitute a significant proportion.

Another relevant visual (eye-music) device is the crossing of vocal lines. The rhetorical term for this crossing is *metabasis* or *transgressio*, the "literal meaning" of which Bartel describes as conveying the sense of "stepping (*basis, gressus*) over or through (*meta, trans*) something else."[19] Both Vogt and Spiess describe the *metabasis* as occurring when

Figure 5.9.   "Excruciating" Intervals for "Crucifixus"

A. Vivaldi (95): Credo RV 591 (ca. 1717)

J. D. Heinichen *(49):* Missa 11 *(ca. 1720)*

Table 5.6. "Excruciating" Intervals for "Crucifixus"

Crucifixus *Setting*	*Composer*	*Intervals*
17	G. P. Colonna	Dim 5 (V), Aug 4 (V)
19	A. Draghi	Dim 4 (H) (see figure 5.8)
20	A. Draghi	Dim 5 (V)
56	G. Legrenzi	Aug 4 (H)
88	G. A. Perti	Dim 4 (H) (see figure 5.8)
95	A. Vivaldi	Dim 4 (H) (see figure 5.9)
98	J. D. Zelenka	Dim 4 (V)
49	J. D. Heinichen	Dim 4 (V), Aug 2 (V), Aug 4 (V), Aug 5 (D) (see figure 5.9)
8	A. Caldara	Dim 7 (H) (see figure 5.8)
90	G. Reutter	Dim 5 (V)
97	J. D. Zelenka	Dim 4 (H), Dim 7 (H) (see figure 5.8)
102	J. D. Zelenka	Dim 4 (V)
4	J. S. Bach	Dim 5 (V), Dim7 (V), Aug 2 (H), Aug 4 (H,V) (see chapter 6 for details)
96	J. D. Zelenka	Dim 4 (H)
3	J. C. Bach	Dim 3 (D)
33	F. J. Haydn	Dim 7 (V)
34	F. J. Haydn	Dim 3 (H), Aug 4 (H—span of motive)
70	W. A. Mozart	Aug 4 (V) (see figure 5.8)
71	W. A. Mozart	Dim 4 (D), Dim 5 (D)
72	W. A. Mozart	Dim 5 (V)
30	F. L. Gassmann	Dim 4 (V), Dim 5 (V)
35	F. J. Haydn	Dim 5 (H)
52	L. Hofmann	Dim 5 (H)
74	W. A. Mozart	Dim 5 (V), Dim 7 (V)
77	W. A. Mozart	Aug 4 (V)
78	W. A. Mozart	Aug 4 (V)
80	W. A. Mozart	Dim 5 (V)
81	W. A. Mozart	Dim 5 (V), Dim 7 (V) (chord of Dim 7th)
82	W. A. Mozart	Aug 2 (V), Aug 4 (V) (augmented chord)
84	W. A. Mozart	Dim 7 (V)
38	F. J. Haydn	Dim 4 (H), Dim 5 (H—span of motive)
43	F. J. Haydn	Aug 4 (H—span of motive)
44	F. J. Haydn	Dim 5 (V)
48	J. M. Haydn	Dim 7 (V)

. . . one voice crosses over the other.

The definition and example which Vogt provides (and Spiess duplicates) reflects the literal understanding of the term rather than its rhetorical content. The voices "step over" each other, creating in fact a two fold "transgression." First, such voice crossing is considered a compositional irregularity in traditional counterpoint. As Bernhard points out, "upper voices must seldom pass under lower ones, and lower ones seldom over higher ones." [The footnote in Bartel's text refers to Bernhard's *Tractatus*, 42.] Second, a visual transgression is created with this device. In the example, the figure is used effectively to vividly illustrate the text, "take me with you; seize me in your [arms]." As the voices intertwine, one voice "seizes" the other and "drags" it along.[20]

The example given by Vogt is used to pictorialize the text and is shown as figure 5.10.[21] This literal crossing of parts occurs in some *Crucifixus* settings. J. S. Bach (4) is one such composer (see chapter 6); Zelenka (100) is another, in his *Missa St. Caeciliae* (see figure 5.11). Caldara intertwines the vocal lines to depict the Crucifixion further in his *Crucifixus a 16 Voci* (see figure 5.8), and Salieri causes the soprano line to cross over the alto in his representative setting (see figure 5.11).[22]

The question remains, however: if only a third of composers set the word "Crucifixus" according to this tradition, what did the others do? The rhythmic qualities of the word seemed to have held a great appeal for composers. Many opted for a four-note motive to accommodate the four syllables of the word. Frequently, the word was set dactylically, with

Figure 5.10.   Example of *Metabasis* (Vogt)

Figure 5.11.   Examples of *Metabasis*

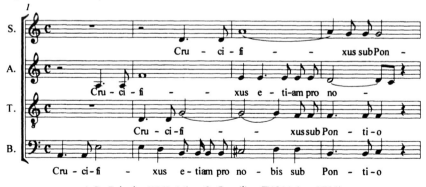

J. D. Zelenka (100): Missa S. Caeciliae ZWV 1 (ca. 1711)

Figure 5.11.   (contined)

A. Salieri (91): Mass in D (1788)

the emphasis on the syllable "Cru-." The emphasis can also be placed on the "-fi-," as in Caldara's *Missa in spei Resurrectionis*: here the syllable "-fi-" is set to a longer note value (see figure 5.12).

The other option was to use four notes of the same value, which also happens. Appendix B is an attempt to organize the many rhythmic variants of setting the word "Crucifixus." Initially, the motives are sorted according to time signature. Then they are organized into families of motives—first the most basic rhythmic pattern and then variants of that pattern. The subscripts attached to each family of motives hold the key to the variants of the original rhythmic pattern. The variants are as follows:

Type 1: The motive in its definitive state for that particular rhythmic family
Type 2: Shortening of the final note of the motive
Type 3: Retaining the underlying basic rhythm (as in type 1) but with decoration

Figure 5.12.   Emphasis on the Penultimate Syllable of "Crucifixus"

A. Caldara (11): Missa in spei Resurrectionis (ca. 1720)

Type 4: Some form of prolongation of the syllable "-fi-" in the form of either a longer note value or a melisma

Type 5: Longer note values for the two last syllables

Type 6: Shorter note values for the two last syllables

Type 7: Extension of the first one or two syllables

This form of analysis has highlighted a number of points:

- There are a significant number of settings in triple meter. Within this group, composers set the word "Crucifixus" as an on-beat motive or as one beginning on the second beat of the bar. There is only one case of a "Crucifixus" motive beginning on the last beat of the bar— Haydn (41).
- With quadruple meter settings, many of the "Crucifixus" motives begin on one of the strong beats of the bar: beat 1 or 3. Fewer begin on one of the weak beats of the bar: beat 2 or 4.
- There is only one setting in compound time—a setting by Mozart in $\frac{6}{8}$.
- The syllable "-fi-" nearly always falls on the strong beat (and in many cases the strong first beat of the second bar of the motive).
- Many settings contain a four-note motive corresponding to the four syllables of "Crucifixus."

Group A, type 1, in appendix B lists those composers who employ a four-note motive consisting of equal note values. There is a sense of uniformity created by employing such a regular rhythm, and often the same device is employed elsewhere in a setting. Vivaldi uses the same underlying "plodding" crotchet rhythm in the bass line and continues this for the duration of the movement.[23] Biffi's setting is similar in this respect.

While composers emphasize the first syllable of the word in various ways (for example, offsetting it on the weak beat by syncopation or by dactylic rhythm), more attention tends to be focused on the penultimate syllable. Settings that focus more on the first syllable are shown in appendix B, group B, types 1, 2, 3, and 6. The basic motive here is a dactylic one, naturally lengthening the first syllable.

What all three figures clearly demonstrate is that the word "Crucifixus" appears to have a hierarchy of stressed and unstressed syllables. Initially, it would appear that the word has two stressed components (the "Cru-" and the "-fi-") and two unstressed syllables. As the word is spoken, it is natural to emphasize the "-fi-" more than the other syllables. So out of the two stressed syllables, the "-fi-" seems to be more even more emphatic than the "Cru-." Perhaps this is because of the peculiar phonetic quality of the syllable. Many settings focus on this syllable, resorting to a variety of devices, from the simple allocation of a longer note value to a longer, more melismatic phrase.

"etiam pro nobis" and "sub Pontio Pilato"

In general, the setting of these two phrases conforms completely to expectation. Composers usually opt for a neutral narrative-type setting, closely linked to the rhythm generated by the words of these two phrases. More often than not, dactylic rhythms are employed to reflect the stressed and unstressed syllables of the text. Sometimes, these phrases are set to downward-moving "small intervals" (tonal or semitonal), which adds pathos to the overall setting (the rhetorical term for semitonal movement is *pathopoeia*). Examples occur in settings by Biffi and Bertoni (in both settings, on "sub Pontio"), Caldara, Gassmann, Haydn, W. A. Mozart, Reutter, Salieri, Schmidt, and Zelenka. Figure 5.13 gives some examples that also illustrate the use of dactylic rhythms to set these two portions of text.[24] These previously mentioned settings are a combination of imitative and chordal settings. The Bertoni (5) setting includes a particularly good example of a

Figure 5.13.   Use of "Sighing" Intervals

F. Bertoni (5): Crucifixus con Organo a 4 Voci *(ca. 1760)*

A. Biffi (7): Credo in D Minor *(ca. 1730)*

A. Caldara (11): Missa in spei Resurrectionis *(ca. 1720)*

sub Pon - ti - o Pi - la - to

A. *Caldara (12):* Mass in A Major *(1732)*

sub Pon - ti - o Pi - la - to

F. J. *Haydn (37):* Missa Brevis Scti. Joannis de Deo *(ca. 1775)*

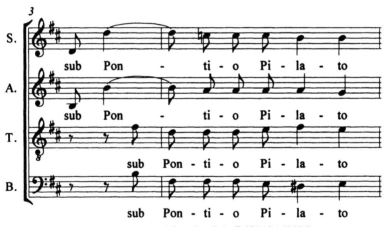

sub Pon - ti - o Pi - la - to

sub Pon - ti - o Pi - la - to

sub Pon - ti - o Pi - la - to

sub Pon - ti - o Pi - la - to

W. A. *Mozart (77):* Missa Brevis in D *KV 194 (1774)*

A. Salieri (91): Mass in D (1788)

F. Schmidt (94): Missa Sanctae Caeciliae (before 1746)

J. D. Zelenka (99): Missa Nativitatis Domini ZWV 8 (1726)

downward phrase treated in imitation. The chordal phrases, while having a leading "voice" that descends, are harmonized appropriately (see W. A. Mozart, *Missa Brevis in D* KV 194, figure 5.13).

With both sections of text, there is also a tendency to set the first part of the phrase syllabically and then have some form of melisma or longer note value for the second part of the phase. For example, with "etiam pro nobis," "etiam pro" may be set syllabically, with prolongation on the "no-," since this is a naturally accentuated syllable. In addition, the actual sound of the word lends itself particularly well to being drawn out. "Sub

Pontio Pilato" is usually set in a speechlike style up to the "-la-" of "Pilato." If any part of this phrase demands to be dwelled or focused on, it is this syllable. As with the "no-" of "nobis," the very phonetic quality of "-la-" lends itself well to prolongation. Attention can be drawn to this part of either phrase in a number of ways. First, the composer may choose to do something as simple as to employ a longer note value for that syllable. A relevant example is the Albrechtsberger setting (2), which does exactly that for both phrases (see figure 5.2). Caldara (11), on "sub Pontio Pilato," and Dittersdorf (18) provide further examples where either or both phrases have a longer note value that emphasizes these parts of the text (see figure 5.14).[25]

Second, the composer may choose to have a simple melismatic decoration on the note that draws attention to the syllable. In Abos's setting (1) (figure 5.15), the composer does this in both cases. He has already emphasized the other strong syllables in these phrases by using longer note values and a dactylic rhythm ("e-" of "etiam" and "Pon-" of "Pontio"), so,

Figure 5.14. Longer Note Values for the Penultimate Syllables of Narrative Phrases

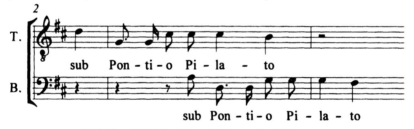

A. Caldara (11): Missa in spei Resurrectionis *(ca. 1720)*

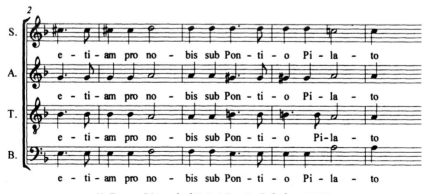

K. D. von Dittersdorf (18): Missa in C *(before 1773)*

to create sufficient focus for these stressed syllables, he uses a lower auxiliary note as a decoration. The auxiliary note, in both cases, is made more unstressed by having the main note value dotted. In addition, the fact that the main note falls on the first beat of the bar (a strong beat—the one strong beat in ¾), together with its property of being dotted, creates the desired effect. Other examples (see figure 5.15) are the following:

Hasse (32), who uses an unaccented lower auxiliary note on the "no-" of "nobis" in the soprano line while drawing out the same syllable in the lower parts by using a longer note value.
Haydn (42), who uses a dotted rhythm together with an arpeggiated note for the same portion of text.[26]

Figure 5.15. Decoration of Penultimate Syllable in Narrative Phrases

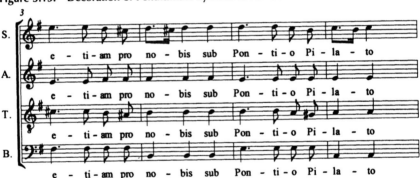

G. Abos (1): Messa a 4 Voci (ca. 1740)

J. A. Hasse (32): Mass in D Minor (1751)

F. J. Haydn (42): Theresienmesse (1799)

L. Leo (57): Messa Completa (ca. 1730–1740)

Leo (57), who uses a passing note between the main note on the first ("no-") and second ("-bis") beats of the bar

Third, the composer may choose to set these syllables melismatically. This occurs a significant number of times (see table 5.7). Examples illustrating this approach are shown in figure 5.16.

"passus" and "et sepultus est"

The word "passus" may be set in a number of different ways. The expected means of musical prolongation, suggested in chapter 4, are very much in evidence in this survey. Composers convey a sense of duration by drawing out the word. In order to do this, such musical devices as syncopation, suspension, melisma, or any combination of these are employed.

Most of the settings prolong the word "passus" by one or more of these methods. However, I discovered another, unanticipated custom: that of setting "passus" strictly syllabically. The resulting two-note motives occurred in many settings (in fact, as many as forty-three of the 102 settings). Frequently, the note values used in the bisyllabic setting of the

Table 5.7.   Use of Melisma for the Penultimate Syllable of Narrative Phrases

Setting	Composer	"etiam"	"sub"
3	J. C. Bach	*	
9	A. Caldara	*	
12	A. Caldara	*	
13	A. Caldara	*	
21	F. Durante	*	
22	J. J. Fux		*
24	J. J. Fux		*
28	B. Galuppi		*
55	J. C. Kerll		*
62	A. Lotti		*
63	A. Lotti	*	
75	W. A. Mozart		*
88	G. A. Perti	*	
89	N. Porpora	*	
97	J. D. Zelenka	*	*
100	J. D. Zelenka	*	*

Figure 5.16.   Use of Melisma for the Penultimate Syllable of Narrative Phrases

e - ti - am pro no - - bis

A. Caldara (12): Mass in A Major (1732)

e - ti - am pro_ no - - - - - bis

G. A. Perti (88): Kyrie, Gloria and Credo (ca. 1700–1720)

word "passus" conform to our expectation of relatively longer note values. Michael Haydn's (48) *Missa St. Francisci* provides an example of this, where the two-note motive for "passus" is generally set to longer note values than have occurred earlier in the setting (see figure 5.17).[27]

Often, a two-note motive will be harmonized with chords that are suitably "agonizing." Many of Mozart's settings illustrate this point. His *Missa in C* KV 259 (82) harmonizes "passus" by introducing a diminished seventh in third inversion. The arrangement of the chord emphasizes the interval of an augmented fourth between the outer voices. His *Missa in B Flat* KV 175 (83) moves through a German sixth for a brief single beat among four (in the vocal parts) for the setting of the word "passus." Zelenka uses grating intervals in his *Missa Circumcisionis* (98), while Heinichen introduces an augmented fourth where the basses are given "passus" in his *Missa 12* (50) (see figure 5.18). A different way of express-

Figure 5.17. Relatively Long Note Values for "passus"

J. M. Haydn (48): Missa S. Francisci (1803)

Figure 5.18.   Use of Dissonance for the Word "passus"

W. A. Mozart (82): Missa in C KV 259 (1775–1777)

W. A. Mozart (83): Missa in B Flat *KV 175 (1777)*

J. D. Zelenka (98): Missa Circumcisionis *(1724)*

ing suffering occurs in Mozart's *Missa in C* KV 337 (85), where the two-note "passus" motive is set as stark, bare octaves in the vocal parts (see figure 5.19).

One of the reasons why so many composers opt for a plain syllabic setting of this word may be to match (and balance) the setting of the word "Crucifixus." As we have already seen, many composers chose also to set

Figure 5.18.   (continued)

J. D. Heinichen (50): Missa 12 (ca. 1720)

Figure 5.19.   Bare Octaves for the Setting of the Word "passus"

W. A. Mozart (85): Missa in C KV 337 (1780)

"Crucifixus" syllabically, responding to the rhythmic properties of the word. In order to maintain the sense of symmetry of this section of the *Credo* text, it is logical to set at least part of the balancing action phrase syllabically. Further, it now becomes clear that the syllabic setting of the two "narrative" phrases can also play a specific role within the larger context of the *Crucifixus*, that is, as a deliberate means of contrast, by pitting their shorter, speechlike rhythms against the longer, albeit equally syllabic, motivic setting of "passus." The use of dissonance, in one form or another, while highly appropriate for expressing suffering, also acts as a counterweight to the opening word, which is commonly set in a similar manner. Here, we are seeing Tarasti's "arch structure" in action.

Many of the examples of melismatic settings of the word "passus" exploit a combination of prolonging qualities, such as syncopation and suspension (figure 5.20). Hofmann's *Crucifixus* from *Missa in Honorem Sanctae Theresiae in C* (51) has "passus" set melismatically: the solo bass is given an arpeggiated sequential line for the first two statements of the word, the third statement being set "bisyllabically."[28] The second example in figure 5.20 illustrates the use of several musical devices to "prolong" this same word. Scarlatti uses syncopation, suspension, and melisma to set "passus." The layering effect of these entries also contributes to the musical "drawing out."[29]

Many settings exhibit an element of stepwise descent or regular downward movement for "et sepultus est." This descent does not always occur in all the vocal parts: often, the topmost parts conform to these expectations, while the function of the remaining parts is to provide the harmony. Perti's *Crucifixus* settings give an example of this (see figure 5.21).

Figure 5.20. Melismatic Setting of "passus"

L. Hofmann (51): Missa in Honorem Sanctae Theresiae in C (before 1760)

Figure 5.20. (continued)

A. Scarlatti (92): St. Cecilia Mass (1720)

The *Crucifixus* from his *Kyrie, Gloria,* and *Credo* exhibits many expected conventions: dactylic rhythms for "sub Pontio Pilato," syncopation and suspension for "passus," and descent in the upper two voices for the first "et sepultus est." Another example of stepwise descent occurs in A. Carl's setting (see figure 5.21).[30] "Et sepultus est" is sometimes expressed by an abrupt drop in pitch: some settings have a distinct drop of register in the bass line at this point (Hofmann's *Missa in Honorem Sanctae Theresiae in C* [51] is one example—see figure 5.20). While many settings depict the burial by some means of musical descent, a number remain more or less static, or else the descent occurs throughout the portion of text that includes "passus" (as, for example, in the Perti settings). Many composers seek no separation between "passus" and "et sepultus est" but treat these

Figure 5.21. Musical Descent to Express "et sepultus est"

G. A. Perti (87): Messa Canone a 3 (ca. 1700–1720)

Figure 5.21. (continued)

G. A. Perti (88): Kyrie, Gloria and Credo (ca. 1700–1720)

words as a single phrase. All the examples given in figures 5.20 and 5.21 illustrate this. One possible reason for this is Tarasti's "arch" effect, which, as we have noted, commonly operates within this short section of text, the two (sets of) action phrases framing the contextual. It may have been an instinctive response from composers to organize the text in this way so as to make "Crucifixus" and "passus et sepultus est" exactly equivalent units despite their disparity in words and syllables. The other contributory factor is suggested by the punctuation of the text: "Crucifixus etiam pro nobis sub Pontio Pilato, passus et sepultus est." "Passus et sepultus est" forms a single syntactic phrase: the dividing comma seg-

Figure 5.21. (continued)

A. Carl (15): Missa Solennis in C *(before 1751)*

regates the text immediately preceding this phrase; it does not separate "passus" from "et sepultus est."

Often, composers employ a distinct concluding statement of "passus et sepultus est" or simply "et sepultus est," as if to confirm and finalize the account of the Crucifixion. Many of the examples in figures 5.20 and 5.21 illustrate this, and some further discussion will follow in the case studies. As will be shown later, the final statement may appear in any one of several guises: a straightforward confirmatory phrase, as already illustrated; a separate statement isolated from the main body of the *Crucifixus* by a rest in all parts; for settings with a fuller scoring, a thinly scored "hushed" final statement; or a pedal cadence.

CONCLUSION

This chapter has discussed many of the most frequent traits that have been observed in the sample of *Crucifixus* settings. There are other overall trends that were brought to light by this study, but it was considered more appropriate to discuss them elsewhere. Hence, the next chapters, which are devoted to individual case studies, will refer to further general conventions of this kind in connection with specific contexts. A detailed discussion of patterns of influence, together with a look at modes of transmission, is deferred to chapter 13.

NOTES

1. Naturally, the evolution of the musical language itself (including, especially, via the use of instruments alongside the voices, the ability to draw music out in an extended time span without creating monotony) and the drift toward secular (operatic) models were factors favoring expression; but these expansive tendencies could always be offset by amalgamating what had previously been separate units, as the transformation of the "cantata" Mass into the "symphonic" Mass in the mid-eighteenth century evidences.

2. Michael Talbot, *The Finale in Western Instrumental Music* (Oxford: Oxford University Press, 2001), 16.

3. Talbot, *The Finale in Western Instrumental Music*, 19.

4. MacIntyre, *The Viennese Concerted Mass of the Early Classic Period* (Ann Arbor, Mich.: University of Michigan Press, 1986), 320.

5. Talbot, *The Finale in Western Instrumental Music*, 19.

6. MacIntyre, *The Viennese Concerted Mass*, M. 3. I am grateful to the author and UMI Research Press/Proquest for granting permission for the use of examples from this publication.

7. Karl Geiringer, "The Church Music," in *The Mozart Companion*, ed. H. C. Robbins Landon and Donald Mitchell (London: Faber, 1986), 368.

8. Leonard G. Ratner, *Classic Music: Expression, Form and Style* (New York:

Schirmer, 1980), 154. Marsh's comment comes from *Hints to Young Composers of Instrumental Music* (London, 1800).

9. Gordon Jacob, *Orchestral Technique* (London: Oxford University Press, 1965), 63.

10. The example by Hofmann is from MacIntyre, *The Viennese Concerted Mass*, M. 27.

11. Alec Harman and Anthony Milner, *Late Renaissance and Baroque Music*, vol. 2 of *Man and His Music* (London: Barrie and Jenkins, 1988), 503.

12. In the whole of Palestrina's sacred music, no section ever employs fewer than three vocal parts.

13. Tharald Borgir, *The Performance of the Basso Continuo in Italian Baroque Music* (Ann Arbor, Mich.: University Microfilms International, 1987), 6.

14. Charles Rosen, *The Classical Style* (London: Faber, 1972), 366.

15. Rosen, *The Classical Style*, 366. This last comment actually explains why so many modern musicologists take the classical era as a starting point for many kinds of historical or analytical investigation. Godt's identification of a bias toward instrumental music means that for many commentators, 1770 or so marks a significant watershed.

16. For an observation on how the steady tread of a *Crucifixus* bass can conjure up the *Via dolorosa*, see chapter 10, in connection with Vivaldi's setting.

17. See chapter 7 (Caldara: *Crucifixus a 16 Voci*) and chapter 11 (Lotti: *Crucifixus* Settings for Six and Ten Voices).

18. The first example in figure 5.8 is reproduced by permission of Akademische Druck und Verlagsanstalt: A. Draghi, *Missa a 9*, in *Denkmäler der Tonkunst in Österreich 46*, ed. Guido Adler (1916; reprint, Graz: Akademische Druck und Verlagsanstalt, 1960).

The extract from Zelenka's *Missa Votiva* ZWV 18, ed. Reinhold Kubik, is reproduced by permission of Breitkopf and Härtel (Wiesbaden, Germany, 1997).

19. Dietrich Bartel, *Musica Poetica: Musical-Rhetorical Figures in German Baroque Music* (Lincoln: University of Nebraska Press, 1997), 319.

20. Bartel, *Musica Poetica*, 320.

21. Figure 5.10 is reprinted from Bartel's *Musica Poetica*, 320, by permission of the University of Nebraska Press. © 1997 by the University of Nebraska Press.

22. Excerpts from the *Mass in D* by Salieri (figures 5.11 and 5.13 and figure 6.4) as published in Antonio Salieri, *Mass in D*, ed. Jane Schatkin Hettrick, Recent Researches in Music of the Classical Era series, vol. 39 (Middleton, Wis.: A-R Editions, 1994). Used with permission. All rights reserved.

23. See chapter 6, note 21.

24. The extract from *Missa Brevis Scti. Joannis de Deo* by F. J. Haydn is used by permission of G. Henle Verlag, München, Germany: Haydn, *The Complete Works*, ser. XIII, vol. II, ed. H. C. Robbins Landon in association with Karl Heinz Füssl and Christa Landon (München-Duisberg, Germany: G. Henle Verlag, 1958). The extract by Schmidt is located in MacIntyre, *The Viennese Concerted Mass*, M. 50.

25. MacIntyre, *The Viennese Concerted Mass*, M. 15.

26. The extract from *Theresienmesse* by F. J. Haydn is used by permission of G. Henle Verlag, München, Germany: Haydn, *The Complete Works*, ser. XIII, vol. III, ed. Günter Thomas (München-Duisberg: G. Henle Verlag, 1965).

27. J. M. Haydn's *Missa S. Francisci* is reproduced by permission of Akademische Druck und Verlagsanstalt: in Denkmäler der Tonkunst in Österreich 62, ed. Anton Maria Klafsky (Graz, Austria: Akademische Druck und Verlagsanstalt, 1960).

28. MacIntyre, *The Viennese Concerted Mass*, M. 27.

29. A. Scarlatti, *St. Cecilia Mass*, ed. John Steele (London: Novello, 1968). Copyright 1968 Novello and Company Limited. All rights reserved. International copyright secured. Reprinted by permission.

30. MacIntyre, *The Viennese Concerted Mass*, M. 14.

Part IV

CASE STUDIES

6

Adaptation of Preexisting Music for a Setting of the *Crucifixus*: J. S. Bach: *Crucifixus* from *Mass in B Minor* BWV 232

Johann Sebastian Bach is well known for his recycling of his own works and, indeed, the adaptation of works by others. Christoph Wolff observes that Bach upheld the "perfectionist" view of the seventeenth century:

> Seventeenth-century scientific and philosophical thought was concerned with the notion of perfection: from the perfection of the world system to the search for the perfect government. . . . [That Bach was a perfectionist was] demonstrated by his habit of constant elaboration as represented, for instance, in parody, revision, correction, and expansion of earlier versions [of music].[1]

Many instances of this process can be identified in the *Mass in B Minor* BWV 232.[2] The *Crucifixus* examined here is one important manifestation, being a parody of the first section of an earlier Bach church cantata, *Weinen, Klagen, Sorgen, Zagen* BWV 12.

Weinen, Klagen, Sorgen, Zagen ("Weeping, lamenting, sorrowing, hopelessness"; see table 6.1) was one of Bach's earliest Weimar compositions in the genre, dating from 1714. The text was by Salomo Franck, secretary of the Protestant Consistory and court librarian at Weimar. Franck was also a respected poet, and it has been claimed that Bach was drawn to his texts by the "deep mystic feeling" that characterized them.[3] The cantata

121

Table 6.1.   The Text for *Weinen, Klagen, Sorgen, Zagen* (Salomo Franck)

Weinen, Klagen,	Weeping, lamenting,
Sorgen, Zagen,	sorrowing, hopelessness,
Angst und Not	anxiety (fear) and despair
Sind der Christen Thränenbrot,	are the Tear-bread of Christians
die das Zeichen Jesu tragen.	who bear the mark of Jesus.

was written for the third Sunday after Easter. The theme for this Sunday is found in Psalm 66, the Epistle (1 Peter 2:11–20), and the Gospel (John 16:16–23), centering on the "need to trust in God in times of trouble."[4]

THE *CREDO*

In Bach's setting of the *Credo* (*Symbolum Nicenum*), the composer's "concern with symmetry" of form is evident.[5] In fact, the compositional process behind this movement further underlines his interest in balance and proportion. The *Symbolum Nicenum* is physically a separate manuscript, distinct from the other movements. Bach made several alterations, adding the *Et incarnatus* on a separate folio between the *Et in unum* and the *Crucifixus*. This addition replaces what was originally the final section of the *Et in unum* (that is, *Et incarnatus*). This change necessitated a new underlay for the vocal parts of the *Et in unum*, which were added on spare paper at the end of the *Credo*.[6] The significance of this amendment can be seen in figure 6.1, which demonstrates the symmetry of the overall design of the *Credo*.[7] It becomes evident that the *Crucifixus* forms a central point for the *Credo*, offset by the two choruses on either side (*Et incarnatus* and *Et resurrexit*).[8] Four bars of instrumental introduction, not present in the cantata or indeed in the original *Crucifixus* setting, were added to the *Crucifixus*; these serve to separate and demarcate the two extended passages of choral writing in the *Et incarnatus* and the *Crucifixus*. In contrast, the vocal passages at the end of the *Crucifixus* and the opening of the *Et resurrexit* are juxtaposed for maximum contrast. The addition of the introductory four bars to the *Crucifixus* increased the total number of bars for that movement to fifty-three. Robin Leaver points out that this is an indivisible prime number—most appropriate for a movement that is central to the entire *Credo*.[9] The tonal plan of the *Credo* is also carefully constructed (see figure 6.1). A similarly chiastic layout is adopted for BWV 4 (see figure 6.2).

Leaver supports this view: he suggests that the composition process of the *Credo* demonstrates Bach's intention to organize music symmetrically around a "focal point" and that the use of the *Crucifixus* as the central

Figure 6.1.   Symmetry and Tonal Plan of the *Credo*

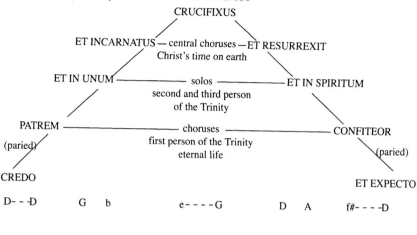

Figure 6.2.   The Chiastic Plan of *Cantata No. 4*

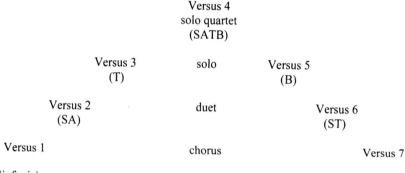

Versus 4
solo quartet
(SATB)

Versus 3   solo   Versus 5
(T)   (B)

Versus 2   duet   Versus 6
(SA)   (ST)

Versus 1   chorus   Versus 7

(Sinfonia)
key throughout = e minor

movement of the *Credo* was logical in a religious sense: "Theologically . . . the work of the cross stands at the very center of the Christian faith."[10] The underlying theory in Leaver's contribution concerns number associations in the *Credo*. He has looked closely at the number of bars of all the *Credo* movements and has attempted to relate these numbers to biblical/ theological associations. If the Crucifixion is considered in terms of number associations, it would appear that Bach had a further reason for moving the *Crucifixus* to the position of movement number 5:

> Bach's revision of the structure of the *Credo* led to some interesting numerical associations with regard to the sequence of sections. . . . It is interesting to note that traditionally 5 has been understood as a symbol of the cross (4 plus

the intersection), and there were 5 wounds of the cross (hands, feet and side).[11]

The *Credo* contains contrasting styles of movement, but these are carefully organized in order to preserve the sense of symmetry, order, and conclusion. One such example of this is the unifying effect created by setting the first movement of each of the paired choruses that frame the *Credo* in *stile antico*:

> The return to the *stile antico* at the *Confiteor* creates the impression that the movement picks up the threads of the opening *Credo in unum Deum*.[12]

BACH'S ADAPTATION OF THE OPENING CHORUS OF CANTATA BWV 12

What were the reasons for Bach's choice of the first part of this opening chorus as the basis for his setting of the *Crucifixus*? Obviously, it is impossible to state authoritatively what Bach's criteria were when he selected BWV 12 for this part of the Mass. However, I would suggest that his prime reason was the congruence of the overall mood between *Weinen, Klagen, Sorgen, Zagen* and the *Crucifixus*. Another factor was the ground bass of a descending chromatic fourth (*passus duriusculus*). This bass line was commonly recognized as an emblem of lament, a fact that made the original setting even more appropriate for adaptation:

> During the fourth and fifth decades of the seventeenth century, a particular bass-line pattern, the descending minor tetrachord, came to assume a quite specific function associated almost exclusively with a single expressive genre, the lament.[13]

The term *passus duriusculus* appears in the treatises of Christoph Bernhard:

> *passus duriusculus*, einer Stimmen gegen sich selbst, ist, wenn eine Stimme ein *Semitonium* minus steiget oder fället. [The somewhat hard passage of one voice against itself (that is, consecutive notes in a melody, not intervals between two voices) is when a voice rises or falls a minor semitone.]

> Evidently, it was the minor semitone in the chromatic fourth that prompted Bernhard's term. *Passus* (for a melody that moves "by step") is a conscious antithesis to *saltus* (one that "leaps"), found elsewhere in the treatise: it is a musical distinction of greater importance to composers and singers than to rhetoricians. If only because of this, it could well be that Bernhard's idea of

passus, saltus, or *duriusculus* was his own and did not come from earlier books on rhetoric. So far, no evidence has been found that it did.[14]

Peter Williams also comments that Bach probably recognized this device as an emblem of lament:

> When the chromatic fourth was used for the bass of a familiar chorale [the last chorale from Cantata BWV 105, *Herr, gehe nicht ins Gericht* (1723)] . . . it would be a conventional means of drawing attention, at that particular moment, to texts that concerned sin, strife or sorrow.[15]

The *passus duriusculus* in its chromatic fourth guise is no stranger to *Crucifixus* settings:[16] it appears in the bass line at the opening of G. P. Colonna's setting and also in Zelenka's *Missa S. Caeciliae* (see figure 6.3).

To return to the subject of Bach's choice of model, the musical quality of the cantata section was high, and the genre of the model was appropriate. According to Christoph Wolff, the choice of style for the model appears to have been deliberate as well. Its conservative idiom, juxtaposed to the progressive style of the *Et incarnatus,* enabled Bach to "underscore what he unquestionably perceived as the universality and timeless validity of the liturgical and dogmatic meaning of the ancient Mass text."[17]

However, the model would not have been selected for its potential for

Figure 6.3.   Use of *Lamento* **in** *Crucifixus* **Settings**

G. P. Colonna (17): Messa Concertati a 5 Voci (ca. 1680 [?])

Figure 6.3. (continued)

J. D. Zelenka (100): Missa S. Caeciliae ZWV 1 (ca. 1711)

melodic embellishment or because of its prosodic similarities. The two texts are extremely dissimilar in terms of meter (that is, one is poetry, the other prose). The problems of accommodating this new text are discussed in the next section. Robin Leaver suggests a further reason for Bach's choice of the model. This is that the original text (*Weinen, Klagen, Sorgen, Zagen*) is about the cross but only in an indirect way since it is never clearly stated ("das Zeichen Jesu"). Leaver suggests that in the same way, the sign of the cross appears in a "disguised" manner on the score at the second set of entries of the first four words (bars 5–9), where the order of the voices changes to a zigzag arrangement (tenor, soprano, bass, alto).[18]

If the score of *Weinen, Klagen, Sorgen, Zagen* is examined in greater detail with this suggestion in mind, it becomes apparent that there is in fact more than just this one subtle reference to the sign of the cross. For example, a crossing of vocal parts occurs in bar 4 between the bass and tenor; further on, at bar 39, the bass has an arrangement of notes that is clearly recognizable as a "musical sign of the cross."[19] These "hidden" signs of the cross made *Weinen, Klagen, Sorgen, Zagen* ideal for use as a model for the *Crucifixus*, where the text centers around images of Christ on the cross; so a work with built-in references to the cross would be an obvious candidate.

Our knowledge that the *Crucifixus* from the *Mass in B Minor* BWV 232 is a parody of an earlier work renders a self-contained analysis of the movement inadequate. It is also vital to examine in detail how Bach adapted *Weinen, Klagen, Sorgen, Zagen* before considering whether the amendments made can be used to support a general theory that there was a widely accepted tradition for setting the *Crucifixus* to music.

Appendix C attempts a detailed comparison of the *Crucifixus* and the related section in *Weinen, Klagen, Sorgen, Zagen*, listing all the changes that Bach made in the process of adaptation. This analysis takes the form of a straightforward comparison between the model and its parody. Rhetorical figures are commented on where they arise as a result of the adaptation process. While the issue of rhetoric should not be ignored, great care needs to be exercised when examining the parody and its model in this light. Bach may well have made deliberate use of rhetorical devices in BWV 12, but it is essential to remember that when accommodating a new text (with no metrical similarities, let alone congruent phrases), he had to fit the new text to the original melodic lines, come what may. While the rhetorical devices might remain appropriate to the parody, they might equally lose the precise significance they had in the model. It is therefore important not to read too much into the unavoidable reuse of these figures. One such instance of overinterpretation occurs in a recent study by Lisa Szeker-Madden where a musical-rhetorical analysis of BWV 12 and its parody was undertaken. The stated aim of this analysis was to prove that "Bach's borrowings from the opening chorus of Cantata 12 are actually musical-rhetorical figures" and that "his application of the parody procedure thus represents the re-use of specific musical-rhetorical gestures which are suitable for the embellishment of a particular *topos*."[20] It is far more important to look for the creation of new rhetorical figures through the adaptation process and then to examine their significance in relation to the tradition of the *Crucifixus*.

Bars 1 to 29: The *Crucifixus* begins with a four-bar introduction (one statement of the ground: see chapter 6 for the reasons behind this). The number of notes in the bass line of the *Crucifixus* has been doubled via note repetition to create a slow, throbbing effect (a typical characteristic of both *lamento* and *Crucifixus* settings).[21]

The first two changes to the music serve to alter the interval of vocal entries above the bass line: the alto entry at bar 6 and the soprano entry at bar 10 are amended to enter a minor instead of a major third above the bass line (compound intervals are treated for analytical purposes as the equivalent of simple intervals). This change has the "vertical" effect of producing an augmented fourth between the sopranos and altos in bar 6 and a diminished fifth between the tenors and sopranos in bar 10; these altered intervals are used to create an anguished effect, illustrating the word "Crucifixus" in time-honored fashion.[22] The rhetorical term *parrhesia* is used in baroque treatises to describe a dissonance of this kind between two voices.[23] The horizontal effect of the alteration is to create downward semitonal movement within the phrase: small, falling intervals were commonly employed in baroque music to express weeping.[24] At bar 13, the sopranos are given the awkward, poignant interval of an augmented second to sing (on the word "Crucifixus"), where Bach originally had a smooth major second. The relation of this altered interval to the traditional treatment of the *Crucifixus* (and, especially, of its opening word) has already been mentioned; it is also recognizable as the rhetorical figure *saltus duriusculus*.[25] The alto entry, in imitation directly after this, retains the augmented second. The next changes that appear (bar 16, alto, tenor; bar 18, bass; bar 19, soprano; bar 19, tenor; bar 27, alto, creating an *exclamatio*) serve the purpose of accommodating the new text.[26] The exception during this section of music is the bass in bar 20, which Bach recomposes to make a decorative arch, motivated, perhaps, by the greater urgency of motion brought about by splitting the original instrumental bass notes.

Bars 29 to 36: At bar 31, one notices the addition of a passing note to the tenor line. This is probably a simple refinement aimed at creating a smoother vocal line. In bar 35, the soprano line leaps down an octave instead of remaining static; this appears to be another refining touch.[27] The leap again introduces the rhetorical figure *exclamatio*. It is interesting to note where the sections of text end and begin within these bars. BWV 12 ends one section at bar 28 ("Angst und Not"), the new section beginning on beat 1 of bar 29 ("sind der Christen Tränenbrot"). BWV 232 ends on the first beat of bar 33 and starts the next phrase on the second beat of the same bar. If the texts are compared (table 6.2), it can be seen that in BWV 12 the line break in the poem demands a more clear-cut break than does the prose of the *Crucifixus*; within these bars, Bach is setting only the short phrase "passus et sepultus est," with the result that the antecedent (bars 29–32) and consequent (bars 33–36) phrases are set to the same portion of text. Since continuity is now desirable, Bach bridges over the origi-

Table 6.2.   Comparison of Use of Texts

Bars	BWV 232	Bars	BWV 12
5–13	Crucifixus	1–9	Weinen, Klagen, Sorgen, Zagen,
13–29	crucifixus etiam pro nobis sub Pontio Pilato,	9–25	Weinen, Klagen, Sorgen, Zagen,
29–36	passus et sepultus est.	25–32	Angst und Not / sind der Christen Tränenbrot,
37–49	crucifixus etiam pro nobis sub Pontio Pilato, passus et sepultus est.	33–45	Angst und Not / sind der Christen Tränenbrot.

nal caesura (between bars 28 and 29 in BWV 12, equivalent to bars 32–33 in BWV 232).

Bars 37 to 49: In BWV 232, Bach returns to the beginning of the text and works through it; at the same point, BWV 12 is still developing the second part of the text. The alteration to the soprano line at bar 40 appears to be another refinement, although it hardly makes the line easier to sing (*exclamatio*). However, the changes to the soprano and alto parts at bars 42 and 43, respectively, have clearly been effected in order to accommodate the new text. As already mentioned, the existing bass part in BWV 12 at bar 39 takes the form of the *crux*. The alteration to the alto part creates another *crux* and also a rhetorical figure: the *fauxbourdon*, where two or more parts move in thirds or sixths. The same applies to the addition to the tenor part in bar 45 and to the loss of an upper auxiliary note for the alto in bar 46. A number of changes are evident in the last three bars of this section, where Bach seems to be attempting a musical expression of the "lowering" of the body into the grave by means of descents in the vocal lines and low tessituras (recognized by baroque theorists as *catabasis*).

Bars 49 to 53: This is an addition, having no equivalent in BWV 12. Within these bars, the key changes magically from the mourning of E minor to the peace of G major. The parts once again descend but are this time unaccompanied, except by continuo. The effect of contrast that Bach creates here by employing this virtually *a cappella* postscript to an instrumentally accompanied chorus was not unprecedented in the baroque; it appears, for instance, at the end of Handel's *Acis and Galatea* ("Mourn all ye Muses") to the words "Ah, the gentle Acis is no more."[28] The prototype is probably to be found in Lully's *Atys* (1676), where, likewise, a simple, block-chordal *a cappella* mode of narration is used to express collective grief over a death. Several other *Crucifixus* settings share this method of contrast for the concluding statement of "et sepultus est."

Albrechtsberger (2) omits the violins and *organo* that have accompanied throughout, leaving only the four voices to complete the setting. Dittersdorf (18) does exactly the same; the sense of contrast is even greater here since oboes are also included in the orchestration. Salieri employs a fairly full orchestra for the *Crucifixus* from his *Mass in D* (91). For the two statements of "et sepultus est," he reduces the scoring to voices alone (see figure 6.4). Zelenka's setting of the *Crucifixus* from *Missa Omnium Sanctorum* ZWV 21 (96) also uses this device to good effect. Here, most of the setting is contrapuntal, the vocal lines supported by strings and woodwind. Zelenka achieves contrast in the last few bars by omitting all instruments except *organo* and by switching from contrapuntal writing to near chordal for this concluding statement. The "stillness" of death is expressed by use of pedal in the upper voices (see figure 6.4).[29]

Returning to Bach's setting, a pivotal chord leading to G major occurs at bar 51[3] as the bass unexpectedly moves up through c♯ to d (the dominant of G). A pungent German sixth occurs over the c♯, resolving to V (with a 4–3 suspension) in preparation for I, the sopranos, altos, and tenors being forced down to the extreme lower limits of their registers. The final chord is a full one, skillfully voiced in such a way as to be clearly audible, even if sung at the lowest possible dynamic level.

THE TEXTS

Bach's adaptation of music originally composed for a poetic text to a prose text seems on the whole to be very successful. It is easy to be hypercritical and judge the *Crucifixus* setting as the inferior of the two, especially in the light of some received opinions about parody and self-borrowing. The task Bach set himself was not a straightforward one. When recycling the music, he had to ensure that the new words did not disrupt the flow of the music. The scale of the two texts was different so that the pattern of distribution of the words in the parody had to be considered very carefully. Moreover, the phonetic quality of the two languages was sufficiently different to be a relevant factor.

The parallelism within the text of *Weinen, Klagen, Sorgen, Zagen* is reflected in the music. The opening words have a similar phonetic quality: they are all bisyllabic verbal nouns, expressing cognate manifestations of grief. Bach creates subtle differences when setting each to music, most notably in the opening section. These bars are loosely imitative; the rhythmic pattern is identical for the first eight entries (see figure 6.5). However—and this is the vital point—in their melodic aspect the phrases are varied. "Weinen" is based on a falling minor second (downward semitonal movement was often used to express weeping). Both "Klagen" and

Figure 6.4. *A cappella* Conclusions to *Crucifixus* Settings

Figure 6.4. (continued)

A. Salieri (91): Mass in D (1788)

Figure 6.4. (continued)

J. D. Zelenka (96): Missa Omnium Sanctorum ZWV 21 (1741)

Figure 6.5.   Rhythmic Pattern for Opening Entries

"Zagen," perhaps in order to draw attention to their rhyme, are based on a descending major second. "Sorgen," in contrast, is built on a falling arpeggiated phrase that spans a diminished fifth. Obviously, four words as different as these (at least phonetically) need a measure of individual treatment *in contrast* to a single word (that is, "Crucifixus") that, if repeated in imitation, would in theory require a less differentiated approach. The possible reasons why Bach changed the melodic shape of the alto and soprano entries in the *Crucifixus* (bars 6 and 10) have already been discussed, but a further possible reason for this alteration now presents itself: faced with imitative statements of the same word, Bach perhaps aimed to make the musical phrases more alike. By chromatically altering these two entries (originally both set to "Klagen"), he creates *exact* imitation (falling minor seconds) of the opening phrase. True, the remaining entries in each set (originally set to "Sorgen" and "Zagen") are not adapted in any way, but it remains significant that the second phrase is modified. It is less important than previously to make the second and fourth entries match (originally "Klagen" and "Zagen") because the factor of rhyme has been replaced by that of word repetition.

In the next section (*Weinen, Klagen, Sorgen, Zagen*, bars 9–25 [corresponding section in the *Crucifixus*: bars 13–29]), Bach continues to set the words contrapuntally. In general, "Klagen" and "Zagen" are treated melismatically, while "Sorgen" is usually accorded a more syllabic treatment. The opening statements of "Weinen" in this section are heard in imitation. They employ a new motive based on a rising third (g'–a'–b' / f#'–g#'–a' / e-f#-g / a-b-c'). This motive is treated imitatively in inverted form in bars 13 to 16. The opening (*Seufzer*-like) subject from the first section reappears in both original and elaborated forms in the upper three voices, when "Weinen" returns (see figure 6.6). Unfortunately, the unifying and cumulative effect of this treatment is sacrificed in the process of adaptation since in the *Crucifixus* Bach has at this point finished setting the word "Crucifixus" and has already moved on to "etiam pro nobis" and "sub Pontio Pilato."

At bar 25 in *Weinen, Klagen, Sorgen, Zagen*, Bach arrives at a new section of text: "Angst und Not sind der Christen Tränenbrot." The initial statement is treated syllabically (bars 25–32). In the corresponding section of the *Crucifixus*, the opposite is true, notably in connection with the word

Figure 6.6.   Reappearance of the Opening Subject in *Weinen, Klagen, Sorgen, Zagen*

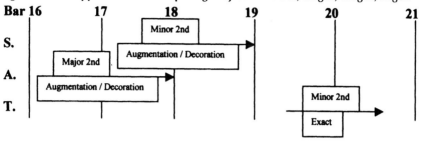

"passus." The difference possibly indicates Bach's awareness and acceptance of an established *Crucifixus* tradition.

At bar 33 in *Weinen, Klagen, Sorgen, Zagen*, the music once again becomes more contrapuntal, "Angst und Not" being treated in imitation. At this point in BWV 232, Bach returns to the beginning of the text so that the word "Crucifixus" becomes set to the imitative phrase originally used for "Angst und Not." Here, one typical problem with imposing a new text on music originally written for a different text becomes apparent: "Angst und Not" comprises three syllables, whereas "Crucifixus" has four; some adjustment is therefore needed in order to fit the new text to the music. The naturally accented syllables of "Crucifixus" are "Cru-" and "-fi-," so, although the number of notes in the subject (four) might initially suggest that the word would fit the original music, the accentual structure of the new word prevents this. The "-fi-" of "Crucifixus" must unavoidably fall on the strong beat of the bar.

Further statements of "Angst und Not" are set to paired crotchets (S, bar 35; A, bar 37; S, bar 38; B, bar 39; T, bar 40); the unifying effect of this rhythmic pattern applied to the same words is regrettably lost in the reworking, where Bach has set himself the task of working again through the entire text during this section.

IMPROVEMENT—OR ACCEPTANCE
OF A TRADITION?

Three processes were doubtless happening concurrently in Bach's adaptation of BWV 12:

1. Adaptation to accommodate new words
2. Improvement (or refinement) of the original
3. Minor alterations in conformity with the established tradition of *Crucifixus* settings

Table 6.3 attempts a summary of all the amendments and additions made in the process of adaptation (see appendix C) by categorizing them under these three heads. The specific amendments that suggest that Bach was aware of existing traditions when he set the *Crucifixus* appear in the final column (3).

The changes within bars 5 to 14 are very subtle (alteration of a note by a semitone here or there), but they effectively describe the pain and suffering of the word "Crucifixus" by creating augmented seconds, augmented fourths, and a diminished fifth. These alterations can be understood as stemming from Bach's awareness of existing conventions of word painting for the word "Crucifixus." The other amendments that suggest Bach's familiarity with standard expressive devices in settings of the *Crucifixus* are those occurring on the words "et sepultus est," namely, the "directional convention," here in its descending guise (the rhetoricians' *catabasis*). Bach certainly seems to be expressing the sense of "sepultus" by the changes he makes (bars 37–49) and even more so in the newly composed final bars.

There is one further piece of evidence to support the view that Bach had a close knowledge of the central Italian-German *Crucifixus* tradition. His setting of the word "passus" conforms fully to our expectation of long-drawn-out notes or (as here) melismatic phrases in illustration of the idea of "suffering" (as mentioned in this chapter).[30] Long note values are thus able to convey the sense of exceptional duration both visually and aurally.

What is admirable is the fact that Bach has managed to interweave these conventions into a composition originally conceived for a different text. True, the shadow of this text imposed rigid constraints. But Bach's creativity was nevertheless able to flourish and develop within those confines. My view that the *Crucifixus* was no mechanical contrafactum but a profound and ingenious act of reconception conforms to the spirit of Malcolm Boyd's comment about the *Mass in B Minor* in his book on Bach:

> No other work more convincingly demonstrates that at the highest level Bach's process of parody, adaptation and compilation must be accepted as a creative act almost on a par with what we normally think of as "original composition."[31]

At the same time, the nature of this reconception—particularly where it goes beyond the strictly necessary—illuminates and validates the idea of a *Crucifixus* tradition (a set of *topoi*) received and transmitted by a long line of composers, which included J. S. Bach.

Table 6.3.   Summary of Amendments and Additions

Bar	Part	Nature of Amendment/Addition	1	2	3
6 (2)	A	Alto entry placed at a minor third above the bass line instead of a major third			*
10 (6)	S	As for A, bar 6			*
13 (9)	S	a' has been changed to an a♯' to create an augmented second in the melodic line			*
14 (10)	A	f♯' has been changed to an f' for the same reason as S, bar 13			*
15 (11)	A	a' has been changed to an a♯'		*	
16 (12)	T	The addition of a g on the first beat of the bar	*		
16 (12)	A	The addition of an upper auxiliary note c''		*	
16 (12)	A	The addition of a b'	*		
18 (14)	B	The addition of an a on the first beat of the bar	*		
19 (15)	S	The addition of a g' on the first beat of the bar	*		
19 (15)	T	The addition of an unaccented anticipatory note	*		
20 (16)	B	The addition of an f♯ on beat 1 and accented passing notes on beats 2 and 3	*	*	
27 (23)	A	The addition of an a'	*		
31 (27)	T	The addition of a passing note		*	
33 (29)	S	The addition of a crotchet on beat 1 with an octave leap downward			*
40 (36)	S	The two crotchets on beat 3 now read d''–a' instead of b' – c''		*	
42 (38)	S	The addition of an extra note, a'. Change in pitch of the following note to b' to give a smoother melodic line	*	*	
43 (39)	A	The addition of f♯'-g'-e'-f♯' in sixths with the bass	*	*	*
45 (41)	T	The addition of an e on beat 2	*		
46 (42)	A	The omission of the anticipatory f' to beat 3	*		
47 (43)	S, T	The b' in the soprano line is suspended to create a seventh with the bass line. In consequence, the tenor line has to remain on a g♯ instead of moving immediately to an a. The prolonged soprano note helps create a greater sense of ''descending'' (''sepultus'' = burial).	*	*	
(47–49) (43–45)	all	All adjustments serve to illustrate the word ''sepultus.'' In bars 48 to 49 the bass moves up a fourth to make a perfect cadence rather than descending a fifth (this is more conclusive in its effect and is not required here because of the addition of a final section).			*

The categories are as follows:
1 adaptation in order to accommodate new words
2 improvement or refinement of the original
3 minor alterations in conformity with the tradition of *Crucifixus* settings
Bar numbers in brackets refer to the corresponding bars in *Weinen, Klagen, Sorgen, Zagen.*

NOTES

1. Christoph Wolff, "J. S. Bach and the Legacy of the Seventeenth Century," in *Bach Studies*, vol. 2, ed. Daniel R. Melamed (Cambridge: Cambridge University Press, 1995), 200.

2. For a listing of adaptations see George B. Stauffer, *Bach: The Mass in B Minor* (New York: Schirmer, 1997), 48–49. Stauffer's book should also be referred to for an in-depth account of the composition of the Mass.

3. Karl Geiringer, *Johann Sebastian Bach: The Culmination of an Era* (London: Allen and Unwin, 1966), 149.

4. Stephen Daw, *The Music of Johann Sebastian Bach: The Choral Works* (Rutherford, N.J.: Fairleigh Dickinson University Press, 1981), 94.

5. John Butt, *Bach: Mass in B Minor* (Cambridge: Cambridge University Press, 1991), 94.

6. Friedrich Smend, *Kritischer Bericht, Messe in H-Moll* (Kassel, Germany: Bärenreiter-Verlag, 1956), 152–53. Robert L. Marshall, *The Compositional Process of J. S. Bach: A Study of the Autograph Scores of the Vocal Works*, vol. 1 (Princeton, N.J.: Princeton University Press, 1972), 57–58.

7. Figure 6.1 is from Butt, *Bach*, 94.

8. Christoph Wolff points out that Bach has placed the earliest (*Crucifixus*) and latest (*Et incarnatus*) settings of the *Mass in B Minor* side by side. He suggests that Bach's reasons for revising the *Credo* were that it was "lacking a genuine forward looking dimension" and that the result of the reorganzation of the *Credo* created a "refocused architectonic center as well as an unprecedented pinnacle of cultivated musical modernity." "'Et Incarnatus' and 'Crucifixus': The Earliest and Latest Settings of Bach's B-Minor Mass," in *Eighteenth Century Music in Theory and Practice: Essays in Honor of Alfred Mann*, ed. Mary Anne Parker (New York: Pendragon Press, 1994), 17.

9. Robin A. Leaver, "Number Associations in the Structure of Bach's *Credo* BWV 232," *Bach* 7, no. 3 (1976): 19.

10. Leaver, "Number Associations in the Structure of Bach's Credo," 18.

11. Leaver, "Number Associations in the Structure of Bach's Credo," 20.

12. David Humphreys, "The Credo of the B Minor Mass: Style and Symbol," *The Musical Times* 140, no. 1867 (1999): 55.

13. Ellen Rosand, "The Descending Tetrachord: An Emblem of Lament," *The Musical Quarterly* 65 (1979): 346.

14. Peter Williams, *The Chromatic Fourth during Four Centuries of Music* (Oxford: Clarendon, 1997), 61–62. Bartel informs us that the term *passus duriusculus* is "only encountered in Bernhard's *Tractatus*" in *Musica Poetica: Musical-Rhetorical Figures in German Baroque Music* (Lincoln: University of Nebraska Press, 1997), 357.

15. Williams, *The Chromatic Fourth during Four Centuries of Music*, 77.

16. It is important to remember that *passus duriusculus* was a term used to describe a passage "realized through various uses of the semitone" (Bartel, *Musica Poetica*, 357). A *passus duriusculus* may rise or fall. The chromatic fourth is confined by the boundaries of its namesake interval but again may occur in

ascending or descending form. Where the chromatic fourth appears (particularly) as a descending bass line, it is often described as a lament.

17. Wolff, "The Earliest and Latest Settings of Bach's B-Minor Mass," 17.

18. Robin A. Leaver, "Parody and Theological Consistency: Notes on Bach's A-Major Mass," *Bach* 21 (1990): 32.

19. The arrangement of notes is A–B–G–A. See appendix C, bar 39, bass.

20. Lisa Szeker-Madden, "*Topos*, Text, and the Parody Problem in Bach's Mass in B Minor, BWV 232," *Canadian University Music Review* 15 (1995): 125.

21. A regular "trudging" movement was sometimes used in *Crucifixus* settings to create a tragic, processional effect (the road to Calvary). One such example is the *Crucifixus* movement in Vivaldi's *Credo* RV 591; see chapter 10. Other examples are found in Caldara's *Mass for 4 Voices* (9), Heinichen's *Missa 12* (50), Albrechtsberger's *Missa Annuntiationis* (2), and Zelenka's *Missa Circumcisionis* (98).

22. Examples of *Crucifixus* settings employing these kinds of intervals for effect on the word "Crucifixus" are Perti, *Messa Canone a 3*—diminished fourths (87), Hofmann, *Missa in D*—diminished sevenths (52), and Caldara, *Mass in F*—diminished fifths (10).

23. *Parrhesia* is described by a number of theorists. Burmeister (Rostock, 1606) is more specific in his description ("a mingling of a single dissonance among consonances, the dissonance being equal to one half of the whole tractus") than Kircher (Rome, 1650), who refers to it as "a false relation, a stark dissonance, especially a tritone between parts." George J. Buelow, "Rhetoric and Music," in *The New Grove Dictionary of Music and Musicians*, vol. 15, ed. Stanley Sadie (London: Macmillan, 1980), 798.

24. These small, falling intervals used to express anguish and suffering are a common occurrence in settings of the *Crucifixus* and are also known as the rhetorical figure *pathopoeia*, for example, in Bertoni, *Crucifixus con Organo a 4 Voci* (5), on the words "sub Pontio Pilato," and Hasse, *Mass in D Minor* (32), on the word "passus."

25. *Saltus duriusculus* was a rhetorical term used to denote any chromatically altered (diminished, augmented) leap.

26. *Exclamatio* was used to describe a leap greater than a third—literally, an "exclamation."

27. Once again, the alteration generates greater rhythmic activity, as in bar 20 earlier.

28. Handel employs the same *topos* of collective mourning in *Saul* ("thy choicest Youth on Gilboa slain" from "Mourn, Israel") and *Semele* ("is lost in smoke" from "Oh terror and astonishment").

29. Salieri: see chapter 5, note 22. The extract from Zelenka's *Missa Omnium Sanctorum* ZWV 21 (1741), ed. Wolfgang Horn, is reproduced by permission of Breitkopf and Härtel (Wiesbaden, Germany, 1989).

30. Suffering differs from ordinary pain, as we said earlier, through its duration (a sharp stab does not qualify).

31. Malcolm Boyd, *Bach* (London: Dent, 1983), 172. Other commentators who perceive Bach's parody process in a similar way include Alfred Mann: "It is evi-

dent that the creative process does not cease when Bach begins to 'copy'—that is, when he returns to an old score in order to modify it for a new purpose. Transcription leads to revision and revision to the expression of totally new ideas. . . . The composer's memory of his own works extends from the more obvious to the remote—and practical necessity merges with critical choice, 'borrowing' with abiding inspiration." "Bach's Parody Technique and Its Frontiers," in *Bach Studies*, vol. 1, ed. Don O. Franklin (Cambridge: Cambridge University Press, 1989), 124.

Organization of Texture and Text: Caldara: *Crucifixus a 16 Voci*

Caldara's *Crucifixus a 16 Voci* is unusual for the size of the vocal ensemble it employs. The use of sixteen voices (four each of SATB) provides the composer with a number of musical possibilities but also brings disadvantages. The greatest potential that this combination of voices offers lies in the great variety in density of texture and the timbral diversity obtainable. Different vocal registers can be emphasized by combining selected voices. With sixteen voices, an almost limitless number of different vocal combinations become possible, and the overlap of phrases can occur with great ease. However, writing "correct" counterpoint for this number of voices is no easy task, most notably in passages where all the voices are employed at once. Moreover, with so many voices being used, there is a danger that the setting can become fragmented rather than being projected successfully as a unified whole. However, in the hands of a skillful and experienced composer such as Caldara, a *stile antico* setting can reap the benefits and avoid the pitfalls of a multivoice composition.

ORGANIZATION OF TEXTURE

Caldara has organized this setting into three distinct sections, plus a final cadence comprising four bars (see appendix D). Each section begins with a light scoring that builds up gradually to a *tutti* for all sixteen voices. This fuller scoring characterizes the final bars of each section and also the four-bar cadential phrase concluding the setting. This four-bar cadence is separated from the preceding part of the setting by a bar's rest. In order to highlight this bar of silence to its fullest effect, it was vital to use the full complement of voices both immediately before and immediately after it. Such a collective silence was symbolic of death—theorists of the day referred to it as the musical-rhetorical figure *aposiopesis*.[1]

Table 7.1 gives the approximate dimensions of each section. Within these sections, the proportion of music devoted to the tuttis is shown in table 7.2 (where "tutti" is defined as the simultaneous employment of all sixteen voices together). Here we witness an unusual distribution of full and lighter scoring. Within the first section, approximately half the music is scored for all sixteen voices. The second section has a lower proportion—approximately a third—while the third section has the largest: about two-thirds. The second section is notable, however, for containing two passages of relatively heavy scoring, including bars 28 to 29, not long after the start. This initial climax arises from the rapid cumulative effect of imitative entries at the outset of the section. The careful planning extends to both the contrapuntal motives and the treatment of the text (these two factors being inseparable), as we shall see later on. However, what is already evident even at this stage of the analysis is that the systematic underlying framework has the effect of creating a unified "whole."

There are local climaxes (that is, where Caldara uses all sixteen voices) in each section. This "decentralized" form of organization, as opposed to working toward a single climax, may have been used for a number of reasons:

Table 7.1. Organization of Sections

Section	Bars	Length
1	1–23	23 bars
2	23–39	17 bars
3	39–53	15 bars
Cadence	55–58	4 bars

Table 7.2. Incidence of Full Scoring within Sections

Section	Bars	Length
1	12–23	12 bars
2	34–39	6 bars
3	43–53	11 bars

1. The large scale of the setting, while in one way advantageous since it affords scope for creativity and development, would make it difficult to sustain a lengthy buildup to a final section where all sixteen voices were used for the first time.
2. The unusual combination of so many voices requires the composer to employ a dense texture frequently in order to make the most of his resources and justify their exceptionality.
3. There is an intrinsic appeal in contrasting thinner and thicker textures.

So, leaving aside the passages of full scoring, how exactly does Caldara utilize the voices in this setting?

Frequently, there is a "cascade effect" of successive entries created at the opening of a section. This is most evident at the outset of sections 1 and 2. The first section very literally has a downward "cascade" of vocal entries (beginning with the sopranos, followed by the altos, tenors, and finally the basses) over eight bars (Bach uses a similar "cascade" organization at the beginning of his *Crucifixus*, with successive entries of SATB). At the same time, Caldara cleverly organizes this section to create an opposition of upper voices (sopranos and altos alone in the first six bars) to lower voices (tenors and basses alone in the two following bars). A similar process occurs in the second section, where entries cascade from soprano through the middle voices to the bass. However, this time there is no such neat opposition of voices. The entries are packed together much more tightly, and, as already mentioned, the voices build up to make a cumulative effect. In the third section, there is no literal "cascade" since the order of entries is ASTB. It is interesting to see that Caldara gives each group of voices a clear identity; the four soprano voices are employed as a distinct group, as are the other groups of like voices, and they retain this group identity, in particular for the imitative entries on the word "Crucifixus."

ORGANIZATION OF THE TEXT

Before a discussion about the actual organization of the text can take place, it is necessary to examine the way in which Caldara sets different sections of text.

The Motives

The classic musical sign of the cross is used as the basis for the word "Crucifixus." The motive incorporates a leap of a minor sixth upward (*exclamatio*), followed by a descent of a diminished seventh (*saltus durius-culus*), before returning to the opening note (see figure 7.3). The third note of the motive is a sharpened note (to correspond with the "-fi-" of "Cruci-fixus"), which likewise conforms to our expectations of a "Crucifixus" motive. Rhythmically, this phrase employs four even notes (four minums), so there is no rhythmic emphasis on the third syllable of the word but only the "natural" strong inflection of this note as it falls on the first beat of the second bar. However, Caldara highlights this syllable not by making it the local high point of this phrase (that honor falls to the second syllable) but, instead, by making it the lowest point of the phrase. Attention is drawn away subtly from the preceding note (the actual high-est note of the phrase and what one would expect to be the climactic point of the phrase) by leaping down a diminished seventh and sharpening the note on the syllable "-fi-." The use of this anguished interval naturally focuses the musical attention on the third note of the phrase. Another dimension to the musical symbolism of the cross occurs as the *Crucifixus* subject "crosses" over its associated countersubject (an example of *meta-basis*). Here, we also have an example of a chromatic *Crucifixus* subject being offset against a diatonic countersubject (although that countersub-ject does not always remain diatonic, as the phrase in S_4, bars 2^4–3^4, shows). As Caldara progresses through this setting, this opening subject is adjusted according to the tonal center and underlying harmonic struc-ture (see table 7.3). Some of the chromatic impact is lost, but Caldara still attempts to retain, as best he can, the overall cross shape of the subject.

This countersubject on the words "etiam pro nobis" is contained within the compass of the subject (that is, within the span of the initial minor sixth). It is set dactylically and always appears in association with the partner word, "Crucifixus." It retains its diatonic character despite the fact that since the *Crucifixus* subject eventually loses its chromaticism, there is no longer any need to maintain the strict diatonicism of the count-ersubject as a means of contrast. An occasional prolongation on the "no-" of "nobis" occurs, for example, in S_3, bars 25^3 to 29. The other neutral phrase contained within the text of the *Crucifixus*, "sub Pontio Pilato," is likewise set dactylically.

"Passus" conforms to the general expectation of a setting in longer note values. It is set to a two-note motive of minims that occurs on both the strong and the weak beats of the bar (where it is set on the weak beat, the second note is shortened to a crotchet). There is a general similarity to the "Crucifixus" subject, both motives employing long note values. The use of longer note values for "passus," in relation to the preceding "contex-tual" words, has the desired effect of expressing duration.

"Et sepultus est" employs two motives that are used in combination with each other. Caldara tends to use only the first two words of the

Table 7.3. *Crucifixus* **Motives**

Bar	Voice	Motive	Rhythmic Grouping (Appendix B)[1]
1 (4) (7) (41)	S.I (A.IV) (T. I) (A.III)	 Cru - ci - fi - xus	A_1
2 (5) (8)	S.II (S.IV) (B.III)	 Cru - ci - fi - xus	A_1
9	T.II	 cru - ci - fi - xus	
10 (25) (28)	A.IV (A.I) (B.IV)	 cru - ci - fi - xus	A_1
11	T.IV	 cru - ci - fi - xus	
11	S.IV	 cru - ci - fi - xus	A_4
23	S.III	 cru - ci - fi - xus	
26	T.I	 cru - ci - fi - xus	A_1

[1]Where applicable.

Table 7.3.   (Continued)

Bar	Voice	Motive	Rhythmic Grouping (Appendix B)

27	S.IV		A_1 offset
29	B.I		A_2
32	A.III		A_5
37	S.IV		A_6
40	S.I		A_2
42	S.III		A_2

phrase to form the second of these motives, reserving the impact of a complete full statement for cadence points alone.[2] In the third section, he deliberately avoids the total use of the concluding "est" directly before the *aposiopesis* so that it has the desired clinching effect in the final cadential statement that follows. The two motives are as follows:

1. A falling stepwise phrase with trochaic rhythms, commencing on either a strong or (with syncopation) a weak beat of the bar. The regular repetition of the dotted-crotchet-plus-quaver rhythmic cell con-

veys a sense of deliberate, ritualistic motion, as would apply to the bearing of a coffin or (especially in the view of the descending motion) to the lowering of a coffin into a grave.

2. A four-note motive in crotchets, comprising a leap upward followed by a larger leap downward (for example, bar 43, T_1, T_2).

While the final cadence after the fermata does not literally express a descent, the bars immediately preceding the fermata very clearly do (bar 47 on), with the downward sequence of motive 2 (basses) added to the effect of motive 1, together with the sustained notes in the upper voices. In addition, while descent is expressed at the end of first two sections, it is the third section that expresses it in a more emphatic manner.

As already discussed, the general pause or *aposiopesis* is symbolic of death. It proves a useful device for this section of text, where death is only implied, not directly stated. By building in a general pause toward the end of this setting Caldara is using musical rhetoric to symbolize death— the last five bars can be read almost linguistically as "dead and buried." This adds an extra semantic dimension to the setting. Where the text is not explicit, the music (or pause in the music) makes it clearer.

The musical imagery in this setting reaches a density that is extreme. Each motive is clearly designed to express the text and, with sixteen voices participating, the bars in which all the voices participate certainly conform to what Irving Godt describes as "Gross Effects," the fifth level of word painting; there is a complete saturation of imagery.

The Text as a Whole

It is now time to focus on the text as a whole. There is a definite sense of progression in the organization of the text. As we have already seen, the setting has three distinct sections. This organization into sections affects many aspects, not just the vocal texture. The tonal plan of the setting follows (or, more accurately, probably initially determines) this structure, as does the organization of the text. Caldara creates an overall framework that gives a clear beginning and end to the setting. As already discussed, the sequence of the text is important since it lays down a sequence of events—the cause (crucifixion) and consequent effects (suffered and was buried) are important here. So we see a clear opening ("he was crucified") and also a clear ending ("and was buried") in the appropriate places. The first two subsections also have a similar organization of text: the third actually commences with two statements of "sub Pontio Pilato" before the "Crucifixus" motive is introduced. However, the text still reads "well" as a logical statement. "Passus" occurs after "Crucifixus" is introduced, so the "cause" and "effect" order of text is preserved; there is no suffering without cause. The sectioning of the portions of text and their subsequent more complex use is extremely interesting. The various motives described in the previous section are used in combination; Caldara displays a personal approach to working through the text. He builds up musical-semantic associations between different motives by using them as a composite "unit" of text, where the unit may be a combination of textual components. For example, "sub Pontio Pilato, passus" is used as a discrete unit (reading linearly as a complete phrase) in all three sections. However, "passus et sepultus est" is also treated as a unit in sections 2 and 3. This flexibility in the combining of motives helps create seamless transitions throughout this setting. Table 7.4 gives the organization of words within the setting, showing the combinational effect of the various motives. Caldara succeeds, marvelously, in presenting the *Crucifixus* text both as a historical, temporal sequence and as a conglomerate of images in which the component events fuse into a single composite image. In other words, he uses the power of counterpoint—in the simultaneous presentation of contrasting (potentially) differently texted lines—to compress the sequential into the ever-present.

CONCLUSION

As we have seen, Caldara's setting of the *Crucifixus* conforms in many ways to our expectations of the musical representation of this text. It also demonstrates that while it is possible to portray the text with motives that describe that text, the underlying musical structure may in some form contradict this portrayal of the text. Here I am referring to the tonality of this setting with the move to the relative major (reached by bar 23). In doing this, Caldara creates an opposition. The tonality is no longer acting to support the musical motives, which are still being used in an attempt

Table 7.4.   Organization of Key and Text in Caldara's *Crucifixus a 16 Voci*

Structure	Section 1	Section 2	Section 3	Aposiopesis	Final Cadence
Key	A minor- C major-	C major- E minor	→ V^7 A minor		A minor
Text/ motives	1. Crucifixus etiam pro nobis 2. sub Pontio Pilato/passus 3. et sepultus [est]	1. Crucifixus/ etiam pro nobis 2. sub Pontio Pilato/passus 3. passus/et sepultus [est]	1. sub Pontio Pilato/passus 2. Crucifixus/ etiam pro nobis/et sepultus 3. passus/et sepultus		et sepultus est.

to pictorialize the text. The major key appears to contradict the tragedy of the words and also has an effect on those motives used to portray the words. These motives have to be amended in order to conform to the constraints of the new (major) key. This affects particularly the "Crucifixus" motive, where, as figure 7.3 shows, the anguished diminished seventh becomes a much less "tortured" minor seventh. However, in terms of overall structure, the aim to express the Crucifixion is not lost, partly as a result of the overall tonal structure (that is, the framework of A minor) and partly in consequence of consistent use of motives to convey meaning. Caldara manages to succeed in expressing the text by using what we may recognize as a "standard" use of motives appropriate to the *Crucifixus* text and additional rhetorical figures and yet manages to place this in context of a complex overarching musical framework (that is, minor, with an excursion to the relative major) without losing the overall intended effect.

NOTES

1. Frits Noske describes the *aposiopesis* as "a general pause, mostly connected with death or eternity," in *Saints and Sinners: The Latin Musical Dialogue in the Seventeenth Century* (Oxford: Clarendon Press, 1992), 23. According to Bartel, most authors of the time describe the figure as a general pause: "an intentional and expressive use of silence in a composition." Bartel also mentions that the figure tends to appear most often in "compositions whose texts deal with death or eternity" and cites J. Hassler as an example: "J. Hassler expresses the text: 'I depart and die,' in which all the voices are silenced," *Musica Poetica: Musical-Rhetorical Figures in German Baroque Music* (Lincoln: University of Nebraska Press, 1997), 203. In late Baroque music, a general pause just before a closing phrase lost any specific connection with the idea of death but retained a generalized sense of apocalyptic drama, as many movements by Handel, a devotee of the device, illustrate.

2. The three sources used for the purposes of appendix D conflict with each other with regard to the underlay and extent of the text used for the first of the "et sepultus est" motives. Appendix D is an edition created with reference to all three sources. It should be noted that the source from Münster, Santini Sammlung der Bischöflichen Bibliothek D-MÜs SANT Dr 127, ed. G. W. Teschner (Berlin: Trauwein, 1840), and the version in Caldara's *Kirchenwerke*, ed. Eusebius Mandyczewski (Denkmäler der Tonkunst in Österreich, 1906; reprint, Graz, Austria: Akademische Druck und Verlagsanstalt, 1959), offer identical readings of this phrase and one that is offered in my edition. Here the tendency is to complete the statement of "et sepultus est" (for example, as for tenor entries, bars 35–36), whereas Charles H. Sherman's edition (Stuttgart, Germany: Carus-Verlag, n.d.) consistently uses only the first two words for this phrase (for example, as for S IV, bars 52–53).

8

A Semiotic Analysis: Bertoni: *Crucifixus con Organo a 4 Voci*

As chapter 3 shows, there are many parallels between semiotic and rhetorical analysis. The following two chapters start from the premise that, to a certain extent, these two analytical methods will reveal the same features. Both techniques are particularly appropriate for the *Crucifixus* settings that are being analyzed for this study. Semiotic analysis demands the "sectioning" of the music into paradigms and proves to be appropriate for the analysis of vocal music, where the sections of text are often a factor in determining musical paradigms. Agawu recognizes that a semiotic analysis of vocal music is possibly more enlightening than one performed on an instrumental work because of this added verbal dimension:

> An application of a semiotic approach to vocal genres such as opera, oratorio and lieder is not only conceivable, but potentially illuminating. At the same time, the added complexities of other systems—language, drama—should discourage a premature application of semiotic principles. Since instrumental music forms the common denominator in all these genres, the approach developed toward it may serve as a model for the development of other analyses.[1]

At this stage, another premise is that these paradigms might be considered the equivalent of musical-rhetorical figures. However, paradigmatic semiotic analysis does prove to operate in a single dimension when compared with rhetorical analysis. This analytical method is very much a "linear" process that does not take into account harmonic or structural devices such as *metabasis*. What is also evident from this study is that semiotic analysis in its "standard" form is actually very difficult to apply to some of the settings, particularly to those that employ imitative or contrapuntal writing.

These limitations cast doubt on the value of semiotic analysis for music of this type—and, indeed, on the application of other twentieth-century analytical techniques. However, a justification for the use of both "immanent" and "transcendent" critique has been made in the preface and in subsequent chapters. Moreover, this case study makes it possible to state more specifically what the advantages of the chosen modern analytical method are. Paradigmatic semiotic analysis is useful in being able to highlight a family of melodically and/or rhythmically related phrases that may then, in turn, be identified as generic rhetorical devices. It can provide clear evidence that a particular sequence of notes is being used to express something definite: in this case, the words. It may also draw attention to less well known devices or to a device that is specific to a particular composer.

ANALYSIS

In order to perform a semiotic analysis on Bertoni's setting of the *Crucifixus* (appendix E), the following principles have had to be observed. These guidelines had to be set up in order to address various issues that arose from the contrapuntal nature of the music.

1. In general, the vocal line carrying the "subject" is represented in the analysis.
2. Where the countersubject is deemed to contain notably important motivic material, this, too, is represented in the analysis.
3. The analysis is not exhaustive. It does not include every single detail of this setting. This has occurred mainly for the reason that a semiotic analysis of a contrapuntal work proves difficult to organize because of the overlapping of material.
4. It has not been possible to represent the order of the motives exactly as they appear, again as a consequence of the fugal writing. Therefore, it is important that the analysis should not be read as a typical paradigmatic model, which orders the paradigms as they appear within the setting, but rather as a grouping of similar themes.

Hence, figure 8.1 is the closest to a paradigmatic model of this *Crucifixus* setting as is possible to achieve. The paradigms have been grouped and labeled from A to F, with one miscellaneous group (G) at the end. This final group has been sorted by virtue of sharing the same segment of text

Figure 8.1. Semiotic Analysis: Paradigmatic Model

A

B

C

D

E

F

G

Figure 8.21. (continued)

A   B   C   D   E   F   G

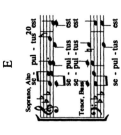

rather than through any musical relation and therefore has been labeled "miscellaneous." Bertoni's setting is fugal in style, except for the final few bars, where the texture suddenly becomes chordal. Surprisingly, these bars prove problematic to place within this semiotic scheme, and it is these that are grouped as "G."

However, it must be remembered that any analytical technique employed is there to serve a purpose. One of the aims of this analysis is to support the theory that a series of *topoi* existed in connection with the words of the *Crucifixus*. This paradigmatic analysis supports the theory admirably. The "Crucifixus" motive, while not displaying any of the most "obvious" modes of expression, employs one of the more frequently used rhythmic patterns (appendix B, group B_1), while "etiam pro nobis" is more or less syllabic—confirming our expectations. The third motivic group gives evidence of the syllabic setting of "sub Pontio Pilato," which also includes the stepwise falling interval that is so often used to express pathos (*pathopoeia*). Bertoni also uses this semitonal descending movement in both the "Crucifixus" and the "etiam pro nobis" motives. "Passus" is both syncopated and drawn out, and again we witness descending stepwise motion in this motive together with many of its variants (group D). Group E motives are based on the rhythmic design of group A, while those in group F have been placed together because of rhythmic similarity. Descent to express burial is not as obvious here as it is in settings by some other composers. Bertoni seems to rely on the octave leap downward in the bass to give the impression of descent, that is, by change of register in the bass. The same happens with all three "et sepultus est" phrases. In bar 17, the bass leaps down at the beginning of the phrase (c'-c); in bar 19, the octave jump occurs in the middle of the phrase (g-G), as it does in the final phrase (again, g-G).

The second stage of semiotic analysis involves the formulation of the rules that govern the organization of the different motivic units: this operation is known as syntagmatic analysis. In the case of the Bertoni setting, the following procedure has been undertaken in order to achieve this analysis: the units within each of the paradigmatic groups have been categorized, where the principles for these groupings are taken from appendix B. The following rule may be formulated as an outcome of this analysis. For each vocal entry,

$$A_1 + B_1 + C_1 + \{C_1\}$$
$$C_5$$

This rule shows that, in this particular setting of the *Crucifixus*, for every appearance of the "Crucifixus" motive, the following will occur: the "Crucifixus" motive, followed by the "etiam pro nobis" motive and then a statement of "sub Pontio Pilato" in its fundamental form. The last part of the formula (the part enclosed in braces) states that C_1 and C_5 are interchangeable, so the last part of this *Crucifixus* exposition may use "sub Pontio Pilato" once again in its defining state (that is, type 1) or else in an amended version (that is, type 5, where type 5 features the lengthening of the two last notes of a motive). The tenor and bass entries follow the C_5 version of the formula, while the soprano and alto entries follow the C_1 version. It is possible to formulate further distributional rules for this setting, but before I embark on this, there are a number of points that have already arisen as a result of this procedure.

1. First, the rules that are being generated here are dependent on my own particular analysis of this setting. Another analyst might have arrived at a different result. However, having said this, if rules are being generated by motives, which in turn are inseparable from the sections of text, then a similar formula may very well have been generated by another analyst.
2. Further, these rules are based on certain decisions made during the course of the analysis, which might involve the selection of one musical feature in preference to another. For example, my decision to categorize group C motives into types 1 and 5 (based on prior criteria set up in chapter 5) is based on rhythmic rather than melodic or intervallic patterns.

The relevance of an analysis such as this needs to be considered once again. Paradigmatic analysis clearly highlights the families of motives and has already shown itself to be a useful tool in the argument of this thesis. Syntagmatic analysis is probably less clear in this respect. However, what it does help support are the theories of organization and ordering of text and also the beginning–middle–end paradigm. It is at this point that we really start to see an overlap between introversive and extroversive semiosis. This question is explored in greater detail later in the case study.

To return to the syntagmatic analysis. From the formula quoted previously, it is possible to see a logical ordering of text: A, B, C. Because of the contrapuntal nature (see figure 8.2 for a summarization of the distribution of motives) of the setting, it is impossible to formulate a "concrete" general rule that can be applied to all four voices to summarize the organization of the entire setting. As with most analytical methods, danger arises when the analyst tries to "force" the issue, that is, to apply analytical rules where it is inappropriate to do so. Therefore, I have deliberately not formulated complete overall rules from the distributional patterns. However, the distribution that is represented in figure 8.2 is nevertheless significant. It supports the theory of a beginning–middle–end paradigm.

Figure 8.2. Distribution of Motives

Soprano:	A B C$_1$ C$_1$ D C$_1$ D D G/Misc.
Alto:	A B C$_1$ C$_1$ D$_{INV}$ D$_7$ G/Misc.
Tenor:	A B C$_1$ C$_5$ C$_1$ D D C$_8$ C$_8$ D$_5$ D E G/Misc.
Bass:	A B C$_1$ C$_5$ D E F D F F D$_7$ D G/Misc.

Where C$_8$ has the last note of the motive rising by a semitone rather than falling.
Where D$_{INV}$ is an inverted version of D.
Where D$_7$ has a lengthened first syllable.

All four voices begin with "Crucifixus" (A) and work their way through the text until they reach the end. All voices have a penultimate statement of "passus" (D or E) and complete the setting with "et sepultus est" (G/ Misc.). The organization of this setting further supports my discussion since it shows clearly that although the middle of the setting may "jumble" the order of the sections of text, there remains a distinct sense of sequence through the text.

"Introversive" semiosis is described as the analysis of the deeper structural level of the piece. The overlap with "extroversive" semiosis occurs with regard to the syntagmatic analysis, which, in the case of *Crucifixus* settings, provides support for the beginning–middle–end paradigm. If the overall structure of the piece is examined, a threefold type structure becomes apparent. The initial three entries of the subject display the typical fugal oscillation between tonic and dominant keys and constitute the first part of the setting. The fourth entry is in the relative major and initiates the middle section. The segregation of sections is by no means as distinct as in Caldara's *Crucifixus a 16 Voci*, yet there is a strong sense of order in this setting. The final section works through only the last portion of text, "et sepultus est," and is again in the home key of C minor.

CONCLUSION

This case study provides some proof that there is a positive argument for the application of semiotic analysis to music of this period and genre. The findings from this analysis, while producing no groundbreaking new results, nonetheless support and emphasize all the approaches and theories advanced in this thesis. It is possible to argue that one need not first jump through the "hoops" of semiotic procedure to draw the conclusions that have arisen from this chapter, but semiotic analysis is at the very least a useful tool for enabling the evidence to be presented in a standardized and more formal manner. Obviously, being a "transcendent" rather than an "immanent" critique, it is not comprehensive as a method when used in isolation. It is often the case with analysis that a fusion of several methods, particularly a combination of contemporary and modern methods, yields better results than the exclusive use of just one technique.

The main drawback that I see with the analysis performed on this setting in the context of the thesis is that the existence of some nonlinear rhetorical devices (and indeed other devices) is left unacknowledged. One such device is the *aposiopesis* that appears before the final statement of "sepultus est" in bar 20. In addition, the way in which a paradigmatic analysis is laid out can hinder the immediate recognition of some structural rhetorical figures, such as the *climax* or *gradatio*, that occur in connection with the successive sequential statements of "sub Pontio Pilato."[2]

NOTES

1. V. Kofi Agawu, *Playing with Signs: A Semiotic Interpretation of Classical Music* (Princeton, N.J.: Princeton University Press, 1991), 128.

2. *Climax* is defined by Burmeister as "that which repeats a similar pitch [patterns] on gradations of pitch levels." *Musical Poetics*, trans. Benito V. Rivera (New Haven, Conn.: Yale University Press, 1993), 181.

9

A Rhetorical Analysis: Zelenka: *Crucifixus* from *Missa Paschalis* ZWV 7

The following case study is an attempt to discover exactly how heavily steeped in rhetoric the music of the chosen period was. After just one analysis, it is naturally impossible to draw any definite conclusions, but, nonetheless, this is a useful exercise since it highlights both the advantages and the pitfalls of an "immanent" analysis of this type. At this point, it is important that the distinction between word painting and rhetorical figures be reiterated. Musical rhetoric is similar to "linguistic" rhetoric in that it actually employs structural devices in order to create the desired effect. For example, in language, rhetorical effect might be achieved by repetition of a particular word or phrase: maybe directly after the first statement, maybe at some later stage in the text (see figure 2.1 for examples of these figures of speech). A similar effect might be attained in music by applying the same principles. Word painting, however, is concerned with the more literal expression of the text. Structural rhetorical devices, as we shall see, may or may not contribute to word painting in part or as a whole.

ANALYSIS

Zelenka's *Crucifixus* from his *Missa Paschalis* ZWV 7 (see figure 9.1) is typical of the genre in many ways. The mode selected is minor, as befits music that attempts to describe the tragedy of the Crucifixion (B minor

Figure 9.1.   J. D. Zelenka (101): *Crucifixus* from *Missa Paschalis* ZWV 7 (1726)

Figure 9.1. (continued)

moving to F-sharp minor). The open tonality of this section arguably creates the impression of incompleteness: it implies that the Crucifixion, death, and burial of Christ was not final but that there was something more to happen—the death of Christ was a starting point for another event. The setting as a whole is chromatic in nature, bordering at some points on the extremes of dissonance. The tempo is slow, and the vocal scoring for this setting is SATB, constituting a collective comment as might be expected for this section of text. The choice of many of the motives is, again, typical for a setting of the *Crucifixus*; these are discussed in more detail at a later stage of this analysis.

I have attempted to carry out a rhetorical analysis on this setting. The analysis is not intended to be exhaustive, and there are reservations about this analytical method that will need to be expressed as an integral part of this case study. Some of these caveats have already been mentioned in chapter 2, while others have come to light only through the practical application of the analytical procedure.

Deep Level: Analysis of Rhetorical Structure

This proved very difficult to apply to a mere section of a whole Mass. Even given an understanding of the classical structure of an oration and a knowledge of how music theorists of the day based their methods of structure on it, it proved difficult to relate the discrete stages specifically to this setting (or other settings) of the *Crucifixus*. The *exordium* and *peroratio* stages were fairly straightforward to pinpoint within the setting: naturally, the beginning and the end (the *peroratio* is here most definitely the concluding statement following the rest in all parts in bar 11). However, any attempt to match the various structural middle stages to the content of this *Crucifixus* proves very difficult indeed, especially if, for example, Burmeister's guidelines are employed. Here, Burmeister refers to the structure of a piece being governed by fugal style and proceeds to describe the various sections in this light. Mattheson's schema, having six sections, is equally difficult to apply, but I think that this is largely because such a short section of music has been put under the microscope. Mattheson refers to six "sections" of compositional structure: in a piece consisting of a mere thirteen bars, it will be difficult to accommodate all these sections. It is impossible to find all the traits that Mattheson describes, such as "the entrance or beginning of the vocal part," which signifies the *narratio*, or the "well-conceived repetitions" that constitute the *confirmatio*. This setting is simply not on a scale capable of accommodating either of these elements. It is interesting that of the two descriptions of rhetorical structure, Burmeister's is the more straightforward and, interestingly, matches the concept of tripartite structure: the beginning–middle–end paradigm. In addition, the fact that this is a vocal piece that is bound so closely to the word setting obviously has an effect on the musical-rhetorical structure of the piece since the organization of the music is driven, to a large extent, by the words. Conversely, the rhetorical structure and organization of the words cannot dominate the setting completely since the musical organization and structure also have a major role to play. A certain amount of common sense needs to be exercised when carrying out an analysis of this kind, and the analyst must be prepared to use his or her discretion and apply what is sensible and also to ignore anything that would cause the entire analytical procedure to become distorted—by attempting to "see" what does not actually exist.

Surface Level: Analysis of Rhetorical Figures

Again, this part of the analysis highlighted some interesting points. The analysis succeeded in proving that the music was steeped in rhetorical devices that would cumulatively "affect" the listener. In the following text, I have used the more general descriptions of various musical figures given by Bartel in his *Musica Poetica*. The justification for this, together with other relevant discussion, is presented after the analysis itself. Figure 9.1 provides a labeled version of this setting.

1. *Exclamatio/salto semplice*: Bar 1, bass, notes 2 to 3, to the "-ci-fi-" of "Crucifixus." The *exclamatio* was literally a musical exclamation, the *salto semplice* a consonant leap. Here the leap in the vocal line occurs in conjunction with "he was crucified."

2. *Syncope*: For example, bar 2, soprano, notes 1 to 2; bar 3, tenor, notes 1 to 2; bar 4, alto, notes 2 to 3. The term *syncope* was used to describe an ordinary suspension.

3. *Saltus duriusculus*: Bar 2, bass, notes 2 to 3, bar 3, notes 2 to 3. A dissonant leap: in this case, a leap of a diminished fourth.

4. *Heterolepsis* and *hyperbaton/exclamatio/salto semplice*: Bar 2, tenor, notes 2 to 3. Here, Zelenka writes another musical exclamation underlining the word "Crucifixus." The leap of an octave can be described as the musical-rhetorical figure *hyperbaton*, which Bartel describes as "the transfer of notes or phrases from their normal placement to a different location."[1] It can also be described as the *salto semplice*. This leap also causes an overlap between the alto and tenor ranges; this is known as *heterolepsis*.

5. *Palilogia/mimesis*: This occurs between the initial bass statement of "etiam pro nobis" in bar 2 and the appearance of the same words in the tenor in bar 3. *Palilogia* is the reiteration of a phrase, either at the same pitch in the same voice or a phrase that is passed to different voices to appear at different pitches. *Mimesis* or *imitatio* is, literally, the imitation of a phrase, where that imitation is not exact, so both the bass and the tenor statements of "etiam pro nobis" on the third beat of bar 3 could be classed as this. *Mimesis* also occurs between the upper voices, the alto echoing the soprano on the second beat of the third bar. The first two syllables of this statement of "etiam pro nobis" are an augmentation of the rhythm of this motive in the bass. The effect that Zelenka creates in this setting, by using these devices, is one of overlap. He makes a point of overlapping each of the motives in different ways.

6. *Epizeuzis*: The general description for this is "an immediate and emphatic repetition of a word, note, motif or phrase."[2] *Epizeuzis* is evident throughout this setting but more in the context of a literary-rhetorical device. There are many repetitions of various parts of the text; "etiam pro nobis" is repeated, and so is "passus." The concluding statement (bars 11–13) of "passus et sepultus est" is an evident *epizeuzus*. The quasi-responsorial setting of "sub Pontio Pilato" (bars 4–6), the soprano leading the lower three voices, is another instance of emphatic repetition.

7. *Noema*: A *noema* is described as a chordal passage that appears within the context of a contrapuntal section or piece of music. The responsorial imitation of the lower three voices in bar 5 might be

described in this sense as a *noema*. However, this is not a strict *noema* since not all the voices participate in the homophonic texture.

8. *Palilogia*: This occurs exactly between the soprano and alto statements of "sub Pontio Pilato" at bars 4 and 5.

9. *Passus duriusculus (pathopoeia)*: The *passus duriusculus* consists of a passage of stepwise chromatic movement (or contains some element of chromatic alteration). There are two examples of the rising *passus duriusculus* evident in Zelanka's *Crucifixus*.[3] The soprano begins this passage on a c♯″ on the third beat of bar 3, rising to an f♯″ in bar 7, beat 4. The bass begins on an f♯ (bar 5, beat 2) and rises via a series of semitones to b in bar 8. The chromatically rising bass line offers many opportunities for colorful harmony, which Zelenka proceeds to exploit. The two lines overlap, the soprano beginning the *passus duriusculus* on the words "sub Pontio Pilato," which, as we have already noted, acts as a "call" to the lower voices, which then respond. The bass has exactly the same rhythm as the soprano but with a delay of half a bar. The passage that makes up the *passus duriusculus* also fits the description of *pathopoeia*: a passage that uses chromaticism to express the words or, according to Burmeister, "a figure suited for arousing the affections, which occurs when semitones that belong neither to the mode nor to the genus of the piece are employed and introduced in order to apply the resources of one class to another."[4] It is interesting to note that most of this *passus duriusculus* is used to set the word "passus," and the chromatic harmonies that are a result of this figure likewise express the word "suffering." Does Zelenka intend, perhaps, a subtle pun between the two meanings of "passus": "suffered" and "step"?

10. *Synaeresis*: The musical-rhetorical term for syncopation. Although syncopation is abundant throughout this setting (as a result of the overlapping techniques that Zelenka uses), its most notable occurrence is in bars 6 to 8, mainly in the soprano line, where it is used to express the word "passus." As we have already seen, syncopation has the effect of prolonging a line, which is eminently suitable for the musical depiction of a word that invites a representation of the passing of time.

11. *Syncope/prolongatio*: A 4–3 suspension occurs between the soprano and bass at bar 10, beat 1. This suspension, in addition to being a *syncope*, is also a *prolongatio*. The latter was a term used to describe a suspension where the duration of the dissonance is longer than that of the resolution—here a ratio of two beats to one.

12. *Aposiopesis*: This silence, considered to be representative of death, occurs in all parts on the first beat of bar 11. This musical-rhetorical

figure appears in a number of *Crucifixus* settings. The preceding two case studies have shown it to good effect, and Haydn employs it in his *Missa Brevis in F* (33).

13. *Epizeuzis* and *catabasis*: Bars 11 to 13, all parts: an emphatic reiteration of the text that has just appeared before the *aposiopesis* forms the *peroratio* of this *Crucifixus* setting. *Catabasis* is evident in the soprano line—a descent from a b' to an f♯' over these two bars—to express the burial of the body. Another *syncope/prolongatio* occurs between the alto and bass, from bar 12, beat 4, to bar 13, beat 2.

14. *Cadentiae duriusculus*: This figure was used to describe cadences where dissonance occurred in the approach chord to the cadence. Here it occurs in the form of an unstable 6/4 chord on the fourth beat of the twelfth bar and the addition of a dissonant passing note in the tenor line (note 5 in this bar).

15. *Paragogue* or *supplementum*: These were terms to describe some form of elaboration in the upper voices over a pedal point at the end of a piece of music. Zelenka introduces a pedal note, c♯, which is held for four beats, while the upper voices have changing harmonies over this.

For a setting of this length, there are an exceptionally large number of musical-rhetorical figures present. As stated at the outset, the figures identified here are not intended to be an exhaustive list.

This analytical procedure has uncovered a number of interesting points. When I embarked on this analysis, I was all too aware of the profusion of rhetorical terms in existence. This proliferation of terminology proved problematic for the development of an analytical strategy for a rhetorical study. One salient problem was that a single term would be used to describe more than one figure. Figure 2.2 gives examples of this. The opposite problem, of there being many different terms used to describe a single figure, also existed. An example is the word *hypotyposis*, which Burmeister uses as a generic term for word-painting devices (in this case, I have drawn on a term that is used in connection with a group of devices). Other terms used to refer to the same family of figures are *assimilatio* and *homoiosis*:

> The *homoiosis* or *assimilato* is a musical passage through which the attributes of a certain thing are actually expressed, for example when individual voices in a passage depict different elements as in the text "Tympanizant, cytharizant, pulsant nobis fulgent stolis coram summa Trinitate." In such a composition the bass represents the mighty tympanum while the other voices represent all kinds of other instruments. (Kircher, *Musurgia*)[5]

Hypotyposis is that ornament whereby the sense of the text is so depicted that those matters contained in the text that are inanimate or lifeless are brought to life. (Burmeister, *Musical Poetics*)[6]

Thus, the most straightforward approach for this analysis was to adopt Bartel's general descriptive overview of various terms and to analyze the music using this system. It must be emphasized that the resultant analysis is therefore a general one. If one were to be more accurate in a rhetorical analysis, one would perhaps attempt to conform strictly to the rhetorical terminology or system of a single theorist contemporary with the composer examined. One might even establish which particular theoretical texts the composer in question knew and then proceed to carry out an analysis on that basis. Table 9.1 lists the relevant theorists of the period, together with their dates.[7] Note that these overwhelmingly come from the German-speaking areas of Europe.

There remains the issue of how musical conventions change over time. It is possible to witness the changing nature of rhetorical terminology if the different treatises are compared. Over time, theorists observed that certain devices were widely used and would then attempt to document them. This shows that the musical vocabulary was never static but was constantly evolving. One case in point is Burmeister's and Nucius's descriptions of "fugal" figures, which tend not to feature in later treatises:

During the course of the eighteenth century, *fuga* is dropped from the lists of musical-rhetorical figures. Not only is the device increasingly understood as an independent musical genre, but it no longer fits into the affection-oriented emphasis of the late-Baroque concept of the figures. As the figures are increasingly understood and defined according to their text expressive and affective potential, *fuga* loses its place to more expressive, rhetorical devices. The class of figures which were *minus principales* and *superficiales* in the seventeenth century now become the more significant ones.[8]

This exercise has also illustrated some of the parallels between rhetorical and semiotic analysis. One striking similarity is the relation of surface musical figures to a deeper "whole," which can be likened to the relation of extroversive (surface) to introversive (deep) semiotic analysis. In the case of semiotics, the two are interdependent. With rhetoric and music, the surface devices are likewise inseparable from a deep underlying structure. Musical figures have a specific musical function and therefore play particular roles within the music: some devices are purely structural and therefore will naturally have a correspondence to the structure of the piece. Examples of this are the cadential figure *paragogue*, which theorists describe as appearing at the end of a composition, and the "fugal" devices, which are employed at particular stages in a composition. There

Table 9.1.   Musical-Rhetorical Theorists

Name and Dates	Title of Treatise	Date of Treatise
Joachim Burmeister (1564–1629)	Hypomnematum musicae poeticae Music autoschediastike Musica Poetica	Rostock, 1599 Rostock, 1601 Rostock, 1606
Johannes Nucius (1556–1620)	Musices poeticae sive de compositione cantus	Neisse, 1613
Joachim Thuringus (dates unknown)	Opusculum bipartitum	Berlin, 1624
Athanasius Kircher (1601–1680)	Musurgia Universalis sive ars magna consoni et dissoni	Rome, 1650
Christoph Bernhard (1628–1692)	Tractatus compositionis augmentus; Ausführlicher Bericht vom Gebrauche der Con- und Dissonantien	Not printed in Bernhard's lifetime
Wolfgang Casper Printz (1641–1717)	Phrynis Mytilanaeus oder Satyrische Componist	Dresden/Leipzig, 1696
Johann Georg Ahle (1651–1706)	Musicalisches Frühlings-, Sommer-, Herbst-, und Winter- Gespräche	Müllhausen, 1695–1701
Mauritius Johann Vogt (1669–1730)	Conclave thesauri magnae artis musicae	Prague, 1719
Johann Gottfried Walther (1684–1748)	Musicalisches Lexicon Praecepta der musicalischen Composition	Leipzig, 1732 Ms. 1708
Johann Mattheson (1681–1764)	Critica Musica Das neu-eröffnete Orchestre Der vollkommene Kapellmeister	Hamburg, 1722–1725 Hamburg, 1713 Hamburg, 1739
Meinrad Spiess (1683–1761)	Tractatus musicus compositorio-practicus	Augsburg, 1745
Johann Adolf Scheibe (1708–1776)	Compendium musices theoretico-practicum Der critische Musikus	ca. 1730 Leipzig, 1745
Johann Nikolaus Forkel (1749–1818)	Allgemeine Geschichte der Musik	Göttingen, 1788

is also evidence in the writings of theorists that the art of rhetoric was applied to music as a "whole" in this respect. The terminology that Burmeister and, more important, Mattheson use in their application of the structure of an oration to music confirms this (see chapter 2). Burmeister refers to "fugue," which naturally relates to the fugal figures that he has already described. Mattheson uses terms such as "repetition," "dissonance," "syncopation," and "emphatic impression" to describe the characteristics of various sections of musical-rhetorical structure. The figures that appear in Zelenka's setting of the *Crucifixus* can be classed as representatives of the various groupings of these figures.[9] *Palilogia* and *mimesis* are examples of repetition. The humble *syncope* is a figure of dissonance. *Synaeresis* is an example of syncopation, while *epizeuzis* gives "emphatic impression." The use of *paragogue* at the end of the setting certainly conforms to our expectations of a *peroratio* figure, as does the *cadentiae duriusculus*. Interestingly, Burmeister calls the *paragogue* "supplementum" and classes it not as a figure as such but rather as part of the structure.

CONCLUSION

There are a number of questions raised by this case study. First, it is clear from our analysis that rhetorical figures and structure came instinctively to a composer of the time. These features formed an inherent part of the musical language of the day. It is interesting to discover that our modern-day understanding of compositions of Zelenka's time does, to a certain extent, recognize these rhetorical devices—maybe not in terms of the exact rhetorical description that composers of the day used but rather in our own terms. For example, bars 4 to 5 provide us with an example of responsorial imitation (see chapter 5), where the soprano begins a phrase and is responded to by the lower three voices. In rhetorical terms, the contrast of a chordal texture with mainly imitative technique is described as *noema*, and the repetition of this motive in different voices but at different pitches is known as *palilogia*. The use of a suspension, which occurs many times in this setting, is recognized by us as such but was known in the eighteenth century by a different term, *syncope*. A comment that Hans Heinrich Unger made about the Italians springs to mind here: did they compose "with their rhetoric [texts] in their hands?"[10] This speculation applies equally to the German tradition. How mechanical and calculated was this compositional process? From the examples that I have collected, it really does seem that the inclusion of rhetorical devices was so innate that the seemingly rule-bound compositional process in no way detracted from the level of inspiration or musicality of these settings.

The second point is more specific to this study. This analysis has established that rhetorical figures are clearly evident within this setting. But, however prolific they are as individual figures, they rarely make up a complete set of *topoi* that form the *Crucifixus* tradition. So it is impossible to state that the word "Crucifixus" would or should have been set exclusively as a *pathopoeia* or as an *exclamatio* or a *saltus duriusculus*. It is in practice most likely to be a combination of these. For instance, the "Crucifixus" subject at the opening of the Caldara's sixteen-voice setting is a "composite" rhetorical figure consisting of an *exclamatio* between the first and second notes, a *saltus duriusculus* between the second and third notes, and the use of *pathopoeia* between the third and fourth notes. A similar comment can be made about the word *"passus."* The section of text "et sepultus est," however, can be equated with one specific device, the *catabasis*, which appears to have been reserved specifically for passages of music expressing some element of downward movement. That figure would be classed as a word-painting rhetorical figure (*hypotyposis*). This finding highlights the fact that the use of rhetoric in music was very much a unified, integrated operation, the aim of which was to create an *overall* effect that would "move" the listener in such a way that the whole became more significant than the mere sum of its parts.

NOTES

1. Dietrich Bartel, *Musica Poetica: Musical-Rhetorical Figures in German Baroque Music* (Lincoln: University of Nebraska Press, 1997), 441.

2. Bartel, *Musica Poetica*, 441.

3. Janice B. Stockigt comments that the *"passus duriusculus* descending over the interval of a perfect fourth" was "a figure that Zelenka usually attempted to incorporate into 'Crucifixus' settings." See *Jan Dismas Zelenka: A Bohemian Musician at the Court of Dresden* (Oxford: Oxford University Press, 2000), 255.

4. Joachim Burmeister, *Musical Poetics*, trans. Benito V. Rivera (New Haven, Conn.: Yale University Press, 1993), 175.

5. Bartel, *Musica Poetica*, 208.

6. Burmeister, *Musical Poetics*, 175.

7. Compiled from Bartel, *Musica Poetica*.

8. Bartel, *Musica Poetica*, 283.

9. Both George J. Buelow and Dietrich Bartel attempt to group musical-rhetorical figures into various categories, such as "repetition," "silence," and so on.

10. Hans Heinrich Unger, *Die Beziehungen zwischen Musik und Rhetorik im 16.–18. Jahrhundert* (Würzburg, Germany: Triltsch, 1941), 124. Quoted in Irving Godt, "Italian Figurenlehre? Music and Rhetoric in a New York Source," in *Studies in the History of Music*, vol. 1, ed. Ronald Broude and Ellen Beebe (New York: Broude Brothers, 1983), 179.

10

Textual Influence: Vivaldi: *Crucifixus* from *Credo* RV 591

This case study uses an analytical method that is based largely on Irving Godt's system of identifying and classifying textual influences described in chapter 3. Like any of the analytical methods that have been applied so far, this approach contributes its own perspective toward building an overall picture of a *Crucifixus* tradition. There are overlaps with both semiotic and rhetorical analysis but also aspects that neither of those approaches covers.

Godt points out that a composer often began work by studying the text and that this is something frequently overlooked in modern analyses of vocal music. As we have already seen from the previous case studies, the text can control the music to a large extent. This analysis now looks more closely at the relationship between text and music and at how one shapes the other.

My analytical framework is loosely based on figure 3.1.

ANALYSIS

The first part of this analysis examines the way in which the text affects the structure of a piece of music, exploring the realm of linguistic properties—how the words "drive" the music—and covers the "formal" and "rhetorical" branches of the structural section of figure 3.1.

General Comments and Structural Analysis

Many of the conventions already described in the general analytical account in chapter 5 are evident in Vivaldi's setting of the *Crucifixus* (appendix F). This movement, as one might expect, is separate from the rest of the *Credo*. The only other textual passage to be treated similarly in isolation is the section immediately preceding the *Crucifixus*, the *Et incarnatus*, which also conforms to expectations by being tonally open. The shift of tonality in this movement serves two purposes: first, the underlining of the mystery of the Virgin birth, and, second, the linking of the lengthy opening section of the *Credo* (ending in E minor) to the opening of the *Crucifixus* (A minor—note here the typical choice of the minor mode for this movement). The tempo is *Largo*, and the setting is for all four voices, providing the collective commentary that the text itself suggests. One interesting feature of this setting is the accompanimental pattern established in the continuo. Throughout the movement, there is a constant "trudging" pulse of quavers, falling on each beat of the bar and separated by quaver rests: a pulsing accompaniment such as this is typical of both *lamento* and *Crucifixus* settings. It has a relentlessness and inevitability about it that lend a further dimension of expression to the movement—what I would term "indirect expression" of the text. The only points at which this constant rhythm ceases are significant cadence points (bars 11, 24, and 31–33). These cadence points (and the consequent disruption to the relentless bass line) mirror the organization of the text:

Bars 1 to 12: "Crucifixus—et sepultus est"
Bars 12 to 25: "Crucifixus—et sepultus est"
Bars 25 to 33: "passus et sepultus est"

The movement has three distinct sections. The entire text is worked through in each of the first two sections, with only the last two segments of text used for the third. This is a tripartite structure with a clear beginning, middle, and end. The repetition of the entire text in the second section is important in rhetorical terms since this is the amplification of the opening idea. The order of the text within each section is also carefully organized, supporting my comment that the events of this section of text need to be arranged in some clear kind of sequence. "Crucifixus" and "etiam pro nobis" are worked through at the outset of both the first and second sections before the composer embarks on "sub Pontio Pilato" and then moves on to "passus" and "et sepultus est." "Sub Pontio Pilato" is used as a linking device between the first two sections of text and the last two. This is particularly noticeable in the first section, where, in bars 6 to 7, the soprano has a solo rendition of this section of text before continuing to the final two statements. When the other voices are brought in, "passus" and "et sepultus est" are the only portions of text that are set. In the second section, "sub Pontio Pilato" (in a different guise from its first appearance) is used twice in order to bridge between the opening and concluding sections of text. This time, there is a significant overlap with "pro nobis" in the soprano, alto, and bass and with "sub Pontio Pilato" in the tenor. The bass then imitates (rhythmically) the tenor's "sub Pontio Pilato" while the tenor has a rising *passus duriusculus* set to the word "passus" (bars 16–18). Vivaldi has organized the text itself into three parts, mirroring the overall tripartite structure:

1. a) "Crucifixus"
   b) "etiam pro nobis"
2. "sub Pontio Pilato"
3. a) "passus"
   b) "et sepultus est"

Repetition of text occurs mostly on "passus et sepultus est." "Crucifixus" is also repeated; one of the reasons for this is the imitative style introduced at the outset. As we have already seen, "sub Pontio Pilato" appears only three times in the entire setting. The action phrases of this section of the *Credo* carry greater significance (and potential for word painting, as we will see), for which reason composers were accustomed to lavish more musical attention on them. Further, in terms of linguistic rhetoric, these are the words that demand amplification and so will naturally be repeated for optimum effect. However, "etiam pro nobis" (a contextual phrase) is used significantly more than its neighboring narrative phrase. Vivaldi pairs this section of text with the opening word "Crucifixus," and there is a good reason for this. In true *Crucifixus* tradition, this short, neutrally set narrative phrase is used to balance the "melodic dissonance" of the "Crucifixus" motive. The other reason is that to organize the five sections of the *Crucifixus* as $2 + 1 + 2$ makes symmetrical sense.

The organization of the text is underpinned by the musical structure. The first section begins in A minor but moves to the relative major before concluding in G major. The next section moves from G major via its relative minor to D minor. The last section moves back first to E minor and then to the home key of A minor. The textual and tonal organization are summarized in figure 10.1. This diagrammatic representation highlights several interesting features, such as the number and position of cadence points in each section. There are *three* main points of cadential repose in every section. The first two sections have an initial cadence at the end of the first two portions of text ("Crucifixus" and "etiam pro nobis"). The second cadence occurs after the first set of statements of "passus et sepultus est," followed by the final cadence of the section (and it is only at these two points that the pulsing *organo* line is broken) after reconfirming statements of the same sections of text. The cadences in the last section are again positioned to coincide with the final statement of the *Crucifixus*.

Figure 10.1. Textual and Tonal Organization

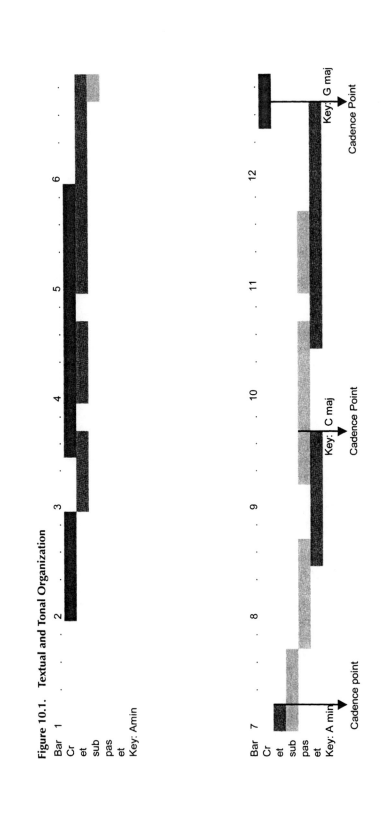

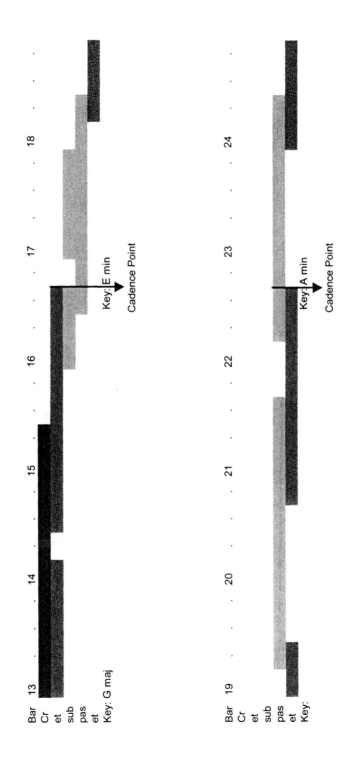

Figure 10.1. (continued)

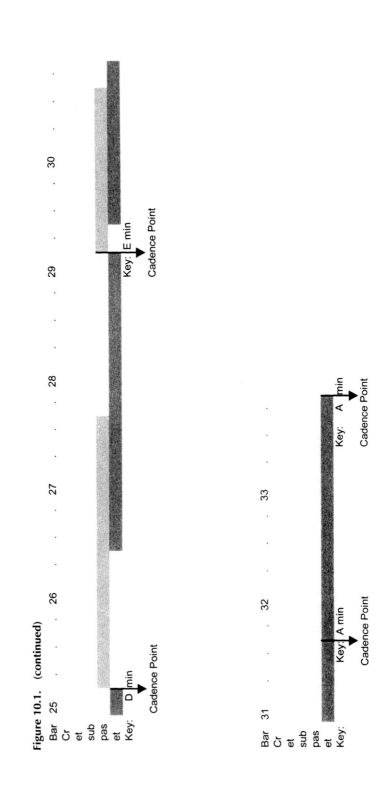

An overlap occurs between the first and second sections in the form of the "Crucifixus" motive, initiating the second section. No such link occurs between the second and third sections, but this omission is needed to distinguish between the end of that section and the next since the same two lines of text ("passus" and "et sepultus est") are being reiterated.

Vivaldi's choice of keys to visit is typical for a composer of his time: the dominant, subdominant, and relative major and, in addition to these, the relative major of the dominant key, which happens also to be the dominant key of the relative major of the home key. Table 10.1 summarizes the use of key in this movement.

Classification of Textual Influences

Up to this point, the focus has been on the structural level of the setting: examining how the text influences the "deep" structure of the music. Now we move on to an analysis of the "surface" level. This analysis is now concerned with the semantic properties of the text—how the words themselves influence the nature of the music. The subdivisions of the referential branch of the textual influence diagram (see figures 3.1 and 3.2) are now being explored, namely, the symbolical and pictorial properties.

The first category in this analysis is sound. Vivaldi's setting of the *Crucifixus* features a number of these conventions. Silence, in the form of a short rest in the vocal lines, was often used to depict a sigh (the rhetorical device *suspiratio*). Scoring for a larger number of voices has already been identified as a "standard" feature of *Crucifixus* settings, but the claim is further strengthened by Godt's argument that this "numerical convention" was a standard means of expressing multitude.

Table 10.1.   Tonal Structure of Vivaldi's Setting of the *Crucifixus*

Key Status	Key	7^1	9^3	12^3	16^3	22^3	25^1	29^1	31^3	33^4
Tonic	A minor	*				*			*	*
Dominant	E minor				*			*		
Subdominant	D minor						*			
Relative major	C major		*							
Relative of the dominant/ dominant of the relative of the tonic	G major (the role here is that of a "pivot" key)			*						
Section		1	1	1	2	2	2	3	3	3

Dissonance is used to express pain—it occurs here as part of the motive for the word "Crucifixus" and is also closely associated with the depiction of the word "passus." Chromaticism (in terms of harmony) is another traditional means of expressing pain and grief, both of which are intrinsic elements of the *Crucifixus* text, and again figures prominently in Vivaldi's setting. Key conventions also operate, the use of a minor key matching the overall mood of the textual subject. Common features such as suspensions were often used to express some form of delay, cadences being, as one might expect, indicative of completion. In Vivaldi's setting, both the intermediate and the final cadence points arrive at points in the text where some form of closure is semantically appropriate. The intermediate cadences coincide with the completion of a section of text, for example, where statements of "Crucifixus" and "etiam pro nobis" have been exhausted. Where there is repetition of sections of text, arrival at a more definite feeling of closure makes the repetition of the same statement(s) more effective.

Many of the melodic conventions that appear in Godt's classification system are evident in Vivaldi's *Crucifixus* and will be recognized as some of the conventions shared by several other *Crucifixus* settings. The "altitude" convention of low notes is used here to represent the grave and also the rest that death brings. The "directional" convention is particularly evident in the third section of the setting, where the downward motion of (particularly) the soprano line conspicuously expresses the phrase "et sepultus est." Such downward movement is commonly associated with texts that feature death or defeat and is thus appropriate here. The melismas that appear in conjunction with the word "passus" are what we have come to expect in the textual expression of the *Crucifixus*. They are used as a prolongation device to express the durational quality of the word. Disjunct motion occurs as part of the "Crucifixus" motive, creating a tension that is fitting for a musical phrase attempting to depict this word. Chromaticism in the melodic lines was an accepted tradition for expressing pain and lament, again a feature wholly apt for this setting. Vivaldi uses the *passus duriusculus* in both ascending and descending form in the melodic lines, sometimes spanning a fourth, which, as we have seen, "completes" the emblem of lament. His handling of this device produces a climactic masterstroke: it is used to express the word "passus." There is no appearance of it in the first section. The second section contains two appearances, both in descending form and spanning the characteristic lament interval of a fourth (tenor, bars 16^4–18^1; alto, bars 20^2–21^3). The third section employs the rising form of the device in close imitation between parts (alto, bar 25^2; soprano, bar 25^4; bass, bar 26^2), leading to the soprano's highest note since bar 7 and the climax of the setting. The soprano line eventually moves down via a descending *passus duriusculus* (extended, unexpectedly and poignantly, beyond a fourth). Again, the word "passus" is associated with the device. This descent, used to express burial, is not confined to "et sepultus est" but characterizes the whole phrase "passus et sepultus est." As we have already seen, it is a fairly common occurrence in *Crucifixus* settings.

The setting of words to a monotone was generally used for text that communicated some form of physical or emotional inactivity. The most obvious form of physical inactivity is that caused by death, so the final bars in the soprano remain static for the last statement of "et sepultus est," expressing the stillness of the body as it is buried. Many of the narrative phrases are fairly static in this respect, too: for example, the first few notes of each "etiam pro nobis" are monotonal. As these are neutral, non-emotional statements of fact, they do not demand the "specialized" treatment that the action phrases of the passage do.

Some of the rhythmic conventions that Godt recognizes as influenced by particular words or subjects of the text appear in Vivaldi's *Crucifixus*. The tempo convention was commented on at the outset of this analysis. The regularity of the continuo line has also been mentioned as an expression of the "continuity" of the march to Calvary. Godt observes that the use of triple meter is used to express joy; in this case, it is reserved for the *Et resurrexit*, which expresses the triumph of life over death, setting up a strong contrast with the preceding movement, with its quadruple meter and monotonous "tread." Any metrical change was potentially indicative of a change of mood, which again is true of what is witnessed here.

The next category that Godt addresses is growth. Here, any return or repetition in the text is interpreted as indicative of an affirmation in the text or of some form of increase, a common rhetorical feature. The repetition of words in the *Crucifixus* is used for emphasis and intensification: note here particularly the repetition of the final part of the text that occurs only in the third section (see figure 10.1). This amplification serves to add a deliberate emphasis to the most poignant section of the text: "suffered, and was buried." The process becomes even more effective when the ensuing *Et resurrexit* provides a strong contrast. The direct repetition of only the last portion of the text, at the very end of the setting, is again a common tradition in *Crucifixus* settings. One last feature from this group is ostinato, which was often associated with tragedy. In Vivaldi's setting, there is a form of ostinato (nonexact and rhythmic rather than melodic) at the beginning—again highly appropriate.

The final category is that of indirect applications. Here we have the use of preexistent musical emblems, such as ostinato and the chromatic fourth, and (possibly) the *Via dolorosa* accompaniment. We may include in this category *Augenmusik*, evident in the zigzag arrangement of vocal entries for "Crucifixus."

PROBLEMS WITH THE ANALYSIS
OF TEXTUAL INFLUENCES

Many of the problems that occur with this type of analysis are evident here. First, there is inconsistency within the setting. Vivaldi does not always use the same musical motive for a particular section of text—but this is typical of most of the settings in the survey. The inconsistency is often caused by the underlying musical structure of the setting, which does not permit the unaltered reuse of each motive. Even though the structure of the setting appears to have been influenced by the organization of the text (as with the Caldara setting), there are points where the musical structure simply will not permit a consistent reuse of motives and may even contradict the meaning of the words. Like Caldara, Vivaldi ends up setting a section of text that expresses excruciating pain ("Crucifixus") in a major key (tenor, bar 12^3). Despite this, Vivaldi manages to retain the underlying shape and structure of the motive. Again, for many composers, the identity of the "Crucifixus" motive seems to be more important than the remaining sections of text. "Etiam pro nobis" retains its syllabic, speechlike setting, too, but since it is associated with a motive that largely remains unchanged, this is not surprising. "Passus" is the one section of text that is given several distinct motives, ranging from bisyllabic settings to a melismatic statement set to rising or falling *passus duriusculus* lines.

However, such interference causes no great problem in this setting.[1] Vivaldi is receptive to the text and attempts to depict it in many different ways. This setting is saturated with musical meaning, to the point that it is characteristic of the fifth level of word painting (figure 3.4): an estimate of the image density for this setting is probably around 85 percent. The style of the composition also allows for this degree of freedom in the expression of text, unlike, for example, the *stile antico*, which is far less accommodating toward such imagery.

As we have seen, the structure of the setting is constructed in response to and organized around the text. However, while this method of organization gives scope for comprehensive expression of the words, the needs of musical structure do not permit absolute consistency.

CONCLUSION

While certain branches of Godt's textual influence diagram have been covered in detail here, others have not. The acoustical considerations of the text are discussed in chapter 5 and have in fact been included, to a certain extent, in the analysis in this chapter (in particular, the rhythmic subdivision of acoustical properties). Very often, with a narrative analysis like this, it is difficult to segregate details in strict accordance with a template; in consequence, there arises a certain amount of overlap between the different areas.

What this analysis has at least demonstrated is the saturation of imagery that can be achieved in a setting of text by direct or indirect reference. This property could not have been shown by either semiotic or rhetorical analysis in isolation. Godt's method has established various conventions through a "transcendent" rather than rhetorical ("immanent") approach; this has entailed first establishing, via observation, the recognized conventions of the time. It presents us with a surprisingly broad range of conventions, gained with the benefit of hindsight. These devices are concerned primarily with imagery, irrespective of the place of that imagery within the semantic (or rhetorical) scheme. Godt's method also highlights the influence that words can have on the overall shaping of the structure of the setting. The starting point here lies squarely with text rather than music, whereas a semiotic procedure, for instance, demands that both be considered initially on an equal footing, followed by a categorization according to shape of motive or rhythm.

NOTE

1. There are examples of *Crucifixus* settings that demonstrate a composer blocking the response to the text. One such example is by Cimarosa and will be discussed in chapter 13.

11

Constraints of Style: Lotti: *Crucifixus* Settings for Six and Ten Voices

In the previous chapter, one of the factors cited as affecting the degree of musical response to the text was the style of a composition. *Stile antico* is an example of a style that might be material in blocking a composer's response to the text since the rules of composition simply do not allow sufficient freedom to express the text at a subtle level. This restriction of expression is certainly true of most strict *stile antico* settings from the sample—for example, Durante's *Messa a 3* (21)—and also of most of the smaller scale settings by Lotti.[1]

Composers followed the guidelines that the Church imposed on the writing of sacred music to varying degrees, depending on the attitude of the Church at any given point. We know that, from time to time, the Catholic Church condoned completely the influence of secular music, but equally, it

> [could not] afford to ignore the great appeal of secular style. In the end the uninspired reforms advocated by the Council of Trent [fell] by the wayside as religious leaders utilize[d] the novelties of rhetorical music for their own catholic purposes.[2]

While it is beyond the scope of this thesis to examine the *Crucifixus* tradition in any great detail before 1680, a cursory glance at two earlier settings will demonstrate that some of the conventions were already in existence. Palestrina's *Missa Papae Marcelli* of 1567 begins a new section for the

184

Crucifixus. The natural sequence of the text is carefully preserved—which is no surprise, given the Church's emphasis at the time on the importance of the words. Despite the strict use of counterpoint (there is very little melisma) and the conciseness of this setting, some recognizable *Crucifixus* conventions are evident. A two-note motive is employed to set "passus" (using relatively longer note values), and a musical descent occurs for "et sepultus est," expressed mainly via the fall of the bass line (see figure 11.1).[3]

Monteverdi's *Crucifixus for 4 Voices* (which can be used interchangeably with the *Crucifixus* from the *Missa a 4* in his *Selva morale e spirituale,* published in 1640) is a fairly lengthy setting in a somewhat "evolved" *stile antico,* and extremely chromatic. The opening "Crucifixus etiam pro nobis" is set to a descending *passus duriusculus* (more specifically, a chromatic fourth) that is heard in imitation, while the closing "et sepultus est" expresses descent, using a low register for most of the voices (see figure 11.2).[4] Again, the traditional rules of counterpoint (allowing for the chromaticism) are obeyed, but—a sign of the times—melisma is used much more frequently than in Palestrina's setting.

These two brief examples, picked almost at random from the pre-1680 *Crucifixus* repertory, suffice to show that there would be wide scope for extending backward in time the kinds of analysis performed in this thesis. "Painting" the Crucifixion most certainly did not begin in the generation of Colonna.

Lotti's several large-scale *Crucifixus* settings have established themselves in the choral repertory independently of their parent works. The two settings that are used as case studies in this chapter are the well-known *Crucifixus a 6 Voci* and *Crucifixus a 10 Voci,* each expressing the Crucifixion in a slightly different manner. The setting for six voices is a fairly strict contrapuntal setting, whereas that for ten adopts a wider-ranging compositional style.

ANALYSIS

Crucifixus a 6 Voci

At first glance, this *Crucifixus* does not seem to contain many of the traditions that have been evident in other composers' settings of the *Crucifixus* (appendix G). However, while the expression of text is not so image laden as in some other settings, depiction of the text does take place, sometimes being presented in a most subtle manner.

The opening statement of "Crucifixus" is chordal, employing all six voices and based on a simple I-V progression (C minor). The first two syllables are offset from the first beat (the meter is triple time), and the

Figure 11.1. G. Palestrina: *Crucifixus* from *Missa Papae Marcelli*

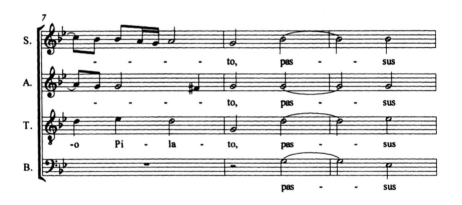

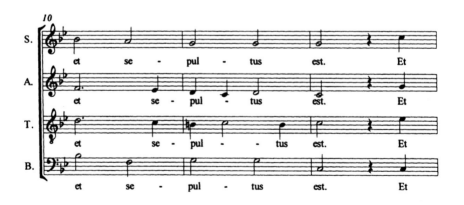

Figure 11.2. C. Monteverdi: Extracts from *Crucifixus for 4 Voices*

"-fi-" falls on the strong beat of the second bar, lending weight to the syllable. After this, the statements of this first word are paired (first soprano and alto, bar 3, then second soprano and first tenor, bar 5), the second tenor and bass providing the harmonic foundation. The "Crucifixus" subject line contains none of the "standard" devices, such as a cross shape, or diminished or augmented intervals in a linear sense. However, the harmony in the fourth bar changes to a diminished seventh (with a suspended sixth on the first beat), which expresses powerfully the agony of crucifixion. This diminished chord returns in bar 6, together with further statements of the word. Throughout this setting, chromatic harmony is used to achieve the textual expression; this is what I refer to as "indirect" expression of the text. This setting also demonstrates that although there can be constraints on the "direct" expression of the text in a situation of this kind, the composer may well resort instead to "indirect" techniques since the text of the *Crucifixus* is such as to demand *some* form of appropriate expression.

"Etiam pro nobis" and "sub Pontio Pilato" are usually set by Lotti mostly in a syllabic manner, the first syllable of "etiam" and "Pontio" being lengthened to give a dactylic rhythm. "Etiam pro nobis" is used in imitation, while "sub Pontio Pilato" is presented in paired entries with an accompanying motive in a third voice.

"Passus" is introduced in bar 22 as a drawn-out phrase, melismatic, employing syncopation and suspensions to give the impression of duration. "Et sepultus est" expresses some descent in the form of two downward leaps (bar 31 on), but this treatment is not consistent. The first and second tenors have an ascending phrase for the same words at bar 36, and the word "passus" is included on the opening two descending notes of the amended phrase at bar 40. The compositional style places constraints on the direct expression of the text, and it is often impossible to conclude whether a musical motive is a direct expression of the text or merely a fortuitous result of applying the stylistic conventions.

So, with the possibilities for direct expression of the text being rather limited, how does Lotti create this wonderfully expressive setting? The answer lies in the harmonic language, which embodies the extreme chromaticism of the late baroque. The harmony arises from the result of the linear properties of the style: the contrapuntal lines lead to much controlled dissonance, which creates the "indirect" expression of, or musical background to, the text. The dissonance that results from the contrapuntal construct permeates the entire setting, but a particularly colorful passage coincides with the numerous repetitions of the word "passus." From bars 30 to 33, there is a chain of suspensions, one per bar, each dissonance carefully prepared and resolved. The final bars of the setting are also highly expressive. The underlying harmonic design is quite straightforward. Bar 37 has chord IV (in C minor), followed by two bars of V, then a pedal C to the end of the setting (five bars). A pedal cadence is a common occurrence at the end of *Crucifixus* settings, frequently used to express the stillness of death. Over this pedal, the harmony is constantly shifting. Lotti moves between 5/3 and 6/4 chords, the latter being unstable and demanding resolution each time. The third degree of the scale is raised (e natural), while the sixth is lowered (a flat), emphasizing the subdominant (from Godt we know that flat conventions were often used to express lamentation). In the penultimate bar, as an addition to the 6/4 chord, Lotti includes the natural seventh degree of the scale. This extra note to the chord adds an even stronger impetus to resolve, the seventh degree pulling toward the tonic, while the flat sixth note needs to resolve to the dominant note. The third note of the chord (the fourth) has an equally strong resolution to the (natural) third of the tonic key.

Some *Crucifixus topoi* are easier to admit to a quasi–*stile antico* setting than others. The "passus" motive, for example, allows the composer to include the standard devices of melisma, suspension, and syncopation in a phrase that obeys the contrapuntal precept of stepwise movement, whereas jagged intervals to express the word "Crucifixus" are more difficult to embody.

There seems to be a definite sense of beginning–middle–end in this setting. The word "Crucifixus" is used only at the outset, and "et sepultus est" is confined to the final fourteen bars.

Crucifixus a 10 Voci

This setting (appendix H) exhibits a much more "direct" musical expression of the text than the *Crucifixus a 6 Voci*. The expression of the word "Crucifixus," for example, conforms much more to expectation. The close proximity of each voice as it enters with the opening motive creates the clash of a second between voices. This opening phrase is subjected to imitation at half-bar intervals. Lotti begins with the tenor voices and builds upward voice by voice (basses excepted—the first bass is given the opening motive in the third bar, but the primary function of these two voices is to support the harmony). The increase in pitch over these first six bars almost "increases" the agony of Crucifixion. Throughout this passage, heavy use is made of suspension and double suspension—for example, alto 2 in bar 4^{3-4} (4–3 suspension), tenor 1 in bar 4^{3-4} (9–8 suspension); this further enhances the expression of the word. The occurrence of *metabasis* (crossing of parts) and *heterolepsis* (overlapping of parts) is almost inevitable, given the closeness of entries, but here becomes a form of *Augenmusik*, as are the sharps appearing in the vocal lines. A cadence point arrives at bar 8. So far, only the word "Crucifixus" has been set. All ten voices are by now being used, but at bar 9 there is a sudden change of texture. Only three voices are now employed, one from each of the lower three voice types. Lotti proceeds to present the first two sections of text in a syllabic setting for the first three words ("Crucifixus etiam pro"), followed by a melismatic/lengthened setting for the "no-" of "nobis." An Italian sixth appears on the fourth beat of bar 9; this can be regarded as an "indirect" expression of the text since it coincides with part of the contextual phrase of this section of text and not with one of the more expressive action phrases. There is a repetition of this same section of text at bar 11, still with three of the lower voices, but with voice exchange occurring between alto and tenor parts. A final statement of "Crucifixus etiam pro nobis" arrives at bar 13, this time for all three soprano lines, with imitation in the first soprano. The key moves to F major and then to B flat for the introduction of the "sub Pontio Pilato" phrase (last beat of bar 15).

"Sub Pontio Pilato" is treated to a syllabic setting on a descending arpeggiated phrase, which is used in imitation and continues to within five bars of the end of the setting. The first imitation occurs at the distance of half a bar, but after this, the rate of imitation increases to four entries per bar: having so many voices makes it possible to create such intensity of imitation. At bar 19, the word "passus" is introduced. In familiar *Crucifixus* style, the majority of motives are expressed in long note values, together with syncopation, suspension, and melisma. This is a motive for three voices; once it appears, Lotti feels a need to balance the "sub Pontio Pilato" phrases, which are appearing at the same time, by pairing voices (for example, bar 22, bass 1 and 2). A second motive associated with "passus" appears at bar 24. This is again a characteristic *Crucifixus* bisyllabic phrase, which then reappears later in the setting.

"Et sepultus est" arrives only toward the end of the piece (bar 37). As in the *Crucifixus a 6 Voci* (and perhaps even more so in this ten-part setting), there is a definite sense of beginning: the opening eight bars are dedicated exclusively to "Crucifixus," followed by a brief section in which only the first two statements appear (bars 9–15). In rhetorical structure, this would constitute the *exordium*. The middle section sets one contextual phrase and one action phrase, one offering a kind of relief for the other. The end of the setting is equally clear-cut—the natural sequence of the text is carefully observed since from the first appearance of "et sepultus est," only "passus" and the final textual phrase appear, "et sepultus est" concluding the setting (*peroratio*). A pedal is used in the approach to and as part of the final cadence. Perhaps unexpectedly, "et sepultus" gives rise to no direct expression of the text. One sees no striking descent in any of the vocal lines, although the style of composition employed would certainly have permitted this.

The *organo* line in this setting has the "trudging" quaver pattern separated by rests that is so typical of so many settings, including Vivaldi's. This bass line underlies the entire setting, broken only at major cadence points and in the final five bars. It is generally a "dependent bass" in Borgir's sense, following the lowest vocal line.[5]

CONCLUSION

A comparison of these two settings demonstrates Lotti's ability to illuminate the text, regardless of the mode of composition in which he is working. It is clear that there are two contrasted methods of expressing the text here, respectively, "direct" and "indirect." In his *Crucifixus a 6 Voci*, Lotti is constrained by the strict style, so he uses indirect expressive methods, such as an appropriate use of harmony, to create a musical background. However, in the second setting, he adopts both methods, relying to a greater extent on "direct" word-painting methods. Most composers use both methods simultaneously, but it is possible to create a *Crucifixus* setting that relies heavily on either of these separately. Lotti's first setting demonstrates how, on occasion, "indirect" expression may be the only option open to a composer who wishes to respond to the imagery of this section of text.

NOTES

1. An exception to this is the *Crucifixus* from Gasparini's *Missa a 4* (29) (identical to the setting attrib. B. Marcello [68]—Godt identifies this as an incorrect attribution). Chiastic organization of *Crucifixus* motives occurs in this setting: "*Chiasmus*, from the Greek word meaning a crossing in the manner of the letter chi (χ) denotes a figure of speech (specifically a figure of position) in which two units of an antecedent phrase are reversed in its consequent. . . . Besides serving as a symbol of the cross, the *chiasmus* may also represent Christ; the letter chi (χ), which begins the Greek name Christos . . . often appears in liturgical manuscripts as an abbreviation of the name (and survives today in our 'Xmas')." Irving Godt, "Italian Figurenlehre? Music and Rhetoric in a New York Source," in *Studies in the History of Music*, vol. 1, ed. Ronald Broude and Ellen Beebe (New York: Broude Brothers, 1983), 188.

2. Maria Rika Maniates, *Mannerism in Italian Music and Culture, 1530–1639* (Manchester, U.K.: Manchester University Press, 1979), 282.

3. The musical extract in figure 12.1 is from Giovanni Pierluigi da Palestrina, *Missa Papae Marcelli*, ed. Henry Washington (London: J. and W. Chester, 1963). Copyright 1963 Chester Music Limited. All rights reserved. International copyright secured. Reprinted by permission.

4. The musical extract in figure 12.2 is from Claudio Monteverdi, *Crucifixus*, ed. Gian Francesco Malipiero (Vienna: Universal Edition, 1968). Reproduced by kind permission of Universal Edition A. G., Wien.

5. "Dependent bass" is a term used by Tharald Borgir to describe the convention of the continuo doubling the lowest vocal part. Borgir's research has revealed that the term commonly used to describe this practice today (*basso seguente*) was simply another name for the *basso continuo*. Tharald Borgir, *The Performance of the Basso Continuo in Italian Baroque Music* (Ann Arbor, Mich.: University Microfilms International, 1987), 13.

12

Orchestral Practice and *Crucifixus* Conventions: Mozart, Haydn, and Beyond

The purpose of this chapter is threefold. First, it aims to ascertain the persistence of *Crucifixus* conventions in settings of the Mass from the classical era. Second, it looks at the role of the orchestra in these settings and at how composers use this resource. Finally, it moves forward from the time frame of this study to explore briefly whether the familiar conventions were transmitted beyond the classical period.

MOZART: *KRÖNUNGS-MESSE* KV 317 (1779)

The *Credo* from Mozart's *Coronation Mass* is a remarkable and, in many ways, a typical example of the genre. Mozart sets the words of the *Credo* in a brisk manner in order to accommodate the lengthy text. The *Credo*, as a continuous text, is treated as an unbroken movement with no clear breaks to disrupt the progress of the text. Musically, this section also runs as a continuous "whole": the framing sections of the *Credo* are marked *Allegro molto*, while the middle section, which begins at the *Et incarnatus* and includes the *Crucifixus*, is a typical *Adagio*. The treatment of the *Et incarnatus* and *Crucifixus* (appendix I) as a single section is typical for both Mozart and Haydn. The *Allegro molto* returns, together with the opening thematic material, at the *Et resurrexit*. Despite the "business-like" approach to the bulk of the text, there is an element of textual imagery in the opening section; for instance, the word "descendit" is set imitatively, using descending scalic figures. However, the exceptionally imaginative treatment of the text is reserved for the middle section. On arrival at the *Adagio*, contrast to the previous section is achieved in a number of ways. The scoring is dramatically reduced: from full orchestra (two oboes, two horns, two trumpets, [three trombones], timpani, violin I, violin II, organ, and continuo instruments) in the bars immediately preceding the middle section to muted violins, continuo, and oboes. The *coro* is pared down from *tutti* to four soloists: soprano, alto, tenor, and bass. The tonality preceding the *Adagio* moves from C toward F major; the music arrives at a dominant seventh of F in first inversion on the first beat of the opening bar of the *Adagio*. The expected key is F major, but Mozart "twists" this into F minor simply by introducing an A flat in the first violin part on the third beat of the bar and then confirming this with an A flat in the soprano part on the final beat. Proceeding from here, the *Et incarnatus* moves through A flat and finishes in E flat—this shift of key conforms exactly to the expected characteristics of an *Et incarnatus* setting.

Although the *Crucifixus* is not separate from the *Et incarnatus*, Mozart does distinguish between the settings of these two sections of text. The *coro* is restored to *tutti* status, which is appropriate for a commentary that calls for a "multitude" narration. The brief link between the two sections of text consists of a dotted figure in the strings, supported by oboes, clearly confirming the key of E flat. Mozart adds trombones to the scoring at this point, doubling the three lower voices and intensifying the marked contrast between *Et incarnatus* and *Crucifixus*. The bass line for the first three bars employs continuous pulsing quaver movement, which, as we have already seen, characterizes many settings. It is equally significant that this is coupled with a rising chromatic fourth in the bass. This might not be the descending *lamento* version of the chromatic fourth, but, as we have already seen, a rising *passus duriusculus* was frequently used also in settings of the *Crucifixus*. The first three bars of this *Crucifixus* are a powerful statement drawing on maximum vocal and instrumental forces. The actual "direct" setting of these first three phrases of the *Crucifixus* (set in a chordal style) is in some ways typical and in others not. The musical setting of the word "Crucifixus" conforms to none of the inherited conventions of word painting or *Augenmusik*. Mozart sets up a chord of E flat on the first beat of bar 65, and the *Crucifixus* motive is brought in on the quaver subbeat. This is the only setting in the survey that uses this unexpected rhythmic pattern, although in many of his settings Mozart sets this word by beginning on a weak beat of the bar. Perhaps the phonetic qualities of the word seemed, here, to suggest to him that the emphasis should be placed on the syllable "-fi-," which is what indeed happens. After two shorter notes, "-fi-" is set to a minim, and the word is completed on the first beat of the next bar. This opening has set up a rhythmic pattern that complements the rising bass line. The syllables that one would expect to be emphasized in the following two narrative phrases are stressed by means of the same procedure—setting the "no-" of "nobis" and the "-la-" of "Pilato" to minims that span the last two beats of each bar (bars 66 and 67). This causes the last syllable of the first three sections of text to fall on the first beat of each bar and the beginning of each new section of text to be "delayed" until the second quaver division of each bar. The effect thereby created is one of urgency—one statement following on directly from the next, with no space between the last syllable of the preceding phrase and the first syllable of the next. It also supports and helps propel the harmonic direction of the *passus duriusculus*. The strings have a chromatically decorated falling phrase on the last two beats of each of these bars—the interest passes to the orchestra, while the *coro* have sustained notes. Simultaneously, the oboes are given a rising phrase, producing the added effect of contrary motion between these instruments and the strings. The narrative phrases are set in the traditional syllabic manner (apart from the lengthening of the penultimate syllable of each phrase). Here, "etiam" is treated to a straightforward, "even"-quaver setting, while "sub" is set dactylically. Both phrases are fairly static in terms of pitch, "etiam" being notably monotonal. The dynamic level and texture are brought down again in bar 68: Mozart marks all parts *piano* and also specifies "tasto solo" for the organ, which helps create a sparser texture.

"Passus" is set to two notes (both quavers). This word is repeated, then repeated again, this time to two crotchets. Again, this is an identifiable *Crucifixus* convention that resorts to the rhetorical technique of amplification to emphasize suffering (emphasis through repetition is another way of stressing a word or concept). The rests that separate these statements are in effect sighs (the rhetorical *suspiratio*). The final statement of "passus" dispenses with trombones, which are not reinstated until the second and concluding statement of "sepultus est."

"Et sepultus est" arrives at bar 70. Over the next two bars, the music depicts the text by means of descending vocal lines. This first statement is accompanied by sustained notes in the horns and oboes, together with a figuration in the strings similar to that heard in the opening bars. The accompaniment also supports the textual imagery (as "indirect" expression of the text) with a descending passage running from the second beat of the bar to the end of the section. The climax of the phrase (*forte*) occurs on this second beat of bar 70, preceded by a brief crescendo marked on the first beat. The writing for strings, horns, and oboes supports this climax, as does the harmonic structure: Mozart introduces a German sixth on the second quaver subdivision of the second beat of this bar. He provides a characteristic concluding statement of "sepultus est" (*peroratio*), beginning on the second beat of bar 71. Here, the trombones return, but the strings, organ, and horns are removed from the texture, and the dynamic level is now *pianissimo*. The vocal line is broken up by rests (the rhetorical figure *tmesis*), which creates a "sighing" effect wholly appropriate for the accompaniment of a burial. This elimination of many of the instruments has an effect similar to the *a cappella* ending of Bach's setting, and it was perhaps intended as such. The last note of the *Crucifixus* becomes the first note of the returning opening *Credo* material, which propels the music directly into *Et resurrexit*.

Many *Crucifixus* conventions put in an appearance during this relatively short setting. The detail applied within a mere seven bars is incredible, but this *Crucifixus* serves once again to illustrate the appeal that this portion of text held for composers. The orchestra provides an extra dimension in its contribution to the atmosphere of the text. However, what is particularly outstanding here is the composer's handling of harmony and how he initiates the change of key. Table 12.1 supplies an analysis of the harmonic structure of this *Crucifixus* setting. The harmonic devices introduced include chromatic chords such as the German sixth, extensive use of diminished sevenths, and at one point a half-diminished seventh chord. Mozart uses second-inversion chords for the deliberate destabilization of the tonal center. The relationship between E flat and C minor is a straightforward one, but Mozart chooses by intention a roundabout way of realizing it. The route that he traverses creates a backdrop of chromaticism to the setting, which adds an extra dimension of pathos to the words. The harmony thus provides "indirect" rather than "direct" expression of the textual imagery.

HAYDN: *MISSA IN TEMPORE BELLI* (1796)

This case study illustrates that many of the *Crucifixus* traditions were still strongly in evidence by the end of the eighteenth century.

In the setting from *Missa in Tempore Belli* (appendix J), there is a contrast between the predominantly solo setting of the *Et incarnatus*, where the final statements of "et homo factus est" are set for the entire *coro*, and the *Crucifixus*, which is predominantly choral but contains a brief solo interlude. As expected, this section of the *Credo* text forms the middle of this section of the Mass. The tempo is *Adagio*. As in Mozart's setting, all available resources are used to describe the Crucifixion in musical terms, whether "direct" or "indirect" (that is, for the creation of an appropriate musical atmosphere). The *Et resurrexit* is, typically, an *Allegro* in C major (the tonic major of the key in which the *Adagio* section ends) and is designed to follow on directly from the *Crucifixus*. The *Et incarnatus* fin-

Table 12.1. Harmonic Structure of Mozart's Setting of the *Crucifixus* from *Krönungs-Messe* KV 317

Bar and Beat	65^1	65^2	65^3	65^4
Text	(rest) Cru-	- ci-	fi -	- -
Harmony	I		6/4 chord of A-flat minor	
Key	E-flat major			

Bar and Beat	66^1	66^2	66^3	66^4
Text	-xus e-ti-	am pro	no -	- -
Harmony	diminished seventh of F minor		6/4 chord of B-flat minor	
Key				
Bass line	e flat	e flat	e flat	e flat

Bar and Beat	67^1	67^2	67^3	67^4
Text	-bis sub	Pon- ti- o Pi-	la -	- -
Harmony	diminished seventh of G		6/4 chord of C minor	
Key			Heralding C minor	
Bass line	e natural	f	f sharp	g

Bar and Beat	68^1	68^2	68^3	68^4
Text	-to,	(rest)	pas- sus,	(rest)
Harmony	diminished seventh of C (third inversion)		i^b in C minor	
Key	C minor			
Bass line	a flat		e flat	

Table 12.1. (Continued)

Bar and Beat	69¹	69²	69³	69⁴
Text	pas- sus,	(rest)	pas-	sus
Harmony	V$^{b(7)}$		i	iii^{cb7}in C minor = dominant seventh of A flat
Key	C minor		C minor	C minor/A flat
Bass line	B (natural)		c	B flat

Bar and Beat	70¹	70²	70³	70⁴
Text	et	se-	pul-	- tus
Harmony	I in A flat I⁷	I⁷ German 6th	i^c	V⁷ 4-3 suspension
Key	A flat major	C minor		
Bass line	A flat	a flat	g	G

Bar and Beat	71¹	71²	71³	71⁴
Text	est,	se-	pul-	- tus
Harmony	i	ii^{b7} (half-diminished seventh)	i^c	V
Key	C minor			
Bass line	c	F	G	G

Bar and Beat	72¹
Text	est.
Harmony	I
Key	C major
Bass line	c

ishes in E-flat major, at which point there is a brief orchestral link to the *Crucifixus*.

Haydn uses responsorial imitation for the first three statements of the *Crucifixus* text. This is a setting in triple meter, a choice that has implications for the placing of the text. Haydn appears to be more interested in

the rhythmic properties of the word "Crucifixus" than in any direct textual association in terms of the melodic line. The basses begin the phrase
on the second beat of bar 67, and the rest of the *coro* respond to this phrase
a bar later. The "-fi-" of "Crucifixus" falls on the strong first beat of bar
68, which is typical of so many settings: the rhythmic properties of this
word have held a strong appeal for composers. The crossing by one vocal
line of the other occurs in the choral response (soprano over alto at bar
69, *metabasis*), which could be viewed as an example of *Augenmusik*. However, since the same effect occurs again in bar 71, I am in this instance
cautious about associating the device specifically with the expression of
the word "Crucifixus," although it could act as a more general symbol of
the cross, in a vein similar to that found in Bach's setting. The harmonization of bar 68 certainly adds pathos to "Crucifixus." Bar 68 begins in E
flat, and the bass line retains an E-flat pedal throughout the first five bars
of the setting. Over these bars, the harmony oscillates between chord I in
E flat (bars 67, 69, and 71) and a diminished seventh over the tonic pedal
(bars 68 and 70). Rather than adding "direct" expression to the text (for
this chord is not reserved exclusively for the word "Crucifixus" but
appears also in connection with "etiam pro" in bar 70), this grating harmony is used in order to color the overall atmosphere of the setting.

"Etiam pro nobis" and "sub Pontio Pilato" have suitably dactylic settings. The bass phrase that initiates this responsorial imitation is aptly set
to a monotone, while the remaining choral parts are likewise relatively
static. By bar 71, Haydn has moved to the relative minor, where he again
prolongs the feeling of noneventfulness by setting up and retaining a
tonic pedal in the bass line for the next four bars. Again, the harmony
oscillates between the tonic and a diminished seventh over the tonic
pedal. The change of key (from E flat to C minor) is carried out swiftly,
on the third beat of bar 71, before we are abruptly launched back into
diminished-seventh harmony. This is a deliberate "ploy": Haydn does
not wish to lose the effect of this particular harmonic ostinato, which has
been set up in the first four bars.

"Passus" is accorded the bisyllabic treatment that we have come to
expect, each statement being separated by a *suspiratio*. The word is
repeated for amplification and on its third appearance (bar 78) is given a
full bar's value. Instead of consisting of two crotchets, this motive is now
given a full minim for the first syllable, followed by a crotchet for the second syllable. This may appear a fairly ordinary setting of the word, but a
number of other musical events conspire to create great contrast between
the first two statements and the third, the whole aim evidently being to
amplify through repetition, lending the third appearance special emphasis. Table 12.2 shows how Haydn achieves this. The introduction of the
Neapolitan key on the third statement is a way of expressing the word

Table 12.2. Contrast between the Statements of "passus" in Haydn's Setting of the *Crucifixus* **from** *Missa in Tempore Belli*

Bar	76	77	78
Text	pas-sus (rest)	pas-sus (rest)	pas- - sus
Vocal scoring	Solo S and A	Solo S and A	Tutti SATB
Orchestra	Vln I, Vln II, Vla	Vln I, Vln II, Vla	Ob I, II, Cl I, II, Fg I, II, Vln I, Vln II, Vla, Org, Vc.
Harmony	C minor - I	C minor - I	Neapolitan (6th)
Dynamics	(p)	(p)	f
Other	Pulsating quavers broken up by use of crotchet on the first beat in the accompaniment		Constant quaver accompaniment returns in the organ and basso. Vln II and Vla have semiquavers. Woodwind accompany with sustained chords

"passus" in the manner that we might expect—via the use of a chromatic chord.

Bar 79 introduces the first of a number of statements of "et sepultus est." The first two are preceded by "passus" (see table 12.3 for a clarification of the organization of the text). The first statement of "et sepultus est" follows on directly from the Neapolitan harmonization of "passus" in bar 78. The soprano line expresses burial via a descending arpeggio at bar 79, followed by all four voices joining in a unison descent to reach (for the soprano, alto, and tenor) the lower depths of their respective registers at bar 80³. This is followed by an upward leap in all but the basses (bar 81). Between bars 80² and 84, the bass has a descending *passus duriusculus*. This emblem of lament subtly underlines the setting of this latter part of

Table 12.3. Organization of Text in Haydn's Setting of the *Crucifixus* **from** *Missa in Tempore Belli*

Bars 67²–69³	*Crucifixus*	responsorial imitation
Bars 69¹–71²	*etiam pro nobis*	responsorial imitation
Bars 71³–75²	*sub Pontio Pilato,*	call and response
Bars 76¹–77²	*passus, passus,*	chordal
Bars 78¹–82³	*passus et sepultus, sepultus est,*	chordal
Bars 83¹–88²	*passus, passus et sepultus est,*	chordal
Bars 88³–93¹	*sepultus est.*	chordal

the *Crucifixus* text in addition providing a sense of continuing harmonic unity between bars 78^1 and 82^3 and bars 83^1 and 88^2. "Passus" is heard again at bar 83 and repeated at bar 84. The first "passus" is set to a grinding diminished seventh on F sharp (first inversion) on the first two beats of the bar, followed by an anguished German sixth of C minor on the last beat. The chromatic harmony here heightens the "suffering." Another statement of "et sepultus" ensues, with a cadence in C minor at bar 88. The last few bars of this setting are marked as pianissimo. The voices move downward by step to express burial, the upper voices finishing at the lower end of their ranges. Haydn eliminates the upper woodwind from the scoring. The bass line has a pulsing-quaver tonic pedal (*paragogue*), supported by a sustained pedal in the *clarini* (trumpets). The opening oscillating harmonic pattern returns to conclude the setting—this is an unusual *Crucifixus* in that respect, but because the harmonic sequence has not been associated with any portion of text at the outset, it works for the concluding bars.

So many of these features are typical of *Crucifixus* settings. Haydn's handling of the orchestra, like Mozart's, adds an extra dimension to the text. The characteristic pulsing bass line is present throughout most of this setting. An obbligato-type melodic line is given to violin I in the first nine bars. This is useful as a linking device and adds interest at a point where the voices express the text in almost monotonal phrases. The change to broken-chord semiquaver motion in the strings at bar 78 supports the unexpected change to a Neapolitan chord at bar 78 by creating a more agitated accompaniment. This underlying accompaniment is maintained up to the antepenultimate bar. Where this pattern ceases, Haydn generates a feeling of repose to highlight the word "est" and the burial of the body. The woodwind section is used to punctuate the texture and often to provide the interest on a beat of the bar where nothing else is happening: for example, from bar 84 to bar 86, the woodwind chords fall on the second beat of the bar, where the vocal parts are static.

THE *CRUCIFIXUS* TRADITION BEYOND HAYDN

This is a logical point at which to examine whether the tradition of the *Crucifixus* was recognized as such beyond the confines of the period that this study encompasses. With romanticism, there was a distinct move away from the literal description of the text. The romantic movement was "characterised by an emphasis on feeling and content rather than order and form"; this manifested itself in music via the "global" expression of an extramusical idea rather than via specific musical description linking text to music or event to music.[1] So one would expect settings of the *Cruci-*

fixus to contain more of an overall atmospheric expression in place of the more specific depiction evident in settings from 1680 to 1800.

Beethoven's *Missa Solennis* (first published in 1827) utilizes many of the *Crucifixus* devices that have been described in this study:

> The *Crucifixus* is a paradigm of rhetorical figures traditional for this text: tmesis, tremolo, syncopation, diminished seventh chords, "crossed" melodic intervals, etc.[2]

One finds the typical change of tempo at the beginning of the *Et incarnatus*. This slow central section is indisputably the centerpiece of the *Credo* (despite a lengthy final section that threatens to disrupt the proportions). The setting itself contains many familiar devices: the use of dissonance as one voice is offset against another for the word "Crucifixus" as well as linear, "excruciating" intervals (see figure 12.1).[3] Warrren Kirkendale mentions that Beethoven makes the following note in his sketchbook for the *Crucifixus*: "*Crucifixus* in ♯ Ton," meaning "*Crucifixus* in sharp key." Kirkendale acknowledges as well the significance of the German word *Kreuz* in relation to Beethoven's annotation.[4] "Etiam pro nobis" and "sub Pontio Pilato" are set in typical narrative fashion, employing syllabic, dactylic, speechlike patterns. "Passus" is accorded suitable melismatic treatment, very often coupled with syncopation. As expected, "et sepultus est" has "downward" tendencies, its final phrase ending on the lowest notes of the soprano and alto range. Beethoven also cuts out most of the orchestra for this final statement, leaving only the strings and organ to accompany.

The *Crucifixus* from Hummel's *Mass in B Flat* op. 77, from 1810 (although records indicate that it may have been composed even earlier) provides further testimony that at least some elements of the tradition lingered on into the beginning of the nineteenth century. While this setting is not as "extreme" in its use of *Crucifixus* traditions as Beethoven's, Hummel responds to the text in the expected manner by employing "excruciating" intervals for the depiction of the word "Crucifixus." The tenor opens with a descending diminished third between its first two syllables of "Crucifixus"; the same interval is used by the other voices as they successively enter with this opening motive. A diminished fifth occurs between the alto and tenor in bar 154, while the second soprano entry at bar 155 introduces a diminished seventh (see figure 12.2).[5]

Schubert's settings (*Mass in A Flat, Mass in G,* and *Mass in E Flat*) demonstrate far less dependence on these traditional devices for the expression of the *Crucifixus*. True, there are many chromatic touches to these settings, but these seem more to belong to an all-encompassing attempt to express the text or else to be an integral part of the harmonic language. Nor does

Figure 12.1. *Crucifixus* Motives in Beethoven's *Missa Solemnis*

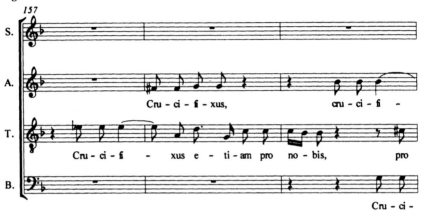

Schumann respond significantly to the textual description in his *Mass* (op. 147). The *coro* remain here in unison (sopranos and altos versus tenors and basses, an octave apart). There is only one complete statement of the text and little depiction of any of the "action" phrases of the text; for instance, "et sepultus est" has no descending line to express burial. Likewise, Liszt's *Missa Solemnis* makes no attempt to "interpret" the text to any degree. The grandeur of the scale of setting appears to have been more important to him than textual expression per se. Rossini, who opts for a quasi-operatic, solo setting of the *Crucifixus* (displaying few of the old conventions) in his *Petite Messe Solennelle* (1864), respects, however, its traditional autonomy: the *Et incarnatus* is included in the first section of

Figure 12.2. **Extract from Hummel's Setting of the** *Crucifixus* **from** *Mass in B Flat* op. 77

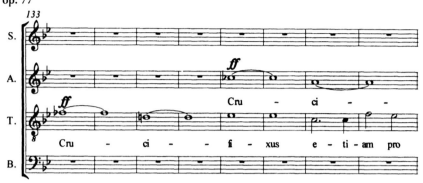

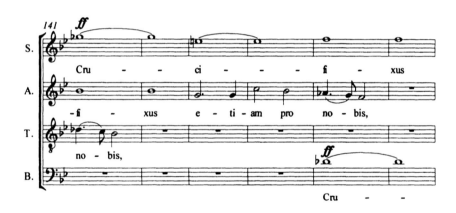

the *Credo*, while the *Crucifixus* is set as a separate, slower movement (*Andantino sostenuto*).

There was fresh interest, even on the part of nonbelievers, in Catholicism and its music during the nineteenth century. The middle of the century witnessed another musical reform within the Church, which generated much interest in the *a cappella* style of the sixteenth century. This reform (the Cecilian), which, at its most extreme, sought to banish orchestral instruments from the Church, had the effect of alienating many composers since it placed major constraints on the music that could be produced and also erected a barrier between liturgical music and mainstream secular music. In general, Church music no longer retained the importance that it held in the baroque period and, to a declining but real extent, in the classical period.

However, the *Crucifixus* as a section of the Mass and also as subject matter has continued to fascinate composers up to the end of the twentieth century. Janáček's setting of the *Crucifixus* in his *Glagolithic Mass* (1927) leads to the structural focal point of the entire work, as in Bach's setting, where the *Crucifixus* acts as a "cornerstone" for the *Mass in B Minor*. John Tavener's *Ultimos Ritos* of 1972 reflects the deeply held religious beliefs of this composer. This work is based on texts by the post-Reformation mystic St. John of the Cross. The work is organized in five movements, designed in the shape of the cross. Five is a number traditionally associated with the cross, so the association here is not fortuitous. Symbolism is highly important to Tavener: the number seven is used by him extensively (for the Seven Last Words from the Cross). It is interesting to see that Tavener uses actual fragments of the Bach setting of the *Crucifixus* throughout most of *Ultimos Ritos*. The sections of Bach's *Crucifixus* are not linked; that is, they do not follow on from each other. Tavener does not hesitate to interrupt a passage taken from the original setting in midword. Here we see a composer whose religious beliefs are as deeply held as those of Bach—Tavener's "parodistic" use of Bach's *Crucifixus* is a way of expressing this. We have, however, moved into a distinctly postmodern age in which the text-music relationship inherited from the Renaissance may give way to new forms of combination and association.

NOTES

1. The description of romanticism is taken from Patrick Hanks, ed., *The Collins Concise Dictionary of the English Language* (London: Collins, 1990), 1010.

2. Warren Kirkendale, "New Roads to Old Ideas in Beethoven's *Missa Solemnis*," *The Musical Quarterly* 56 (1970): 680.

3. The musical example in figure 12.1 is compiled from a number of sources,

including Ludwig van Beethoven, *Missa Solemnis,* op. 123, no editor stated (Leipzig, Germany: Breitkopf und Härtel, 1864; reprint, New York: Dover Publications, 1991); *Missa Solennis* op. 123, no editor stated (Leipzig, Germany: Peters, n.d.); and *Missa Solennis* op. 123, no editor stated (Zürich, Switzerland: Eulenberg, n.d.).

4. Kirkendale, "New Roads to Old Ideas in Beethoven's *Missa Solemnis,*" 680.

5. Figure 12.2 is from Johann Nepomuk Hummel, *First Mass in B Flat* op. 77, ed. Vincent Novello (London: Novello, 1840).

Part V

SUMMARY

13

The *Crucifixus* Tradition: Patterns of Influence and Modes of Transmission

The aim of this chapter is to categorize and summarize the main *Crucifixus* traditions highlighted in this study. The temporal distribution of these traditions is examined, and the likely modes of and influences on transmission are also discussed. Again, it is necessary to issue a caution. The conclusions that will be drawn from this study are obviously based solely on the material examined (that is, the one hundred-odd settings of the *Crucifixus* gathered for the purpose of this research) and are therefore limited in this important respect.

THE *CRUCIFIXUS* TRADITION

The main *Crucifixus* traditions can be examined under four categories: "contextual," "direct," "indirect," and "structural." References have already been made in the later case studies to "direct" and "indirect" expression of the text. These terms concern musical devices that are used either to express specific words or phrases or to contribute to the overall expression of the text. "Structural" refers to the organizational strategies that composers use for the musical setting of this section of text. "Contextual" traditions are those *Crucifixus* conventions that either help provide a background to the setting itself or occur as part of the surrounding *Credo*. This section discusses each of these four areas and also examines the lines and patterns of influence that have become evident as a result of this study.

"Contextual" Crucifixus Traditions

The subject of the *Crucifixus* itself would prompt a composer to use a minor key for the setting. A high percentage of the *Crucifixus* settings are set in the minor mode. Settings dating from the earlier end of the period (around 1680) do not display such an extreme tendency, but from 1710 on, the majority of *Crucifixus* settings are cast in a minor key. There are notable exceptions, such as the setting by Giorgi (31; ca. 1720), which is in C major, and the setting by Cimarosa (16; ca. 1790). However, the majority of settings in the major key tend to be those that are written in the *stile antico*, for example, Durante's *Messa a 3 Voci* (21; ca. 1730) and Legrenzi's *Missa a 5 Voci* (56; 1689). The use of minor keys was far less prevalent in the classical period than formerly, so the fact that so many of the *Crucifixus* settings examined from this period are set in the minor again highlights the significance of this section of text and the appeal that it held for composers. A composer would thwart the expectation of a major key setting in favor of a mode that was clearly better suited to the meaning of the text. Of the forty-three settings that lie within the period 1760–1800, ten are cast in major keys, while eleven begin in the major but modulate to the minor by the end of the section. All the remaining settings are in the minor (see table 13.1).

Chapter 5 comments on the high proportion of tonally open settings. Considering the lack of segregation between the *Et incarnatus*, *Crucifixus*, and *Et resurrexit* in many *Credo* settings, this comes as no surprise: here, the *Crucifixus* is but a passing episode, and the tonal organization reflects this. Further, a tonally open *Crucifixus* setting engenders the feeling of incompleteness—that there is something more to come—which is naturally very appropriate for the account that the text itself delivers: "et sepultus est" is by no means the end of this narrative. Earlier settings imply the autonomy of separate movements by means of some kind of segregating bar line (Colonna, Draghi, Kerll), a tradition that continues through to the late baroque (Caldara, Zelenka). These movements are usually tonally closed. Later, the *Et incarnatus* and *Crucifixus* are often linked, pointing to a growing tendency for settings to be tonally open.

Table 13.1 presents an overall survey of the tonal structure of all the *Crucifixus* settings considered in this survey. While it gives some hint of the distribution of settings in major/minor keys over the period of study, it cannot be taken as an "absolute" benchmark since different numbers of settings were collected for different subperiods. Nevertheless, this table demonstrates some interesting trends. First, the number of tonally open

Table 13.1. Survey of Overall Tonal Structure of *Crucifixus* Settings

	T. C Maj	T. O. Maj: Maj	T. O. Maj: Min	T. O. Min: Maj	T. O. Min: Min	T. C. Min
1680–1700 7 settings	3/7 ~42.9%	1/7 ~14.3%			1/7 ~14.3%	2/7 ~28.5%
1700–1720 15 settings	7/15 ~46.9%		2/15 ~13.4%	1/15 ~6.7%	2/15 ~13.4%	3/15 ~20.1%
1720–1740 28 settings	5/28 ~18.0%	1/28 ~3.6%	3/28 ~10.8%		6/28 ~21.6%	13/28 ~46.8%
1740–1760 9 settings	1/9 ~11.1%		1/9 ~11.1%	2/9 ~22.2%	3/9 ~33.3%	2/9 ~22.2%
1760–1780 29 settings	2/29 ~7.0%		8/29 ~28.0%	1/29 ~3.5%	8/29 ~28.0%	10/29 ~35%
1780–1800 14 settings	4/14 ~28.4%	4/14 ~28.4%	3/14 ~21.3%		1/14 ~7.1%	2/14 ~14.2%
Total	22/102	6/102	17/102	4/102	21/102	32/102

Tonally open (T. O.) = 48
Tonally closed (T. C.) = 52
Major keys only (T. O. and T.C.) = 28
Minor keys only (T. O. and T.C.) = 53
Move from major to minor = 17

settings is close to the number of tonally closed ones. This high incidence is probably due to the continuity of the *Credo* text as a whole, which resists excessive compartmentalization. Second, there were a significant number of settings that began in the major and then modulated to the minor. Often, there is a practical reason for this form of tonal organization (that is, the closing tonality of the *Et incarnatus*), but the strategy of beginning a section such as the *Crucifixus* in the major and then moving to the minor can create a heightened sense of contrast. Some settings move to the minor within the first few bars or even more speedily, as Mozart's *Krönungs-Messe* and Zelenka's *Missa Sancti Spiritus* ZWV 4 (102) show.[1]

A slower tempo marking was frequently used for this section of the *Credo*. This is a convention that remained current throughout the period examined. The transition between old-style baroque scoring governed by the principle of strict part writing and the establishment of a more flexible modern scoring occurs within the frame of this 120-year period and has been discussed in general terms in chapter 5. Effective uses of the orchestra were discussed in chapter 12. It is true to say that the *Crucifixus* tradition tended to employ reduced scoring within the context of the *Credo* and that this custom remained prevalent throughout the period under examination.

"Direct" Crucifixus Traditions

"Direct" traditions are those associated with the words of the *Crucifixus* themselves. These traditions tend to fall into two categories: first, those used to describe the "action" phrases of the text, which, as we have already seen, have more to offer in terms of "text appeal," and, second, the musical setting of the "contextual" phrases of the text. Although these do not offer the composer much potential for word painting, there is nonetheless a "standard" approach to setting these phrases.

These various traditions or *topoi* have been already been examined in detail during an overview of the entire study in chapter 5 and more specifically in the case studies. In this chapter, I examine the patterns of influence that have become evident from this study.

The use of the musical sign of the cross to express the word "Crucifixus" occurs mainly in the late baroque: from Perti (ca. 1710) to Caldara and Zelenka. The incidence of this device was far lower than I originally predicted (table 5.5). The possible reasons for its relative rarity are discussed later in this chapter under "Modes of Transmission." The "excruciating" intervals to express the Crucifixion are a more common form of expression, but it is important to remember that such a device would have been a fairly standard method of expressing a section of text of this kind. On the other hand, the musical sign of the cross is a more specialized device, suited to use only in connection with texts associated with this symbol of Christ's suffering. Indeed, the evidence supports this suggestion, with composers, regardless of period or location, using these intervals to express the specific word "Crucifixus" (see table 5.5). Interestingly, the appearance of a sharp (*Kreuz*) in the vocal lines expressing Crucifixion occurs to a significantly greater extent with Italian composers, rather than with German composers, as one might have expected.

The narrative/contextual phrases are set in a similar manner throughout the period. Dactylic rhythms are used to an overwhelming extent to set the two phrases "etiam pro nobis" and "sub Pontio Pilato," highlighting the natural rhythmic vitality of these sections of text. These phrases harbor little potential for word painting, so most composers, again regardless of period or location, opt for a "neutral," straightforward setting.

The word "passus" has two distinct methods of depiction: first, longer melismatic phrases, often including syncopation, larger note values, and suspensions, and, second, one note per syllable, frequently using longer values for these two notes in relation to what has gone before. Generally, the more melismatic settings tend to occur within the first seventy years of the period, culminating in such flamboyant composers as Zelenka. The peak of this tradition falls in the late baroque.

The final phrase, "et sepultus est," is associated with a number of traditions. The most obvious is the "directional" convention. This is certainly a common method of depiction throughout the period. It was also fairly standard to have a repeated concluding statement of "et sepultus est," as if in confirmation of the biographical fact. This is a common way of rounding off the *Crucifixus* section but is, again, also a fairly universal method of completing *any* section, so extensive use of this device might in any case be expected (it is also part of the rhetorical heritage). Such devices, such as a final *a cappella* statement (in a setting employing instruments), can be included in the same category.

"Indirect" Crucifixus Traditions

These traditions are not linked with any specific portion of the *Crucifixus* text but nonetheless contribute "indirectly" to the expression of the text. Examples include the use of chromatic harmony, of *lamento*, of *Via dolorosa* "plodding" figures, and of pulsating bass lines, plus the "multitude" convention of scoring for several voices.

While the use of chromaticism can hardly be classed as an exclusive *Crucifixus* tradition, some composers employed it to good effect in order to enhance the overall atmosphere of a setting. Recourse to chromaticism reaches extreme heights in the late baroque period and also forms an integral part of the harmonic language of the classical period; thus, underlying chromaticism and dissonance are to be expected in these settings regardless of time or location. Examples include many of the settings by Caldara, Zelenka, Mozart, and Haydn.

The use of the *lamento* bass line is much more limited. There are few examples within this survey, the most obvious being the *Crucifixus* from Bach's *Mass in B Minor*. While the *lamento* bass was often used in baroque opera, it appears to have been employed only occasionally for *Crucifixus* settings. However, while the *lamento* bass itself is not used as frequently as one might have expected, more general forms of the *passus duriusculus* certainly feature prominently. There is a very extensive use of the chromatic fourth and *passus duriusculus* (as already mentioned, the chromatic fourth is regarded as a special case of *passus duriusculus*—for the purposes of this book, *passus duriusculus* is used to refer to a wider or narrower range of ascending or descending stepwise chromatic steps). This remains true throughout the period covered by this survey.

The *Via dolorosa* style of accompaniment is another example of "indirect" expression of the text. Recourse to this device is appears mainly from 1720 on (see figures 5.2, 5.4, and 5.6). Pulsating accompaniments, too, frequently form a backdrop to settings (figures 4.4, 5.17, and 5.18). Again, this style of accompaniment occurs frequently in settings from the last eighty years of the period. Both Mozart and Haydn employ pulsating accompaniments in many of their settings.

The representation of a multitude by the use of several vocal lines is overwhelmingly common. It is interesting to note that the few single solo-voice settings that do exist date mainly from the early classical period (ca. 1750–1770) and belong to the Viennese tradition (with the partial exception of Caldara, who was "Viennese" but not classical). One might speculate whether there was a "localized" fashion for using solo voices in the *Crucifixus* around this time in Vienna.

"Structural" Crucifixus Traditions

The term "structural" is used here in the sense of overall structure and organization of the section and not in connection with structural rhetorical devices. In all the settings, without exception, there is a strong sense of beginning–middle–end. The text presents a narrative, offering a sequence of events, the order of which must to a large extent be preserved. This imperative was recognized by all composers in this study. Each setting opens with the word "Crucifixus"—even where there is an overlap with the end of the *Et incarnatus*, as happens in the case of Haydn's *Missa Sancti Nicolai* (36)—and ends with the phrase "et sepultus est." Admittedly, a musical setting will differ from an oration since the musical text sometimes becomes jumbled—in these settings, where this happens, the jumbled text is enclosed within an outer frame consisting of the opening and concluding words presented in strict sequence. The internal organization of the text depends largely on the length of the section and the style of composition. Longer settings naturally demand a coherent and carefully planned structuring of the words and music, with clear tonal direction and use of musical/textual motives. Both Caldara's setting for sixteen voices and Vivaldi's setting are carefully organized in these respects. Thus, Tarasti's arch structure ("a certain tension between beginning and end") is observable in most settings.[1] There is usually some form of climactic point within *Crucifixus* settings (most notably in the longer settings) so that the setting of the phrase "et sepultus est" signifies completion of (on occasion) a subsection and, ultimately, of the "arch." The structure of most settings is driven mainly by the words since they have such a strong organizational force, and this is true even of *stile antico* movements, where, as we have seen in chapter 11, the composer has to accept the stylistic confines and compose within them.

AN EXCEPTION TO THE TRADITION:
CIMAROSA'S *MESSA A 4 CON STROMENTI*

As with any large collection of material, there will be exceptions to the "rules." There exist rare settings that demonstrate few or none of the traditions discussed in this study. A number of settings, for example, are not written in a minor key, thus setting up a contradiction between the pathos of the words and the semantic implications of a major key. Giorgi's setting from his *Credo a 4 Voci* (31) is one of these, and Galuppi's *Credo Papal in G* (28) is another. Cimarosa's setting of the *Crucifixus* from his *Messa a 4 con Stromenti* (16) is a further example (appendix K). In the key of B flat, this setting is remarkable for its lack of adherence to *Crucifixus* traditions. Whether the composer was aware of the existing traditions (which indeed appears to be the case with many composers) and consciously chose to reject them in favor of an individual style will remain an issue for speculation. Conversely, it would appear that Cimarosa chose to set the *Crucifixus* using codes and conventions peculiar to his own day. He was one of the leading opera composers of his time, and this setting is frankly operatic in nature. It opens with a solo soprano and introduces the full *coro* only after the first twelve bars. The texture is highly fragmented, allowing for many brief orchestral interludes. The writing for solo soprano is operatic in style, opening with a long-held B flat for the syllable "cru-" and then continuing with an arpeggiated sequence of notes to complete the opening word. There are very few devices that could be construed as typical *Crucifixus* conventions, such as the tremolo accompaniment pattern in the strings (bars 6–9). The *coro* enters at the end of bar 12, with chordal interjections, almost incidental to the dialogue between oboe and flute. However, the scoring is scaled down toward the end of this section, which is reminiscent of many *Crucifixus* settings. From bar 20 on (on the words "passus et sepultus est"), the strings double the voices, and the horns alone are permitted to interject dotted rhythms, the entire woodwind section being excluded. This setting truly makes no attempt to depict the words. Here, the composer has chosen to "block the semantic response to the text":[2] there is a conscious interference on the part of composer between the textual influence and the resultant music.

RHETORIC AND THE *CRUCIFIXUS* TRADITION

As this study has repeatedly shown, the influence and presence of rhetoric in music of this period should not be underestimated. The structural *Crucifixus* traditions discussed previously are largely synonymous with rhetorical structure, although cautions about the extent to which one can draw parallels between linguistic rhetoric and musical rhetoric need to be heeded. Certainly the *exordium* . . . *peroratio* organization is evident in the majority of settings, which bears similarity to Tarasti's narrative theory. For the shorter settings (such as the *Crucifixus* from Zelenka's *Missa Paschalis* ZWV 7 (101); chapter 9), it is simply not possible to attempt to impose Burmeister's or Mattheson's elaborate musical-rhetorical structure on the music.

A survey of the more common musical-rhetorical figures used in *Crucifixus* settings is given in table 13.2.[3] While a number of devices are purely structural in musical terms, many of the figures quoted are relevant to the depiction of the text, as we have seen throughout this study. For example, *heterolepsis* often occurs in connection with *metabasis*, where a composer might be trying to express musically the cross or crucifixion. All these devices are used to create effect, the ultimate goal being to persuade the listener of the contents of the text. A composer has a further advantage over the orator: he is able to create a "double narrativity" through use of both linguistic rhetorical devices (for example, repetition of the text) and musical-rhetorical ones.

MODES OF TRANSMISSION

This study has provided evidence that a recognized tradition of setting the *Crucifixus* existed during the period 1680–1800, being handed down from generation to generation of composers. However, how this tradition was passed on must remain an issue for speculation. Was there a conscious handing down of these devices, or was this merely a tradition that was unconsciously absorbed by composers and then reused in an instinctive manner?

First, I would suggest that rhetoric played a major role throughout. As described in the opening chapters, the entire culture of the time was steeped in rhetoric. It would be second nature for a composer to use many devices in the context within the *Crucifixus* (for example, the use of *pathopoeia*) and also to structure the section with a clear opening and conclusion in the manner of a classical oration. Rhetorical figures in isolation did not always form the *topoi* of the *Crucifixus* as such, yet the use of them was pervasive. It would not be difficult for any composer who was responsive to the textual influences to compose a setting employing musical-rhetorical devices that would, in combination, form the *topoi* associated with the *Crucifixus*. So there was an instinctive use of rhetoric to "persuade" the listener.

Obviously, the musical education of composers must have played a major role in the transmission of these traditions. The manner in which a

Table 13.2.   More Common Musical-Rhetorical Figures Used in *Crucifixus* Settings between 1680 and 1800

Figure	Definition
Anaphora (Repetitio)	1. a repeating bass line; ground bass; 2. a repetition of the opening phrase or motive in a number of successive passages; 3. a general repetition.
Anticipatio, Praesumptio	An additional upper or lower neighbouring note following a principal note, prematurely introducing a note belonging to the subsequent harmony or chord.
Aposiopesis	A rest in one or all voices of a composition; a general pause.
Assimilatio, Homoiosis	A musical representation of the text's imagery.
Auxesis, Incrementum	Successive repetitions of a musical passage which rise step by step.
Cadentiae duriuscula	A dissonance in the pre-penultimate harmony of the cadence.
Catabasis, Descensus	A descending musical passage which expresses descending, lowly or negative images or affections.
Climax, Gradatio	1. a sequence of notes in one voice repeated either at a higher or lower pitch; 2. two voices moving in ascending or descending parallel motion; 3. a gradual increase in rise in sound and pitch, creating a growth in intensity.
Corta	A three-note figure in which one note's duration equals the sum of the other two.
Distributio	A musical-rhetorical process in which individual motifs or phrases of a theme or section of a composition are developed before proceeding to the following material.
Emphasis	A musical passage which heightens or emphasises the meaning of the text through various means.
Epanalepsis	A frequent repetition of an expression.
Epizeuxis	An immediate and emphatic repetition of a word, note, motif, or phrase.
Faux bourdon, Carachresis, Simul Procedentia	A musical passage characterized by successive sixth-chord progressions.
Fuga	A compositional device in which a principal voice is imitated by subsequent voices.
Heterolepsis	An intrusion of one voice into the range of another.
Hyperbaton	A transfer of notes or phrases from their normal placement to a different location.

Table 13.2.   (Continued)

Figure	Definition
Hypotyposis	a vivid musical representation of images found in the accompanying text.
Metabasis, Transgressio	a crossing of one voice by another.
Metalepsis	a fuga with a two-part subject (double fugue).
Mimeiss, Ethophonia, Imitatio	an approximate rather than strict imitation of a subject at different pitches.
Noema	a homophonic passage within a contrapuntal texture.
Palilogia	a repetition of a theme, either at different pitches in various voices or on the same pitch in the same voice.
Paragogue, Manubrium, Supplementum	a cadenza or coda added over a pedal point at the end of a composition.
Paronomasia	a repetition of a musical passage with certain additions or alterations for the sake of greater emphasis.
Parrhesia	an insertion of a dissonance, such as a cross relation or tritone, on a weak beat.
Passus duriusculus	a chromatically altered ascending or descending melodic line.
Pathopoeia	a musical passage which seeks to arouse a passionate affection through chromaticism or by some other means.
Polyptoton	a repetition of a melodic passage at different pitches.
Prolongatio	a passing dissonance or suspension of longer duration than the preceding consonance.
Repercussio	1. a modified interval in a tonal answer; 2. a tonal, inverted, or other modified fugal answer.
Retardatio	1. a suspension which is prolonged or which resolves by rising; 2 a delayed rather than anticipatory suspension.
Salto semplice	a consonant leap.
Saltus duriusculus	a dissonant leap.
Suspiratio, Stenasmus	the musical expression of a sigh through a rest.
Synaeresis	1. a suspension or syncopation; 2. a placement of two syllables per note or two notes per syllable.
Syncopatio, Ligatura	a suspension with, or without a resulting dissonance.
Tmesis, Sectio	sudden interruption or fragmentation of melody through rests.
Transistus, Celeritas, Commissura, Diminutio, Symblema	a dissonant or passing note between two consonant ones, either on the strong or weak beat.

composer learned his craft would be material in his absorption of these traditions and in the conscious—or subconscious—reproduction of these conventions in his own work. The learning trajectory of a composer needs to be considered. There would have been the aural and participatory element: many composers began their career in the *cori* and *cappelle* of the churches and cathedrals of the major musical centers of the day and so would have become familiar with the methods of older composers in this very direct manner. If many different Masses displayed similar *Crucifixus* conventions, then a composer-to-be would certainly absorb this. The fact that the *Crucifixus* was so often "remarkable" within a *Credo* setting would also focus his attention on its music. Then, as a composer began to learn his craft, this process invariably involved observing the music around him in a more visual, notation-based manner. Examining compositional methods in detail would bring further *Crucifixus* conventions to light.

Often a composer learned his trade and then either succeeded the older composer as *maestro di cappella* or *Kapellmeister* or moved to another musical center to take up a similar role. With such a mobility of composers, these traditions could end up as "universal property." Each composer, of course, would impose his own personal stamp on the music, which, as we have seen, often reflected the current musical practices of the time, maybe scaled down to suit the conservative tastes of the Church. The political fragmentation of Italy and Germany multiplied the number of courts and institutions, thereby also multiplying opportunities for composers and opening the door to innovations that prevented the ossification of musical style.

There would have been other factors in play, such as the musical treatises of the time. How widely were these in circulation? This same speculation applies to the musical works of the day—how accessible were these to contemporary composers? The state of communications and the distribution of printed matter doubtless affected the transmission of these conventions.

Between 1500 and 1600, much sacred music, including settings of the Ordinary of the Mass (thus of the *Credo* and of the *Crucifixus*), circulated in printed form. It was economical to print Masses because the number of voices (usually four or five) and their specification (as SATB, SSATB, and so on) were relatively consistent and therefore suited to *a cappelle* all over Europe. However, the relatively high cost of printed music must have inhibited its wide circulation to some degree.

The advent of the baroque led to a diversification in the specification of the performing forces for Masses: instruments of various kinds were often added, solo/tutti differentiation was often required, and the vocal layout varied greatly. This both reflected and promoted a great variation in the size and composition of *cappelle*, from the poorly endowed and small (in parish churches) to the richly endowed and large (at courts). This huge variation in size and composition made it necessary to tailor sacred vocal works very precisely to local performance requirements. Printing or engraving the more complex compositions belonging to the sacred repertoire was hence less economical than before, and handwritten copies had the extra advantage of unlimited flexibility (for example, a special part for extra *ripieno* performers could be copied, formed from extracts of the corresponding solo part). The eighteenth century was a "golden age" of music copying as far as vocal music (of all kinds) was concerned.

Despite the need to copy out church compositions by hand, one example at a time, the circulation of such works was surprisingly wide. Institutions and individuals frequently loaned manuscripts to each other (this was particularly true of houses belonging to the same religious order—Franciscan, Benedictine, and so on), and musical visitors often copied manuscripts in the possession of their hosts. On some occasions, commercial copying shops (which, in Italy, were most heavily involved in preparing performance material for operas) dealt in sacred vocal music. Composers might have to act as copyists earlier (or indeed later) in their careers (either as their role dictated or to gather repertory from their peers that they could learn). This would help them broaden their knowledge of repertory and discover how different composers dealt with this same section of the Mass. Often, we find evidence that composers "collected" or copied from existing works in order to study various techniques and styles. Bach often studied other composers' work in detail, before conceiving his own compositions. The adaptations that Bach made to *Weinen, Klagen, Sorgen, Zagen* certainly seem to suggest that he was aware of an existing *Crucifixus* tradition. A comparison between Vivaldi's "collected" and "composed" works shows how a younger composer could imbibe and even literally borrow from (in the spirit of *parodia*) the work of his seniors while not neglecting to update the musical language where necessary.[4]

In the nineteenth century, music publishers gradually began, once again, to bring out sacred vocal music in quantity. One factor was the improvement of printing techniques (via lithography and so on). Another was the widening of outlets for the sacred vocal repertory—a Mass or Magnificat could now be performed not only liturgically but in the concert hall as well and could serve as an object of study for students in newly opened conservatories.

All the works included in the present study, with its time frame of 1680–1800, belong to the era between the Renaissance and romantic periods, when dissemination in manuscript form was the norm for *Crucifixus* settings. To some extent, this inhibited their circulation and therefore their ability to become used as models by subsequent composers but not so much as to prevent the emergence over time of shared conventions applicable to wide areas such as that represented by the present study.

CONCLUSION

To write a conclusion to a chapter that itself is attempting to summarize the *Crucifixus* conventions and their patterns and modes of transmission is a difficult task. So I will end by asking the following hypothetical question. If a composer were to work in isolation, without access to works in a similar genre but having had a musical training similar to that of his peers, would he still be able to create a *Crucifixus* setting containing conventions similar to those that appear in settings conceived amid all these influences? I think that a composer in such a situation might respond to many of the textual influences (as these are usually the starting point for composition) but that some of the more stylized conventions would not appear. For example, the use of grating intervals to express crucifixion might well exist in such a setting, but the musical sign of the cross would not since it would be unlikely to occur spontaneously without exposure to this kind of tradition communicated from composer to composer.

NOTES

1. Zelenka's setting begins in D major but starts to move toward the relative minor within the first bar, arriving there by the third bar. Zelenka makes this tonal shift by employing a *passus duriusculus* as the bass line.
2. Irving Godt, "Music about Words: Madrigalisms and other Text Influences in Music," (unpublished manuscript, 1990), 323.
3. Dietrich Bartel, *Musica Poetica: Musical-Rhetorical Figures in German Baroque Music* (Lincoln: University of Nebraska Press, 1997), 439–43.
4. For a more detailed discussion, see Jasmin Cameron, "Two *Gloria* Settings by Giovanni Maria Ruggieri" (M.Mus. diss., University of Liverpool, 1995).

14

General Overview

The evidence presented in this study shows that the *Crucifixus* was, for many composers, the "crucial" part or focal point of the *Credo*. Composers lavished attention on this section of the text, creating striking and powerful settings. The fact that *Crucifixus* settings have so often been transmitted and performed separately from their parent work or movement serves to highlight their musical quality.

This study has highlighted the major similarities and differences between the areas of word painting, textual influence, rhetorical figures, and semiotics and has then proceeded to relate these to the *Crucifixus topoi* themselves. *Crucifixus topoi* may be made up of several rhetorical devices but not necessarily any of the ones documented by the theorists. Earlier discussion has shown that word painting is not synonymous with either *topoi* or rhetorical devices: the narrative phrases of the *Crucifixus* text are not phrases that are appropriate for this level of musical description, while those musical-rhetorical figures that could be counted as word painting form only a part of the wider "family." The theory of semiotics forms the basis for an analytical technique and is different in this respect from rhetoric. It is true that rhetoric has been applied in this study as an analytical tool rather than being left in its more common passive role as a "theory," but the act of analyzing has helped to bring out the differences between semiotics and rhetoric. The area of textual influence also has many overlaps with the previously mentioned areas but, once again, offers an individual perspective. One interesting point that has emerged from the study is the benefit of using several relevant analytical techniques concurrently. While no one system in isolation is going to provide all the answers in a study like this, the application of several techniques can broaden the range of questions asked.

Another point that the study emphasizes is the present-day lack of interest in the analysis of texted music. All too often, the application of an analytical method has had to be adapted—or developed—in order to be used on the music under scrutiny. Music with words possesses an extra dimension absent from instrumental music. While the musicologist's problem of trying to discover what exactly a composer "meant" is reduced greatly, analysis itself becomes more problematic since it is geared toward instrumental music. It is significant that the rhetorical ("immanent") analysis carried out was in many ways far better suited to the type of music being examined than semiotic ("transcendent") analysis, but not altogether unexpectedly since musical rhetoric is inherited from a linguistic system and is therefore closely akin to music with words. Of course, it is possible to argue that semiosis also derives from a linguistic system and should therefore be as easy to apply to texted music. The difference between the two methods is their locus in time. Musical semiotic analysis was developed as a system focused mainly on instrumental music and performed mostly on music beyond the period of study covered here. On the other hand, a modern approach, such as Godt's, which has an appropriately retrospective viewpoint and is aimed more specifically at texted music, proves how effective a transcendent critique can be. The present study has also drawn attention to the pitfalls of viewing an older system through modern eyes.

So, in summary, the *topoi* of the *Crucifixus* are a combination of many different codes and conventions. The evidence presented in this study suggests that composers collectively developed a set of conventions that combined both age-old customs and contemporary musical practices and were recognized as a "code" to be passed down through the generations. The traditions that resulted were able to serve as a common point of reference for different styles and periods.

While the main aim of the study has been accomplished and many other interesting aspects of this field of study have been discovered, a thesis of this wide scope will leave countless unanswered questions plus the potential for the further development of research. My approach to rhetorical analysis has been a fairly general one, but in chapter 9, I suggested that it might be more appropriate to confine the rhetorical analysis to a system drawn from a source strictly contemporary with the composer in question. It would also be interesting to examine how, exactly, musical-rhetorical devices are documented between 1600 and 1800. From this investigation, it would be possible to see which devices remained popular (or not) throughout the period. If this information could then be related to musical development over this time span, one might be able to work out why rhetorical trends operated in the way that they did. The musical-rhetorical figures that are essentially fugal offer an example of these developments: they feature in earlier treatises (particularly Burmeister's) but are ignored by later theorists, a fact reflecting the general musical practice of the time. It would be interesting to broaden the base of music studied to include examples of Requiem Masses or of other funeral music. From this study, it would be possible to discover whether some of the *topoi* encountered were similar to ones used in the *Crucifixus*, whether, for instance, *lamento* basses occurred similarly in association with mourning. Another task might be to examine a different portion of the Mass (*Et resurrexit*, for example) and to trace its development in a similar manner.

One area on which I was unable to find sufficient information in secondary literature was that concerning Italian theorists of the day. There is relatively little written on this subject, and I feel that it would have been good to have been able to compare Italian and German theorists. There may possibly be documents existing in archives that are not in the public domain but that might help correct this lack of knowledge, but one of the limitations of carrying out this study was not having the time (or money) to investigate such an unknown.

Other issues also emerge from this study. It would be interesting to examine in even greater detail the reasons for the negative attitude shown by many present-day theorists toward texted music (as we have seen, this disposition is probably an amalgamation of many factors). Another question to research in greater depth is why, exactly, so many modern analytical techniques are applied only to classical and later music, largely bypassing earlier music.

Finally, this study has entailed the collection of a considerable quantity of music, a high proportion of which has been drawn from original sources in research libraries. The book draws on a number of *Crucifixus* settings of quality that deserve to be taken into the present-day vocal and choral repertory. The present study is therefore a contribution to knowledge in two respects: academic and musical. Music is, after all, a "living art."

NOTE

1. Eero Tarasti, *A Theory of Musical Semiotics* (Bloomington: Indiana University Press, 1994), 24.

Appendix A
Crucifixus Settings

Setting	Composer	Date (or date grouping)	Name of Work	Source of Reference
1	G. Abos	ca. 1740 (?)	Messa a 4 Voci	Archives of the Cathedral of Malta M-ACM Mus. File 1
2	J. G. Albrechtsberger	1763	Missa Annuntiationis	MacIntyre, The Viennese Concerted Mass, M. 3
3	J. C. Bach	ca. 1758	Credo in C	See Bibliography
4	J. S. Bach	1748/1749	Mass in B Minor BWV 232	See Bibliography
5	F. G. Bertoni	ca. 1760 (?)	Crucifixus con Organo a 4 Voci	London, Royal College of Music GB-Lcm Ms. 1086/5
6	H. I. von Biber	1701	Missa St. Henrici	Messen von Heinrich Biber, Heinrich Schmeltzer, Johann Casper Kerll, ed. Guido Adler (Graz, Austria: Akademische Druck und Verlagsanstalt, 1960)
7	A. Biffi	ca. 1730 (?)	Credo in D Minor	London, Royal College of Music GB-Lcm Ms. 48

Setting	Composer	Date (or date grouping)	Name of Work	Source of Reference
8	A. Caldara	ca. 1730	Crucifixus a 16 Voci	Münster, Santini Sammlung der Bischöflichen Bibliothek D-MÜs SANT Dr 127. See Bibliography
9	A. Caldara	ca. 1720 (?)	Mass for 4 Voices	London, Royal College of Music GB-Lcm Ms. 105
10	A. Caldara	ca. 1720 (?)	Mass in F	London, Royal College of Music GB-Lcm Ms. 789
11	A. Caldara	ca. 1720 (?)	Missa in spei Resurrectionis	Vienna, Gesellschaft der Musikfreunde A-Wgm Ms. A 323
12	A. Caldara	1732	Mass in A Major	Kremsmünster, Benediktinerstift, Musikarchiv A-KR Ms. B17, 353
13	A. Caldara	1729	Missa Laetare	Berlin, Deutsche Staatsbibliothek, Musikabteilung D-Bds Ms. Mus.ms autogr. Caldara A4
14	A. Caldara	1729	Missa Commemorationis	Vienna, Österreichische Nationalbibliothek, Musiksammlung A-Wn Mus. Hs H. K. 207
15	A. Carl	before 1751	Missa Solennis in C	MacIntyre, The Viennese Concerted Mass, M. 14

16	D. Cimarosa	*Messa a 4 con Stromenti*	ca. 1790	London, British Library GB-Lbl Additional Ms. 29275
17	G. P. Colonna	*Messa Concertati a 5 Voci se piace con Stromenti e ripieni a Beneplacito*	ca. 1680 (?)	London, Royal College of Music GB-Lcm Ms. 801
18	K. D. von Dittersdorf	*Missa in C*	Before 1773	MacIntyre, *The Viennese Concerted Mass,* M. 15
19	A. Draghi	*Missa a 9*	1684	See Bibliography
20	A. Draghi	*Missa Assumptionis*	1684	See Bibliography
21	F. Durante	*Messa a 3 Voci*	ca. 1730	London, Royal College of Music GB-Lcm Ms. 856
22	J. J. Fux	*Missa S.S. Trinitatis*	1693	See Bibliography
23	J. J. Fux	*Missa S. Caroli*	ca. 1718	See Bibliography
24	J. J. Fux	*Missa Quadragesimalis*	ca. 1720–30 (?)	See Bibliography
25	J. J .Fux	*Missa Purificationis*	ca. 1720–30 (?)	See Bibliography
26	J. J. Fux	*Mass in D Minor for 10 Voices*	ca. 1730	London, Royal College of Music GB-Lcm Ms. 863
27	B. Galuppi	*Credo a 4*	ca. 1740–60 (?)	London, Royal College of Music GB-Lcm Ms. 865
28	B. Galuppi	*Credo Papal in G*	ca. 1740–60 (?)	London, Royal College of Music GB-Lcm Ms. 866

Setting	Composer	Date (or date grouping)	Name of Work	Source of Reference
29	F. Gasparini	ca. 1710 (?)	Missa a 4	London, Royal College of Music GB-Lcm Ms. 1036/3*
30	F. L. Gassmann	ca. 1770	Missa in C	See Bibliography
31	G. Giorgi	ca. 1720–1730	Credo a 4 Voci	Münster, Santini Sammlung der Bischöflichen Bibliothek D-MÜs SANT Hs. 1695
32	J. A. Hasse	1751	Mass in D Minor	MacIntyre, The Viennese Concerted Mass, M. 15
33	F. J. Haydn	1749/1750	Missa Brevis in F	See Bibliography
34	F. J. Haydn	1766	Missa in Honorem Beatissimae Virginis Mariae	See Bibliography
35	F. J. Haydn	1769/1773	Missa Sanctae Caeciliae	See Bibliography
36	F. J. Haydn	1772	Missa Sancti Nicolai	See Bibliography
37	F. J. Haydn	ca. 1775	Missa Brevis Scti. Joannis de Deo	See Bibliography
38	F. J. Haydn	1782	Missa Cellensis-"Mariazellenmesse"	See Bibliography

	Composer	Date	Title	Source
39	F. J. Haydn	1796	*Missa in Tempore Belli*	See Bibliography
40	F. J. Haydn	1796	*Missa Sti Bernardi von Offida "Heiligmesse"*	See Bibliography
41	F. J. Haydn	1798	*Missa in Angustis "Nelson"*	See Bibliography
42	F. J. Haydn	1799	*Theresienmesse*	See Bibliography
43	F. J. Haydn	1801	*Schöpfungsmesse*	See Bibliography
44	F. J. Haydn	1802	*Harmonienmesse*	See Bibliography
45	J. M. Haydn	1782	*Missa in Honorem Sancti Ruperti*	London, Royal College of Music GB-Lcm Ms. 287
46	J. M. Haydn	1794	*Missa Tempore Quadragesimae*	See Bibliography
47	J. M. Haydn	1794	*Missa in Dominica Palmarum*	See Bibliography
48	J. M. Haydn	1803	*Missa S. Francisci*	See Bibliography
49	J. D. Heinichen	ca. 1720	*Missa 11*	Dresden, Sächsische Landesbibliothek D-Dlb Mus. 2398-D-10
50	J. D. Heinichen	ca. 1720	*Missa 12*	Dresden, Sächsische Landesbibliothek D-Dlb Mus. 2398-D-11
51	L. Hofmann	before 1760	*Missa in Honorem Sanctae Theresiae in C*	MacIntyre, *The Viennese Concerted Mass,* M. 27

Setting	Composer	Date (or date grouping)	Name of Work	Source of Reference
52	L. Hofmann	before 1772	Missa in D	MacIntyre, The Viennese Concerted Mass, M. 29
53	N. Jommelli	1766	Missa a 4 Voci in D	London, British Library GB-Lbl Additional Ms. 14138
54	J. C. Kerll	1687	Missa Cujus Toni	See Bibliography
55	J. C. Kerll	1690	Missa Superba	See Bibliography
56	G. Legrenzi	1689	Missa a 5 Voci	London, Royal College of Music GB-Lcm Ms. 327
57	L. Leo	ca. 1730–1740	Messa Completa	London, British Library GB-Lbl Egerton Ms. 2448
58	L. Leo	ca. 1730–1740	Credo a 4 Voci	Münster, Santini Sammlung der Bischöflichen Bibliothek D-MÜs SANT Hs 2342
59	A. Lotti	ca. 1700–1740	Crucifixus a 6 [Credo a 8]	London, Royal College of Music GB-Lcm Ms. 661/28 GB-Lcm Ms. 1088/1
60	A. Lotti	ca. 1700–1740	Crucifixus a 10	Münster, Santini Sammlung der Bischöflichen Bibliothek D-MÜs SANT Hs 3978
61	A. Lotti	ca. 1700–1740	Missa I	See Bibliography
62	A. Lotti	ca. 1700–1740	Missa II	See Bibliography

63	A. Lotti	ca. 1700–1740	*Missa III*	See Bibliography
64	A. Lotti	ca. 1700–1740	*Missa IV*	See Bibliography
65	A. Lotti	ca. 1700–1740	*Missa V*	See Bibliography
66	A. Lotti	ca. 1700–1740	*Missa VI*	See Bibliography
67	A. Lotti	ca. 1700–1740	*Missa VII*	See Bibliography
68	B. Marcello (attrib.)	ca. 1710–1730 (?)	*Mass in F*	Godt, ed., "Italian Figurenlehre"*
69	L. Mozart	ca. 1764	*Mass in C*	London, British Library GB-Lbl Additional Ms. 32394
70	W. A. Mozart	1768	*Missa Brevis in G* KV 49	See Bibliography
71	W. A. Mozart	1768/1769	*Missa in C Minor* KV 139	See Bibliography
72	W. A. Mozart	1769	*Missa Brevis in D Minor* KV 65	See Bibliography
73	W. A. Mozart	1769	*Missa in C "Dominicus-Messe"* KV 66	See Bibliography
74	W. A. Mozart	1773	*Missa Brevis in G* KV 140	See Bibliography
75	W. A. Mozart	1773	*Missa in C "Missa in Honorem SS^mae Trintatis"* KV 167	See Bibliography
76	W. A. Mozart	1774	*Missa Brevis in F* KV 192	See Bibliography
77	W. A. Mozart	1774	*Missa Brevis in D* KV 194	See Bibliography
78	W. A. Mozart	1775/1776	*Missa in C* KV 220	See Bibliography

Setting	Composer	Date (or date grouping)	Name of Work	Source of Reference
79	W. A. Mozart	1776	*Missa Longa in C* KV 262	See Bibliography
80	W. A. Mozart	1775–1777	*Missa in C Minor* KV 257	See Bibliography
81	W. A. Mozart	1777	*Missa in C* KV 258	See Bibliography
82	W. A. Mozart	1775–1777	*Missa in C* KV 259	See Bibliography
83	W. A. Mozart	1777	*Missa in B Flat* KV 175	See Bibliography
84	W. A. Mozart	1779	*Missa in C "Krönungs-Messe"* KV 317	See Bibliography
85	W. A. Mozart	1780	*Missa in C* KV 337	See Bibliography
86	G. B. Pergolesi (attrib.)	ca. 1730 (?)	*Messa Completa a 4 Voci*	London, British Library GB-Lbl Egerton Ms. 2448
87	G. A. Perti	ca. 1700–1720	*Messa Canone a 3*	London, Royal College of Music GB-Lcm Ms. 661/27
88	G. A. Perti	ca. 1700–1720	*Kyrie, Gloria* and *Credo*	London, British Library GB-Lbl Additional Ms. 14195
89	N. Porpora	1747	*Mass for 4 Voices*	London, British Library GB-Lbl Additional Ms. 14132
90	G. Reutter the Younger	1734	*Missa S. Caroli*	See Bibliography
91	A. Salieri	1788	*Mass in D*	See Bibliography
92	A. Scarlatti	1720	*St. Cecilia Mass*	See Bibliography

93	A. Scarlatti	1703	*Missa Clementina*	London, British Library GB-Lbl Additional Ms. 32071
94	F. Schmidt	before 1746	*Missa Sanctae Caeciliae*	MacIntyre, *The Viennese Concerted Mass,* M. 50
95	A. Vivaldi	ca. 1717	*Credo RV 591*	Turin, Biblioteca Nazionale Universitaria I-Tn Foà 40
96	J. D. Zelenka	1741	*Missa Omnium Sanctorum ZWV 21*	See Bibliography
97	J. D. Zelenka	1739	*Missa Votiva ZWV 18*	See Bibliography
98	J. D. Zelenka	1724	*Missa Circumcisionis*	London, British Library GB-Lbl Additional Ms. 32141
99	J. D. Zelenka	1726	*Missa Nativitatis Domini ZWV 8*	Berlin, Staatsbibliothek zu Berlin Preussicher Kulturbesitzt D-Bsb Mus. ms.23539
100	J. D. Zelenka	ca. 1711	*Missa S. Caeciliae ZWV 1*	Dresden, Sächsische Landesbibliothek D-Dlb Mus. 2358-D-7a
101	J. D. Zelenka	1726	*Missa Paschalis ZWV 7*	Bodleian Library, Oxford GB-Ob Ms. Tenbury 749
102	J. D. Zelenka	1723, rev. ca. 1729	*Missa Sancti Spiritus ZWV 4*	Dresden, Sächsische Landesbibliothek D-Dlb Mus. 2358-D-18, 1–2

*Settings 29 (Gasparini) and 68 (attributed to Benedetto Marcello) are identical. Irving Godt identifies Gasparini as the composer of this Mass, which bears the name of Marcello on the title page of the source in New York Public Library, Mus. Res.*MRD ("Gasparini, Marcello, and New York," *Bulletin of Research in the Humanities* 85 [1982]: 295–321). Godt includes an edited version of this *Crucifixus* setting in "Italian Figurenlehre? Music and Rhetoric in a New York Source," in *Studies in the History of Music,* eds. Ronald Broude and Ellen Beebe (New York: Broude Brothers, 1983), 178–203.

Appendix B

Rhythmic Variants for
Setting the Word "Crucifixus"

Note: The subscripts attached to each family of motives are used to indicate the variants of the original rhythmic pattern as follows: Type 1: the motive in its definitive state for that particular rhythmic famly; type 2: shortening of the final note of the motive; type 3: retaining the underlying basic rhythm (as in type 1) but with decoration; type 4: some form of prolongation of the syllable "fi-" in the form of either a longer note value or a melisma; type 5: longer note values for the two last syllables; type 6: shorter note values for the two last syllables; and type 7: extension of the first one or two syllables.

GROUP A—"CRUCIFIXUS": RHYTHMIC MOTIVES $\frac{4}{4}$ AND $\math혻{\mathtext{¢}}$ (STRONG BEATS)

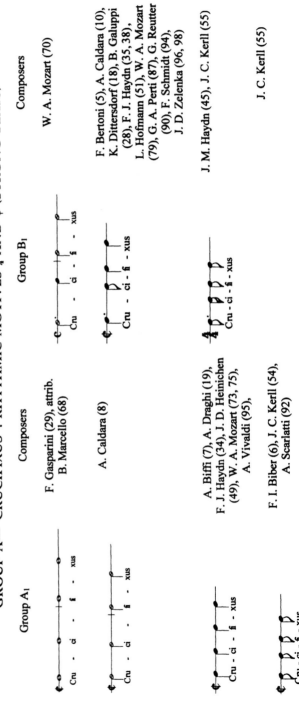

Group A₁	Composers	Group B₁	Composers

(Group A₁)

Cru - ci - fi - xus

(Composers, Group A₁, first)
F. Gasparini (29), attrib.
B. Marcello (68)

(Group B₁, first)
Cru - ci - fi - xus

(Composers, Group B₁, first)
W. A. Mozart (70)

Cru - ci - fi - xus

A. Caldara (8)

Cru - ci - fi - xus

F. Bertoni (5), A. Caldara (10),
K. Dittersdorf (18), B. Galuppi
(28), F. J. Haydn (35, 38),
L. Hofmann (51), W. A. Mozart
(79), G. A. Perti (87), G. Reutter
(90), F. Schmidt (94),
J. D. Zelenka (96, 98)

Cru - ci - fi - xus

A. Biffi (7), A. Draghi (19),
F. J. Haydn (34), J. D. Heinichen
(49), W. A. Mozart (73, 75),
A. Vivaldi (95),

Cru - ci - fi - xus

J. M. Haydn (45), J. C. Kerll (55)

Cru - ci - fi - xus

F. I. Biber (6), J. C. Kerll (54),
A. Scarlatti (92)

J. C. Kerll (55)

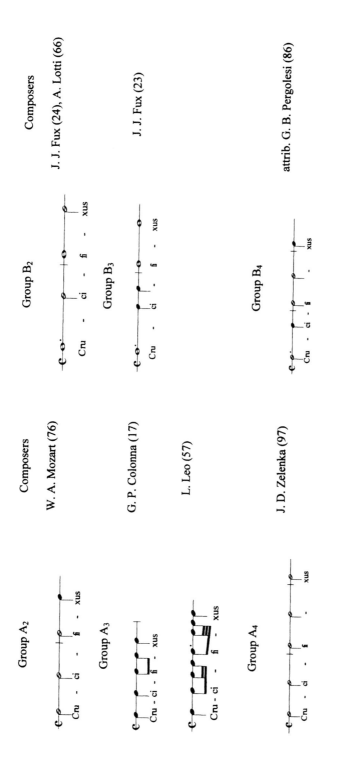

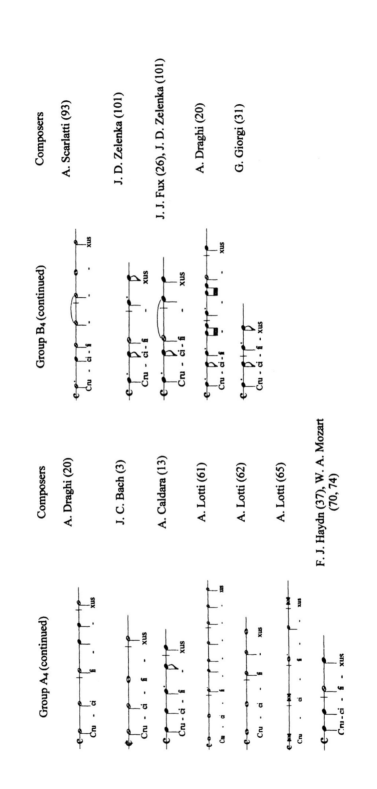

Group A₄ (continued)

Composers

A. Draghi (20)

J. C. Bach (3)

A. Caldara (13)

A. Lotti (61)

A. Lotti (62)

A. Lotti (65)

F. J. Haydn (37), W. A. Mozart
(70, 74)

Group B₄ (continued)

Composers

A. Scarlatti (93)

J. D. Zelenka (101)

J. J. Fux (26), J. D. Zelenka (101)

A. Draghi (20)

G. Giorgi (31)

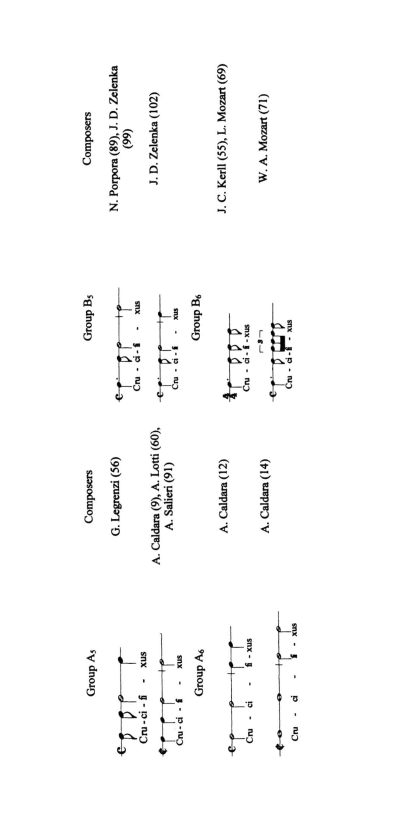

GROUP B—"CRUCIFIXUS": RHYTHMIC MOTIVES $\frac{4}{4}$ AND ¢ (WEAK BEATS)

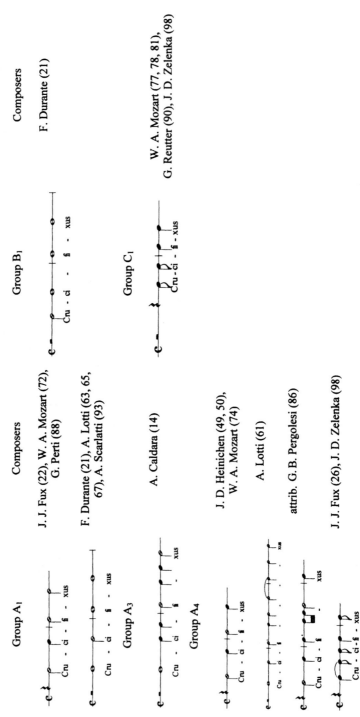

Group A₁

Composers

J. J. Fux (22), W. A. Mozart (72), G. Perti (88)

F. Durante (21), A. Lotti (63, 65, 67), A. Scarlatti (93)

Group A₃

A. Caldara (14)

Group A₄

J. D. Heinichen (49, 50), W. A. Mozart (74)

A. Lotti (61)

attrib. G. B. Pergolesi (86)

J. J. Fux (26), J. D. Zelenka (98)

Group B₁

Composers

F. Durante (21)

Group C₁

W. A. Mozart (77, 78, 81), G. Reutter (90), J. D. Zelenka (98)

GROUP C—"CRUCIFIXUS": RHYTHMIC MOTIVES $\frac{3}{4}$ AND $\frac{3}{2}$ (WEAK BEATS)

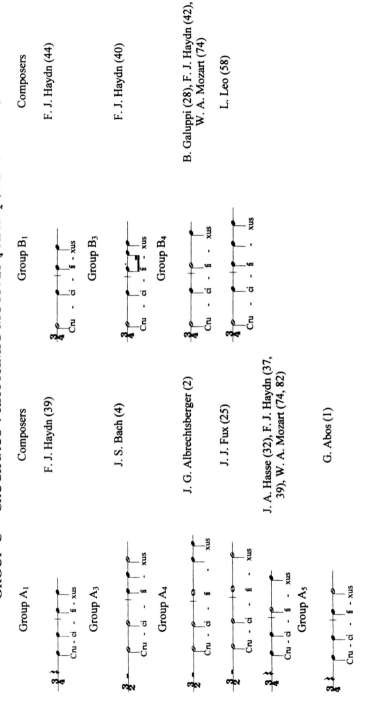

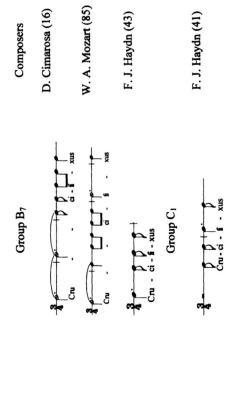

Group B₇

Cru - - - ci - fi - xus

Cru - - - ci - fi - xus

Cru - ci - fi - xus

Group C₁

Cru - ci - fi - xus

Composers

D. Cimarosa (16)

W. A. Mozart (85)

F. J. Haydn (43)

F. J. Haydn (41)

Appendix C

A Comparison of Bach's Setting of the *Crucifixus* from the *Mass in B Minor* BWV 232 and the First Part of the Opening Chorus from *Weinen, Klagen, Sorgen, Zagen* BWV 12

Weinen, Klagen, Sorgen, Zagen (transposed from F minor to E minor)

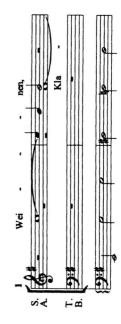

Crucifixus

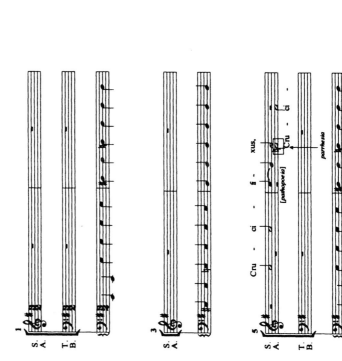

Crucifixus

Weinen, Klagen, Sorgen, Zagen
(transposed from F minor to E minor)

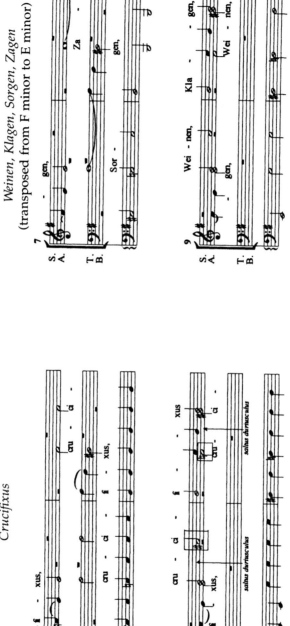

Weinen, Klagen, Sorgen, Zagen
(transposed from F minor to E minor)

Crucifixus

Weinen, Klagen, Sorgen, Zagen
(transposed from F minor to E minor)

Crucifixus

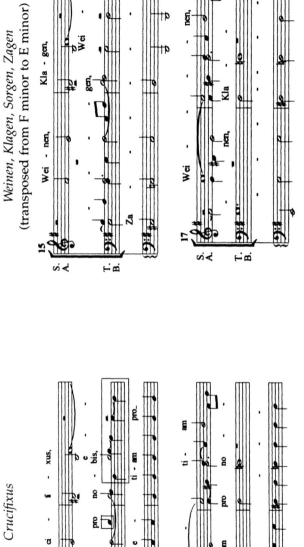

Weinen, Klagen, Sorgen, Zagen
(transposed from F minor to E minor)

Crucifixus

Crucifixus

Weinen, Klagen, Sorgen, Zagen
(transposed from F minor to E minor)

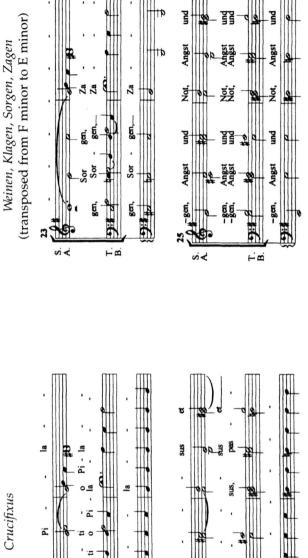

Weinen, Klagen, Sorgen, Zagen
(transposed from F minor to E minor)

Crucifixus

Weinen, Klagen, Sorgen, Zagen
(transposed from F minor to E minor)

Crucifixus

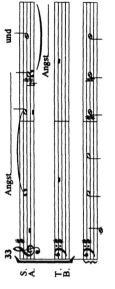

Weinen, Klagen, Sorgen, Zagen
(transposed from F minor to E minor)

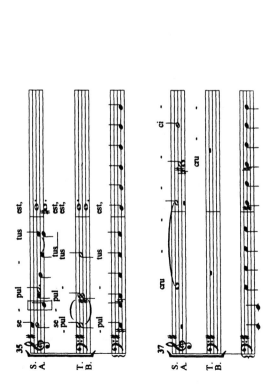

Crucifixus

Weinen, Klagen, Sorgen, Zagen
(transposed from F minor to E minor)

Crucifixus

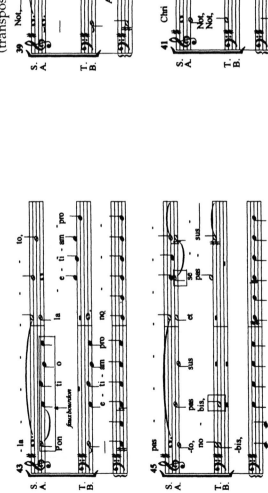

Weinen, Klagen, Sorgen, Zagen
(transposed from F minor to E minor)

Crucifixus

Crucifixus

Weinen, Klagen, Sorgen, Zagen
(transposed from F minor to E minor)

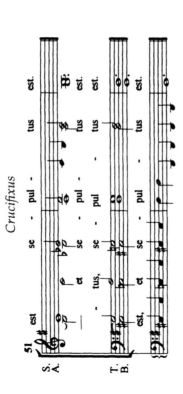

Crucifixus

A. Caldara (8): *Crucifixus a 16 Voci*

Appendix E

F. G. Bertoni (5): *Crucifixus con Organo a 4 Voci*

Appendix F

A. Vivaldi (95): *Crucifixus* from *Credo* RV 591

Appendix G

A. Lotti (59): *Crucifixus a 6*

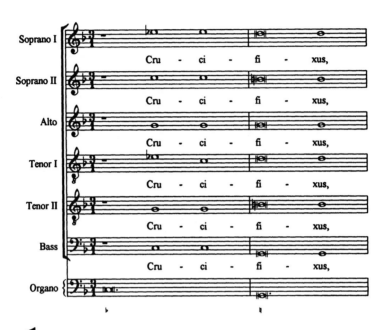

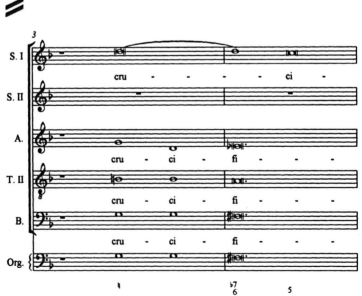

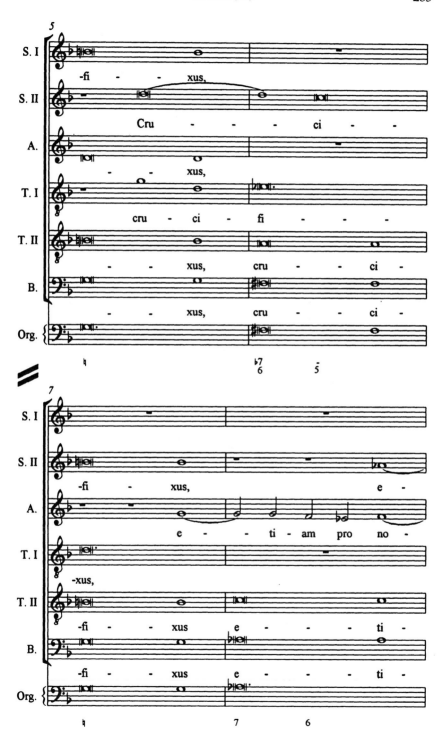

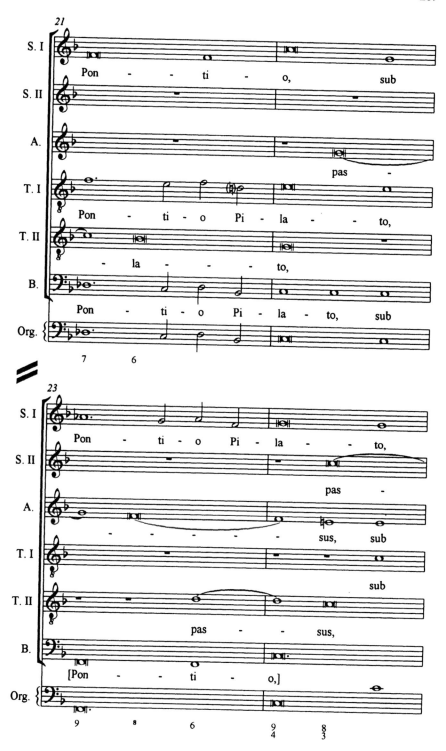

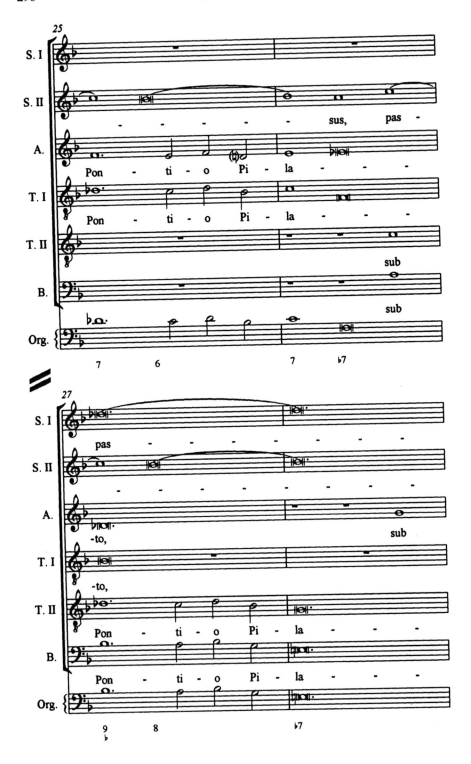

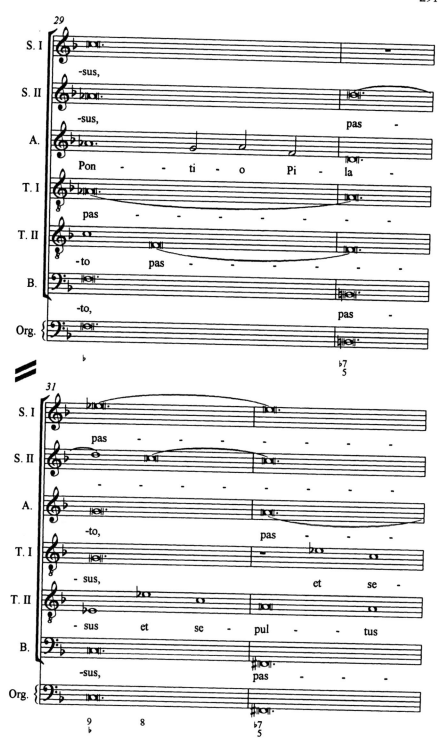

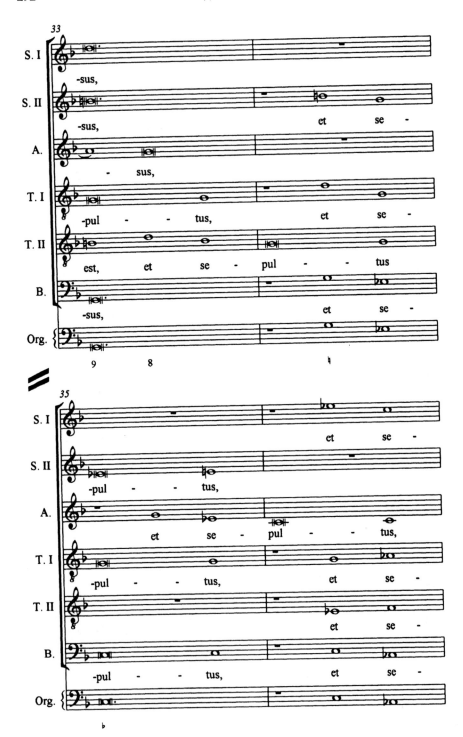

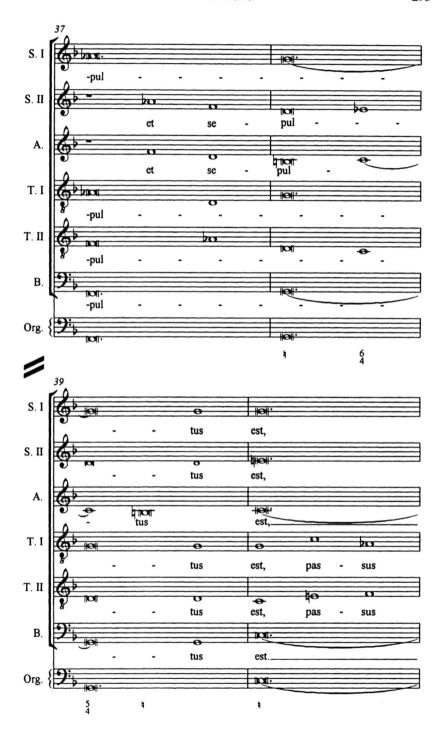

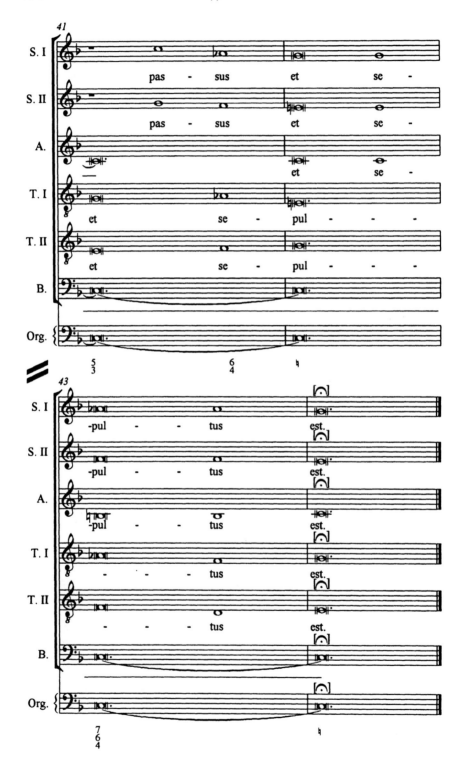

A. Lotti (60): *Crucifixus a 10*

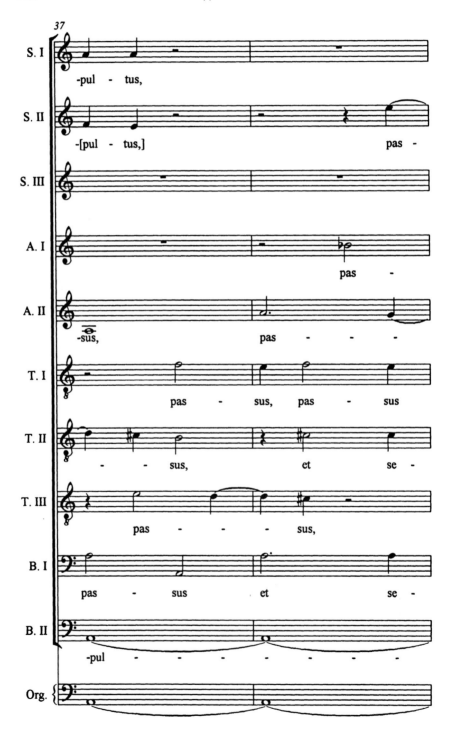

W. A. Mozart (84): *Crucifixus* from
Krönungs-Messe KV 317

Appendix J

F. J. Haydn (39): *Crucifixus* from *Missa in Tempore Belli*

Appendix K

D. Cimarosa (16): *Messa a 4 con Stromenti*

Bibliography

Agawu, V. Kofi. *Playing with Signs: A Semiotic Interpretation of Classical Music.* Princeton, N.J.: Princeton University Press, 1991.

Antonicek, Theophil. "Vienna." [Articles 3, 4] 713–41 in *The New Grove Dictionary of Music and Musicians*, vol. 19, edited by Stanley Sadie. London: Macmillan, 1980.

Apel, Willi, ed. *The Harvard Dictionary of Music.* London: Heinemann International, 1970.

Aristole. *The Art of Rhetoric.* Translated by John Henry Freese. London: Loeb Classical Library, 1926.

Arnold, Denis. "Venice." 614–20 in *The New Grove Dictionary of Music and Musicians*, vol. 19, edited by Stanley Sadie. London: Macmillan, 1980.

Atkinson, Rita L., Richard C. Atkinson, Edward E. Smith, and Daryl J. Bem. *Introduction to Psychology.* Fort Worth, Tex.: Harcourt Brace Jovanovich, 1993.

Audi, Robert., ed. *The Cambridge Dictionary of Philosophy.* 2nd ed. Cambridge: Cambridge University Press, 1999.

Bach, Johann Christian. "Credo in C." 310–14 in *The Complete Works of Johann Christian Bach*, vol. 20, edited by Ernest Warburton. New York: Garland Publishing, 1985.

Bach, Johann Sebastian. *Cantata no. 4 "Christ lag in Todesbanden"* BWV 4. Edited by Arnold Schering. Zürich, Switzerland: Eulenburg, 1932.

———. *Cantata no. 12 "Weinen, Klagen, Sorgen, Zagen"* BWV 12. Edited by M. Hauptmann. Leipzig, Germany: Bach Gesellschaft, 1852.

———. *Mass in B Minor* BWV 232. Edited by Julius Rietz. Leipzig, Germany: Bach Gesellschaft, 1856. Reprint, New York: Dover Publications, 1989.

———. *Messe in h-moll BWV 232.* Facsimile reproduction of the autograph with a commentary edited by Alfred Dürr. Kassel, Germany: Bärenreiter, 1983.

Baker, Nancy K. "Heinrich Koch and the Theory of Melody." *Journal of Music Theory* 20 (1978): 1–48.

Bartel, Dietrich. *Handbuch der musikalischen Figurenlehre.* Laaber, Germany: Laaber-Verlag, 1985.

————. *Musica Poetica: Musical-Rhetorical Figures in German Baroque Music.* Lincoln: University of Nebraska Press, 1997.

Beethoven, Ludwig van. *Mass in C* op. 86 (no editor stated). Leipzig, Germany: Breitkopf und Härtel, 1864. Reprint, New York: Dover Publications, 1996.

————. *Missa Solennis* op. 123 (no editor stated). Leipzig, Germany: Breitkopf und Härtel, 1864. Reprint, New York: Dover Publications, 1991.

————. *Missa Solennis* op. 123 (no editor stated). Leipzig: Peters, n.d.

————. *Missa Solennis* op. 123 (no editor stated). Zürich, Switzerland: Eulenburg, n.d.

Benedetto, Renato di. "Naples." 22–32 in *The New Grove Dictionary of Music and Musicians,* vol. 13, edited by Stanley Sadie. London: Macmillan, 1980.

Benton, Rita, ed. *Directory of Music Research Libraries.* 3 vols. Iowa City: University of Iowa Press, 1970.

Bertini, Argia. "Biffi." 699 in *The New Grove Dictionary of Music and Musicians,* vol. 2, edited by Stanley Sadie. London: Macmillan, 1980.

Biber, Heinrich. *Messen von Heinrich Biber, Heinrich Schmeltzer, Johann Casper Kerll.* Edited by Guido Adler. Graz, Austria: Akademische Druck-und. Verlagsanstalt, 1960.

The Bible. Authorized King James Version. Oxford: Oxford University Press, 1998.

Bockholdt, Rudolf. "Das 'Crucifixus' der h-moll Messe von Johann Sebastian Bach." *Münchner Beiträge zur Geschichte und Theorie Kunst* 2 (1990): 141–64.

Bonds, Mark Evan. *Wordless Rhetoric: Musical Form and the Metaphor of the Oration.* Cambridge, Mass.: Harvard University Press, 1991.

Borgir, Tharald. *The Performance of the Basso Continuo in Italian Baroque Music.* Ann Arbor, Mich.: University Microfilms International, 1987.

Boyd, Malcolm. *Bach.* London: Dent, 1983.

Brainard, Paul. "Bach's Parody Procedure and the St. Matthew Passion." *Journal of the American Musicological Society* 22 (1969): 241–60.

Buelow, George J. "Affections, Doctrine of the." 135–36 in *The New Grove Dictionary of Music and Musicians,* vol. 1, edited by Stanley Sadie. London: Macmillan, 1980.

————. "Expressivity in the Accompanied Recitatives of Bach's Cantatas." 18–35 in *Bach Studies 1,* edited by Don O. Franklin. Cambridge: Cambridge University Press, 1989.

————. "Figures, Doctrine of Musical." 545 in *The New Grove Dictionary of Music and Musicians,* vol. 6, edited by Stanley Sadie. London: Macmillan, 1980.

————. "The *Loci Topici* and Affect in Late Baroque Music: Heinichen's Practical Demonstration." *Music Review* 27 (1966): 161–76.

————. "Music, Rhetoric and the Concept of the Affections: A Selective Bibliography." *Notes* 30, no. 2 (December 1973): 250–59.

————. "Rhetoric and Music." 793–803 in *The New Grove Dictionary of Music and Musicians,* vol. 15, edited by Stanley Sadie. London: Macmillan, 1980.

————. "Teaching Seventeeenth-Century Concepts of Musical Form and Expression: An Aspect of Baroque Music." *College Music Symposium* 27 (1987): 1–13.

————. *Thorough-Bass Accompaniment according to Johann David Heinichen.* Berkeley: University of California Press, 1966.

Buelow, George J., and Hans Joachim Marx, eds. *New Mattheson Studies.* Cambridge: Cambridge University Press, 1983.

Buelow, George J., Peter A. Hoyt, and Blake Wilson. "Rhetoric and Music." 260–75 in *The New Grove Dictionary of Music and Musicians*, 2nd ed., vol. 21, edited by Stanley Sadie. London: Macmillan, 2001.

Bukofzer, Manfred. "Allegory in Baroque Music." *Journal of the Warburg and Courtauld Institutes* 3 (1938–40): 1–21.

Burmeister, Joachim. *Musical Poetics.* Translated by Benito V. Rivera. New Haven, Conn.: Yale University Press, 1993.

Butler, Gregory G. "Fugue and Rhetoric." *Journal of Music Theory* 21, no. 1 (1977): 49–109.

———. "Music and Rhetoric in Early Seventeenth-Century English Sources." *The Musical Quarterly* 66 (1980): 53–65.

Butt, John. *Bach Interpretation: Articulation Marks in Primary Sources of J. S. Bach.* Cambridge: Cambridge University Press, 1990.

———. *Bach: Mass in B Minor.* Cambridge: Cambridge University Press, 1991.

Caldara, Antonio. *Crucifixus a 16 Voci.* Edited by Charles H. Sherman. Stuttgart, Germany: Carus-Verlag, n.d.

———. *Kirchenwerke.* Edited by Eusebius Mandyczewski. Graz, Austria: Akademische Druck-und. Verlagsanstalt, 1959.

Caldwell, John. *Editing Early Music.* Oxford: Clarendon Press, 1985.

Cameron, Jasmin Melissa. "Rhetoric and Music: The Influence of a Linguistic Art." 28–72 in *Music and Words.* Liverpool Symposium III. Liverpool: Liverpool University Press, 2005.

———. "Two Gloria Settings by Giovanni Maria Ruggieri." M.Mus. diss., Liverpool: University of Liverpool, 1995.

———. "Vivaldi's 'Crucifixus' in Its Descriptive and Rhetorical Context." *Studi Vivaldiani* 3 (2003): 133–52.

Cammarota, Robert M. "Review of Eleanor Selfridge-Field, 'The Music of Benedetto and Alessandro Marcello: A Thematic Catalogue with Commentary on the Composers, Repertory and Sources.'" *Notes* 48, no. 3 (1992): 868–71.

Carrell, Norman. *Bach the Borrower.* London: Allen and Unwin, 1967.

Cattin, Giulio. *Music of the Middle Ages.* Vol. 1. Cambridge: Cambridge University Press, 1984.

Clarke, M. L. *Rhetoric at Rome: A Historical Survey.* London: Cohen and West, 1953.

Cook, Nicholas. *A Guide to Musical Analysis.* Oxford: Oxford University Press, 1994.

Cottingham, John. *Descartes.* Oxford: Blackwell, 1986.

Cowart, Georgia. "Critical Language and Musical Thought in the Seventeenth and Eighteenth Centuries." *College Music Symposium* 27 (1987): 14–29.

Crocker, Richard L. "Credo." 29 in *The New Grove Dictionary of Music and Musicians*, vol. 5, edited by Stanley Sadie. London: Macmillan, 1980.

Cross, F. L., ed. *The Oxford Dictionary of the Christian Church.* London: Oxford University Press, 1957.

Cross, F. L., and E. A. Livingston, eds. *The Oxford Dictionary of the Christian Church.* 2nd ed. London: Oxford University Press, 1974.

Dahlhaus, Carl. *The Esthetics of Music.* Translated by William Austin. Cambridge: Cambridge University Press, 1982.

Dann, Elias. "Biber." 678–82 in *The New Grove Dictionary of Music and Musicians,* vol. 2, edited by Stanley Sadie. London: Macmillan, 1980.

Davies, J. G. *The Early Christian Church.* London: Weidenfeld and Nicolson, 1965.

Daw, Stephen. *The Music of Johann Sebastian Bach: The Choral Works.* Rutherford, N.J.: Fairleigh Dickinson University Press, 1981.

Descartes, René. *Passions de l'âme.* In *The Philosophical Works.* Vol. 1. Translated by Elizabeth S. Haldane and G. R. T. Ross. London: Cambridge University Press, 1968.

Dietz, Hanns-Bertold. "Durante." 740–45 in *The New Grove Dictionary of Music and Musicians,* vol. 5, edited by Stanley Sadie. London: Macmillan, 1980.

Dix, Gregory. *The Shape of the Liturgy.* London: Dacre, 1964.

Doctrine Commission of the Church of England. *Christian Believing: The Nature of the Christian Faith and Its Expression in Holy Scripture and Creeds.* London: S.P.C.K., 1976.

Donington, Robert. "Interpretation." 276 in *The New Grove Dictionary of Music and Musicians,* vol. 9, edited by Stanley Sadie. London: Macmillan, 1980.

Drabkin, William. *Beethoven: Missa Solemnis.* Cambridge: Cambridge University Press, 1991.

Draghi, Antonio. *Kirchenwerke.* Edited by Guido Adler. Leipzig, Germany: Breitkopf und Härtel, 1916.

Dunsby, Jonathan. "A Hitch Hiker's Guide to Semiotic Music Analysis." *Music Analysis* 1, no. 3 (1982): 235–42.

Dunsby, Jonathan, and Arnold Whittall. *Music Analysis in Theory and Practice.* London: Faber, 1988.

Eco, Umberto. *A Theory of Semiotics.* Bloomington: Indiana University Press, 1976.

Finscher, Ludwig. "Bach in the Eighteenth Century." 281–96 in *Bach Studies,* vol. 1, edited by Don O. Franklin. Cambridge: Cambridge University Press, 1989.

Forchert, Arno. "Bach und der Tradition der Rhetorik." *Alte Musikals ästhetische Gegenwart.* Bericht über den internationalen musikwissenschaftlichen Kongress Stuttgart 1985 (Kassel, 1987), I/II, 169–78.

Forkel, Johann Nikolaus. *Johann Sebastian Bach.* Translated by Charles Sanford Terry. Leipzig, Germany: Hoffmeister und Kuhnel, 1802. Reprint, London: Constable, 1920.

Freeman, Robert. "Caldara." 613–16 in *The New Grove Dictionary of Music and Musicians,* vol. 3, edited by Stanley Sadie. London: Macmillan, 1980.

Fux, Johann Joseph. *Messen.* Edited by Johannes Evangelist Habert and Gustav Adolf Glossner. Graz, Austria: Akademische Druck-und. Verlagsanstalt, 1959.

Gallo, F. Alberto. *Music of the Middle Ages II.* Cambridge: Cambridge University Press, 1985.

Gassmann, Florian Leopold. *Kirchenwerke.* Edited by Franz Kosch. Vienna: Universal Edition, 1938.

Gaukroger, Stephen. *Descartes: An Intellectual Biography.* Oxford: Clarendon Press, 1995.

Geiringer, Karl. "The Church Music." 361–76 in *The Mozart Companion,* edited by H. C. Robbins Landon and Donald Mitchell. London: Faber, 1986.

———. *Johann Sebastian Bach: The Culmination of an Era*. London: Allen and Unwin, 1966.

Georgiades, Thrasybulos. *Music and Language: The Rise of Western Music as Exemplified in Settings of the Mass*. Cambridge: Cambridge University Press, 1982.

Giebler, Albert C. "Kerll." 874–76 in *The New Grove Dictionary of Music and Musicians*, vol. 9, edited by Stanley Sadie. London: Macmillan, 1980.

Gillies Whittaker. *The Cantatas of Johann Sebastian Bach: Sacred and Secular*. Vol. 1. London: Oxford University Press, 1964.

Godt, Irving. "A Clean Canvas for Word Painting." 105–26 in *Yearbook of Interdisciplinary Studies in the Fine Arts*, vol. 1, edited by Matthew Cannon Brennan. Lewiston, NY: Edwin Mellen Press, 1989.

———. "An Essay on Word Painting." *College Music Symposium* 24, no. 2 (1984): 118–29.

———. "Gasparini, Marcello, and New York." *Bulletin of Research in the Humanities* 85 (1982): 295–321.

———. *Guillaume Costeley (1531–1606): Life and Works*. New York: New York University Press, 1969.

———. "Italian Figurenlehre? Music and Rhetoric in a New York Source." 178–203 in *Studies in the History of Music*, vol. 1, edited by Ronald Broude and Ellen Beebe. New York: Broude Brothers, 1983.

———. "John Bennet and the Directional Convention: An Introduction to Madrigalisms." *Acta* 17 (1993): 121–46.

———. "Music about Words: Madrigalisms and Other Text Influences in Music." Unpublished manuscript, 1990.

Greenberg, Noah, and Paul Maynard, eds. *An Anthology of Early Renaissance Music*. London: Dent, 1975.

Grier, James. *The Critical Editing of Music*. Cambridge: Cambridge University Press, 1996.

Gurlitt, Willibald. "Musik und Rhetorik." *Helicon* 5 (1943): 67–86.

Händel, Georg Friedrich. *Acis and Galatea*. Edited by Wolfram Windszus. Kassel, Germany: Bärenreiter, 1991.

Hanks, Patrick, ed. *The Collins Concise Dictionary of the English Language*. London: Collins, 1990.

Hansall, Sven. "Bertoni." 645–48 in *The New Grove Dictionary of Music and Musicians*, vol. 2, edited by Stanley Sadie. London: Macmillan, 1980.

Harman, Alec, and Anthony Milner. *Late Renaissance and Baroque Music*. Vol. 2 of *Man and His Music*. London: Barrie and Jenkins, 1988.

Harper, John. *The Forms and Orders of the Western Liturgy from the Tenth to the Eighteenth Century*. Oxford: Oxford University Press, 1991.

Harrison, Daniel. "Rhetoric and Fugue: An Analytical Application." *Music Theory Spectrum* 12 (1990): 1–42.

Harriss, Ernest C. *Johann Mattheson's Der vollkommene Capellmeister*. Ann Arbor, Mich.: UMI Research Publications, 1981.

Hastings, Baird. *Wolfang Amadeus Mozart: A Guide to Research*. New York: Garland, 1960.

Haydn, Franz Joseph. *The Complete Works*, ser. XIII, vol. I. Edited by Carl Maria

Brand. Boston: Haydn Society, 1951. Reprint, Leipzig, Germany: Breitkopf und Härtel, 1951.

———. *The Complete Works*, ser. XIII, vol. II. Edited by H. C. Robbins Landon in association with Karl Heinz Füssl and Christa Landon. München-Duisberg, Germany: G. Henle Verlag, 1958.

———. *The Complete Works*, ser. XIII, vol. III. Edited by Günter Thomas. München-Duisberg, Germany: G. Henle Verlag, 1965.

———. *The Complete Works*, ser. XIII, vol. IV. Edited by Irmgard Becker-Glauch. München-Duisberg, Germany: G. Henle Verlag, 1967.

———. *The Complete Works*, ser. XIII, vol. V. Edited by Friedrich Lippmann. München-Duisberg, Germany: G. Henle Verlag, 1966.

Haydn, Johann Michael. *Messen*. Anton Maria Klafsky. Graz, Austria: Denkmäler der Tonkunst in Österreich, 1960.

Herz, Gerhard. *Essays on J. S. Bach*. Ann Arbor, Mich.: UMI Research Press, 1985.

Hilse, Walter. "The Treatises of Christoph Bernhard." *Musical Forum* 3 (1973): 1–196.

Horn, Wolfgang. "Das Repertoire der Dresdner Hofkirchenmusik um 1720–1730 und die Werke Antonio Caldaras." 277–300 in *Antonio Caldara: Essays on His Life and Times*, edited by Brian W. Pritchard. Aldershot, U.K.: Scolar Press, 1987.

———. *Die Dresdner Hofkirchenmusik 1720–1745*. Stuttgart, Germany: Carus-Verlag, 1987.

Hucke, Helmut. "Leo." 668–69 in *The New Grove Dictionary of Music and Musicians*, vol. 10, edited by Stanley Sadie. London: Macmillan, 1980.

Hucke, Helmut, and Marvin E. Payner. "Pergolesi." 394–400 in *The New Grove Dictionary of Music and Musicians*, vol. 14, edited by Stanley Sadie. London: Macmillan, 1980.

Hudson, Richard. "Further Remarks on the Passacaglia and Ciaccona." *Journal of the American Musicological Society* 23 (1970): 302–14.

———. "Ground." 748–50 in *The New Grove Dictionary of Music and Musicians*, vol. 7, edited by Stanley Sadie. London: Macmillan, 1980.

Hughes, Andrew. *Medieval Manuscripts for Mass and Office: A Guide to Their Organization and Terminology*. Toronto: University or Toronto Press, 1982.

Hummel, Johann Nepomuk. *First Mass in B Flat* op. 77. Edited by Vincent Novello. London: Novello, 1840.

Humphreys, David. "The Credo of the B Minor Mass: Style and Symbol." *The Musical Times* 140, no. 1867 (1999): 54–59.

Jackendoff, Ray, and Fred Lerdahl. *A Generative Theory of Tonal Music*. Cambridge, Mass.: MIT Press, 1983.

Jacob, Gordon. *Orchestral Technique*. London: Oxford University Press, 1965.

Jenison, Rick L., and Pavel Zahorik. "Presence as Being-in-the-World." *Presence: Teleoperators and Virtual Environments* 7, no. 1 (1998): 78–89.

Johnston, Gregory Scott. "Protestant Funeral Music and Rhetoric in Seventeenth Century Germany: A Musical Rhetorical Examination of Printed Sources." Ph.D. diss., University of British Columbia, 1987.

Jones, Cheslyn, Geoffrey Wainwright, and Edward Yarnold, eds. *The Liturgy*. London: S.P.C.K., 1978.

Jones, Richard, and Christoph Wolff. "Bach, Johann Christian." 865–76 in *The New Grove Dictionary of Music and Musicians,* vol. 1, edited by Stanley Sadie. London: Macmillan, 1980.

Jungmann, Josef Andreas. *The Early Liturgy to the Time of Gregory the Great.* London: Darton, Longman and Todd, 1960.

———. *The Mass of the Roman Rite.* Vol. 2. New York: Benziger, 1951–1955.

Kelly, J. N. D. *Early Christian Creeds.* London: Longman, 1972.

Kennedy, George. *The Art of Rhetoric in the Roman World 300 B.C.–A.D. 300.* Princeton, N.J.: Princeton University Press, 1972.

Kerll, Johann Casper. *Messen von Heinrich Biber, Heinrich Schmeltzer, Johann Casper Kerll.* Edited by Guido Adler. Graz, Austria: Akademische Druck-und Verlagsanstalt, 1960.

———. *Missa Superba.* Edited by Albert C. Giebler. New Haven, Conn.: A-R Editions, 1967.

Kerman, Joseph. *Musicology.* London: Fontana, 1985.

Kiel, Christian Berger. "Musikalische Formbildung im Spannungsfeld nationaler Traditionen des 17. Jahrhunderts: Das 'Lamento' aus Heinrich Ignaz Bibers Rosenkranz Sonate Nr. 6." *Acta Musicologica* 66 (1992): 17–29.

Kirkendale, Warren. "New Roads to Old Ideas in Beethoven's *Missa Solemnis.*" *The Musical Quarterly* 56 (1970): 665–701.

Kivy, Peter. "What Mattheson Said." *Music Review* 34 (1973): 132–40.

Klafsky, Anton Maria, ed. *Denkmäler der Tonkunst in Österreich* 62. Graz, Austria: Akademische und Verlagsanstait, 1960.

Kordes, Gesa. "Self-Parody and the 'Hunting-Cantata,' BWV 208—An Aspect of Bach's Compositional Process." *Bach* 22 (1991): 35–57.

Krones, Hartmut. "Rhetorik und rhetorische Symbolik in der Musik um 1800." *Musik Theorie* 3 (1988): 117–40.

Landmann, Ortrun, and Wolfram Steude. "Dresden." 612–27 in *The New Grove Dictionary of Music and Musicians,* vol. 15, edited by Stanley Sadie. London: Macmillan, 1980.

Lang, Paul Henry. *Music in Western Civilisation.* New York: Norton, 1941.

Lanham, Richard A. *A Handlist of Rhetorical Terms.* Berkeley: University of California Press, 1991.

LaRue, Jan. *Guidelines for Style Analysis.* New York: W. W. Norton, 1970.

Leaver, Robin A. "Number Association and the Structure of Bach's *Credo* BWV 232." *Bach* 7, no. 3 (1976): 17–24.

———. "Parody and Theological Consistency: Notes on Bach's A-Major Mass." *Bach* 21 (1990): 30–43.

le Huray, Peter. "Music and the Arts in Pre-Renaissance and Renaissance Worship." 156–209 in *Companion to Contemporary Musical Thought,* vol. 1, edited by John Paynter, Tim Howell, Richard Orton, and Peter Seymour. London: Routledge, 1992.

Lenneberg, Hans. "Johann Mattheson on Affect and Rhetoric on Music (I)." *Journal of Music Theory* 2 (1958): 47–84.

Lester, Joel. *Compositional Theory in the Eighteenth Century.* Cambridge, Mass.: Harvard University Press, 1992.

Leventhal, Robert S. "Semiotic Interpretation and Rhetoric in the German Enlightenment 1740–1760." *Deutsche Vierteljahrsschrift für Literaturwissenschaft und Geistesgeschichte* 60 (1986): 223–48.

Liszt, Franz. *Missa Solemnis* (no editor stated). Reprint, Philadelphia: J. Schuberth & Co., 1971.

Littlefield, Richard, and David Neumeyer. "Rewriting Schenker: Narrative–History–Ideology." *Music Theory Spectrum* 14, no. 1 (1992): 37–65.

Lotti, Antonio. *Messen.* Edited by Hermann Müller. Wiesbaden, Germany: Breitkopf und Härtel, 1959.

MacIntyre, Bruce C. *The Viennese Concerted Mass of the Early Classic Period.* Ann Arbor, Mich.: UMI Research Press, 1986.

Maniates, Maria Rika. *Mannerism in Italian Music and Culture, 1530–1630.* Manchester, U.K.: Manchester University Press, 1979.

———. "Music and Rhetoric: Facets of Cultural History in the Renaissance and the Baroque." *Israel Studies in Musicology* 3 (1983): 44–69.

Mann, Alfred. "Bach's Parody Technique and Its Frontiers." 115–24 in *Bach Studies,* vol. 1, edited by Don O. Franklin. Cambridge: Cambridge University Press, 1989.

Mantovani, Giuseppe, and Giuseppe Riva. "'Real' Presence: How Different Ontologies Generate Different Criteria for Presence, Telepresence and Virtual Presence." *Presence: Teleoperators and Virtual Environments* 8, no. 15 (1999): 540–50.

Marshall, Robert L. *The Compositional Process of J. S. Bach: A Study of the Autograph Scores of the Vocal Works.* Vol. 1. Princeton, N.J.: Princeton University Press, 1972.

———. *The Music of Johann Sebastian Bach: The Sources, the Style, the Significance.* New York: Schirmer, 1989.

Mellers, Wilfred. *Bach and the Dance of God.* London: Faber, 1980.

Meloncelli, Raoul, and Nino Pirrotta. "Rome II." 153–62 in *The New Grove Dictionary of Music and Musicians,* vol. 16, edited by Stanley Sadie. London: Macmillan, 1980.

Mitchell, Donald, and H. C. Robbins Landon, eds. *The Mozart Companion.* London: Faber, 1986.

Monelle, Raymond. *Linguistics and Semiotics in Music.* Chur, Switzerland: Harwood Academic Press, 1992.

Monteverdi, Claudio. *Crucifixus.* Edited by Gian Francesco Malipiero. Vienna: Universal Edition, 1968.

Morison, Frank. *Who Moved the Stone?* London: Faber, 1958.

Moule, C. F. D. *The Origin of Christology.* Cambridge: Cambridge University Press, 1977.

Moyer, Ann E. *Musica Scientia: Musical Scholarship in the Italian Renaissance.* Ithaca, N.Y.: Cornell University Press, 1992.

Mozart, Leopold. *Versuch einer gründlichen Violinschule.* Translated by Editha Knocker. London: Oxford University Press, 1945.

Mozart, Wolfgang Amadeus. *Messen* (no editor stated). Leipzig, Germany: Breitkopf und Härtel, 1877–1878.

———. *Missa (Coronation Mass) KV 317.* Edited by Felix Schroeder. Zürich, Switzerland: Eulenburg, 1965.

————. *Neue Ausgabe sämtlicher Werke.* Edited by Walter Senn. Kassel, Germany: Bärenreiter, Werkgruppe I: Messen und Requiem, Band I, 1968; Band 2, 1975; Band 3, 1980; Band 4, 1989.

Muffat, Georg. *Armonico Tributo.* Edited by Erich Schenk. Vienna: Österreicher Bundesverlag, 1953.

Murphy, James Jerome. *Rhetoric in the Middle Ages: A History of the Rhetorical Theory from St. Augustine to the Renaissance.* Berkeley: University of California Press, 1974.

Nash, Walter. *Rhetoric: The Wit of Persuasion.* Oxford: Blackwell, 1989.

Nattiez, Jean-Jacques. "The Contribution of Musical Semiotics to the Semiotic Discussion in General." 121–42 in *A Perfusion of Signs,* edited by Thomas A. Sebeok. Bloomington: Indiana University Press, 1977.

————. *Music and Discourse.* Princeton, N.J.: Princeton University Press, 1990.

Noske, Frits. *Saints and Sinners: The Latin Musical Dialogue in the Seventeenth Century.* Oxford: Clarendon Press, 1992.

————. *The Signifier and Signified: Studies in the Operas of Mozart and Verdi.* Oxford: Clarendon Press, 1990.

Palestrina, Giovanni Pierluigi da. *Missa Papae Marcelli.* Edited by Henry Washington. London: J. and W. Chester, 1963.

Palisca, Claude V. "A Clarification of 'Musica Reservata' in Jean Taisnier's 'Astrologiae,' 1559." *Acta Musicologica* 31 (1959): 133–61.

————. *Studies in the History of Italian Music and Music Theory.* Oxford: Clarendon Press, 1994.

————. "*Ut Oratoria Musica*: The Rhetorical Basis of Musical Mannerisms." 37–61 in *The Meaning of Mannerism,* edited by Franklin V. Robinson and Stephen G. Nichols Jr. Hanover, N.H.: University Press of New England, 1972.

Pantijelev, Grigorij. "Das 'Crucifixus' aus der Messe BWV232 und dessen frühe Variante in der Kantate BWV 12: Ein Vergleich zur kompositorischen Arbeit J. S. Bach." *Beiträge zur Bach Forschung* 9/10 (1991): 214–18.

Pauly, Richard G., and Brian W. Pritchard. "Antonio Caldara's *Credo a 8 voci*: A Composition for the Duke of Mantua?" 46–76 in *Antonio Caldara: Essays on His Life and Times,* edited by Brian W. Pritchard. Aldershot, U.K.: Scolar Press, 1987.

Paumgartner, B. "Zum Crucifixus der h-moll Messe J. S. Bachs." *Österreichische Musikzeitschrift* 21 (1966): 500–503.

Powers, Harold S. "Language Models and Musical Analysis." *Ethnomusicology* 24 (1980): 1–60.

Procter, Paul, ed. *Longman New Generation Dictionary.* Harlow, U.K.: Longman, 1981.

Quintilian. *De Institutione Oratoria.* Translated by H. E. Butler. London: Heinemann, 1921.

Ranum, Patricia. "Audible Rhetoric and Mute Rhetoric: The 17th-Century French Sarabande." *Early Music* 14 (1986): 22–39.

Ratner, Leonard G. *Classic Music: Expression, Form and Style.* New York: Schirmer, 1980.

————. "Eighteenth-Century Theories of Musical Period Structure." *The Musical Quarterly* 42 (1956): 439–54.

Reutter, Georg. *Kirchenwerke*. Edited by P. Norbert Hofer. Vienna: Österreichischer Bundesverlag, 1952.

Riemann, Hugo. *History of Music Theory*. Translated by Raymond H. Haggh. New York: Da Capo Press, 1974.

Rivera, Benito V. *German Music in the Early Seventeenth Century: The Treatises of Johannes Lippius*. Ann Arbor, Mich.: UMI Research Press, 1974.

Robbins Landon, H. C., and John Julius Norwich. *Five Centuries of Music in Venice*. London: Thames and Hudson, 1991.

Robinson, Michael F. "Porpora." 123–27 in *The New Grove Dictionary of Music and Musicians*, vol. 15, edited by Stanley Sadie. London: Macmillan, 1980.

Roche, Elizabeth. "Caldara and the Mass." *Musical Times* 111 (1970): 1101–3.

Roche, Jerome. *North Italian Church Music in the Age of Monteverdi*. Oxford: Clarendon Press, 1984.

Rosand, Ellen. "The Descending Tetrachord: An Emblem of Lament." *The Musical Quarterly* 65 (1979): 346–51.

———. "Lamento" 413–14 in *The New Grove Dictionary of Music and Musicians*, vol. 10, edited by Stanley Sadie. London: Macmillan, 1980.

———. *Opera in Seventeenth-Century Venice: The Creation of a Genre*. Berkeley: University of California Press, 1991.

———. "Venice, 1580–1680." 75–102 in *The Early Baroque Era*, edited by Curtis Price. London: Macmillan, 1993.

Rosen, Charles. *The Classical Style*. London: Faber, 1972.

Rosenthal, Karl August. "The Salzburg Church Music of Mozart and his Predecessors." *The Musical Quarterly* 18 (1932): 559–77.

Rossini, Gioachino. *Petite Messe Solennelle*. Edited by Nancy P. Fleming. Oxford: Oxford University Press, 1999.

Ruffo, Vincenzo. *Seven Masses*. Edited by Lewis Lockwood. Madison, Wis.: A-R Editions, 1979.

Russell, Bertrand. *History of Western Philosophy and Its Connection with Political and Social Circumstances from the Earliest Times to the Present Day*. London: Allen and Unwin, 1961.

Ryott, Paula. "The Lament: The Nature and Background of a Seventeenth-Century Genre." M.Mus. diss., University of Liverpool, 1993.

Salieri, Antonio. *Mass in D*. Edited by Jane Schatkin Hettrick. Recent Researches in Music of the Classical Era, vol. 39. Middleton, Wis.: A-R Editions, 1994.

Samuels, Robert. *Mahler's Sixth Symphony: A Study in Musical Semiotics*. Cambridge: Cambridge University Press, 1995.

Scarlatti, Alessandro. *St. Cecilia Mass (1720)*. Edited by John Steele. London: Novello, 1968.

Schenker, Heinrich. *Five Graphic Music Analyses*. New York: Dover Publications, 1969.

———. *Free Composition*. New York: Longman, 1979.

Schering, Arnold. "Die Lehre von den musikalischen Figuren." *Kirchenmusikalisches Jahrbuch* 21 (1908): 106–14.

Schleiermacher, Friedrich. *The Christian Faith*. Translated and edited by H. R. Mackintosh and J. S. Stewart. Edinburgh: T & T Clark, 1968.

Schmieder, Wolfgang, ed. *Thematisch-Systematisches Verzeichnis der musikalischen Werke von Johann Sebastian Bach*. Leipzig, Germany: Breitkopf und Härtel, 1950.

Schnitzler, Rudolf, and Herbert Seifert. "Draghi." 602–6 in *The New Grove Dictionary of Music and Musicians*, vol. 5, edited by Stanley Sadie. London: Macmillan, 1980.

Schoenbaum, Camillo. "Zelenka." 659–61 in *The New Grove Dictionary of Music and Musicians*, vol. 20, edited by Stanley Sadie. London: Macmillan, 1980.

Scholes, Robert. *Semiotics and Interpretation*. New Haven, Conn.: Yale University Press, 1982.

Schubert, Franz. *Mass in A Flat*. Edited by Friedrich Schreiber. Vienna: Eulenburg, 1880.

———. *Mass no. 2 in G* (no editor stated). Leipzig, Germany: Breitkopf und Härtel, n.d.

———. *Mass no. 6 in E Flat D 950* (no editor stated). N.p.: Eulenburg, n.d.

Schulze, Hans-Joachim. "The Parody Process in Bach's Music: An Old Problem Reconsidered." *Bach* 20 (1989): 5–21.

Sebeok, Thomas A. *Contributions to the Doctrine of Signs*. Bloomington: Indiana University Press, 1975.

Seymour, Peter. "Oratory and Performance." 913–19 in *Companion to Contemporary Musical Thought*, vol. 2, edited by John Paynter, Tim Howell, Richard Orton, and Peter Seymour. London: Routledge, 1992.

Sheldon, David A. "The Galant Style Revisited and Re-Evaluated." *Acta Musicologica* 47 (1975): 240–70.

Sheridan, Thomas B. "Descartes, Heidegger, Gibson, and God: Toward an Eclectic Ontology of Presence." *Presence: Teleoperators and Virtual Environments* 8, no. 5 (1999): 551–59.

Sisman, Elaine R. *Haydn and the Classical Variation*. Cambridge, Mass.: Harvard University Press, 1993.

Smend, Friedrich. *Kritischer Bericht, Messe in H-Moll*. Kassel, Germany: Bärenreiter-Verlag, 1956.

Smith, Peter. "Colonna." 582–83 in *The New Grove Dictionary of Music and Musicians*, vol. 4, edited by Stanley Sadie. London: Macmillan, 1980.

———. "Liturgical Music in Italy, 1660–1750." 370–97 in *The New Oxford History of Music: V: Opera and Church Music 1630–1750*, edited by Anthony Lewis and Nigel Fortune. London: Oxford University Press, 1975.

Sonnino, Lee A. *A Handbook to Sixteenth-Century Rhetoric*. London: Routledge and Kegan Paul, 1968.

Stauffer, George B. *Bach: The Mass in B Minor*. New York: Schirmer, 1997.

Steiner, Ruth, Maurus Pfaff, Richard L. Crocker, Frederick R. McManus, Theodor Göllner, Lewis Lockwood, and Denis Arnold. "Mass." 769–97 in *The New Grove Dictionary of Music and Musicians*, vol. 11, edited by Stanley Sadie. London: Macmillan, 1980.

Steuart, Benedict. *The Development of Christian Worship*. London: Longmans Green, 1953.

Stevens, John. "Music, Number and Rhetoric in the Early Middle Ages." 885–910 in *Companion to Contemporary Musical Thought*, vol. 2, edited by John Paynter, Tim Howell, Richard Orton, and Peter Seymour. London: Routledge, 1992.

———. *Words and Music in the Middle Ages: Song, Narrative, Dance and Drama, 1050–1350.* Cambridge: Cambridge University Press, 1986.

Stockigt, Janice B. *Jan Dismas Zelenka: A Bohemian Musician at the Court of Dresden.* Oxford: Oxford University Press, 2000.

Stopford, John. "Structuralism, Semiotics and Musicology." *Journal of the British Society of Aesthetics* 24, no. 1 (1983): 129–37.

Strunk, Oliver. *Source Readings in Music History: The Renaissance.* Vol. 2. London: Faber, 1981.

Sutcliffe, F. E. "Introduction." In *Discourse on Method and the Meditations*, by René Descartes, translated by F. E. Sutcliffe. London: Penguin Classics, 1968.

Szeker-Madden, Lisa. "Topos, Text, and the Parody Problem in Bach's Mass in B Minor, BWV 232." *Canadian University Music Review* 15 (1995): 108–25.

Tagg, Philip. "Musicology and the Semiotics of Popular Music." *Semiotica* 66 (1987): 279–98.

Talbot, Michael. *The Finale in Western Instrumental Music.* Oxford: Oxford University Press, 2001.

———. "An Italian Overview." 3–17 in *Companion to Baroque Music*, edited by Julie Anne Sadie. London: Dent, 1990.

———. *The Sacred Vocal Music of Antonio Vivaldi.* Florence: Olschki, 1995.

———. *Vivaldi.* London: Dent, 1984.

Tarasti, Eero. *A Theory of Musical Semiotics.* Bloomington: Indiana University Press, 1994.

Taylor, Vincent. *The Cross of Christ.* London: Macmillan, 1957.

Thomas, Downing A. *Music and the Origins of Language: Theories of the French Enlightenment.* Cambridge: Cambridge University Press, 1995.

Unger, Hans-Heinrich. *Die Beziehungen zwischen Musik und Rhetorik im 16.–18. Jahrhundert.* Würzburg, Germany: Triltsch, 1941.

Vickers, Brian. "Figures of Rhetoric/Figures of Music?" *Rhetorica* 2, no. 1 (1984): 1–44.

———. *In Defence of Rhetoric.* Oxford: Clarendon Press, 1988.

Walker, D. P. "Musical Humanism in the Sixteenth and Early Seventeenth Centuries." *The Music Review* 2 (1941): 1–13, 111–21, 220–27, 288–308; 3 (1942): 55–71.

Walker, Paul. "Rhetoric, the Ricercar, and J. S. Bach's Musical Offering." 175–91 in *Bach Studies*, vol. 2, edited by David R. Melamed. Cambridge: Cambridge University Press, 1995.

Walker, Thomas. "Ciacona and Passacaglia: Remarks on Their Origin and Early History." *Journal of the American Musicological Society* 21 (1968): 300–20.

Walther, Johann Gottfried. *Praecepta der Musicalischen Composition.* Translated by Peter Benary. Leipzig, Germany: Breitkopf und Härtel, 1955.

Warburton, Ernest. "J. C. Bach's Latin Church Music." *Musical Times* 123 (1982): 781–83.

Wheelock, Gretchen A. *Haydn's Ingenious Jesting with Art.* New York: Schirmer, 1992.

Williams, Peter. *The Chromatic Fourth during Four Centuries of Music.* Oxford: Clarendon, 1997.

———. "Encounters with the Chromatic Fourth." *Musical Times* 126 (1985): 276–78, 339–43.

———. "*Figurenlehre* from Monteverdi to Wagner." *Musical Times* 120 (1979): 476–79, 571–73, 648–50, 816–18.

———. "The Snares and Delusions of Musical Rhetoric: Some Examples from Recent Writings on J. S. Bach." 230–40 in *Alte Musik: Praxis und Reflektion*, edited by Peter Reidemeister and Veronika Gutmann. Winterthur, Switzerland: Amadeus Verlag, 1983.

Wilson-Dickson, Andrew. *The Story of Christian Music*. Oxford: Lion Publishing, 1992.

Wingfield, Paul. *Janàcek: Glagolithic Mass*. Cambridge: Cambridge University Press, 1992.

Wolff, Christoph. "Bach the Cantor, the Capellmeister, and the Musical Scholar: Aspects of the B-Minor Mass." *Bach* 20 (1989): 55–64.

———. *Bach: Essays on His Life and Music*. Cambridge, Mass.: Harvard University Press, 1991.

———. "'Et Incarnatus' and 'Crucifixus': The Earliest and Latest Settings of Bach's B-Minor Mass." 1–17 in *Eighteenth-Century Music in Theory and Practice: Essays in Honor of Alfred Mann*, edited by Mary Anne Parker. New York: Pendragon Press, 1994.

———. "J. S. Bach and the Legacy of the Seventeenth Century." 192–201 in *Bach Studies*, vol. 2, edited by David R. Melamed. Cambridge: Cambridge University Press, 1995.

Wroe, Ann. *Pilate: The Biography of an Invented Man*. London: Jonathan Cape, 1999.

Young, Percy M. "Leipzig." 634–42 in *The New Grove Dictionary of Music and Musicians*, vol. 10, edited by Stanley Sadie. London: Macmillan, 1980.

Zarlino, Gioseffo. *The Art of Counterpoint*. Translated by Guy A. Marco and Claude V. Palisca (part 3 of *Le Istitutioni Harmoniche* 1558). New Haven, Conn.: Yale University Press, 1968.

Zaslaw, Neal, ed. *The Classical Era*. London: Macmillan, 1989.

Zelenka, Jan Dismas. *Missa Omnium Sanctorum ZWV 21* (1741). Edited by Wolfgang Horn. Wiesbaden, Germany: Breitkopf und Härtel, 1989.

———. *Missa Votiva ZWV 18*. Edited by Reinhold Kubik. Wiesbaden, Germany: Breitkopf und Härtel, 1997.

General Index

Musical Index

Note: Crucifixus *settings are listed here (by composer), together with more general references to other composers. Music theorists who were also composers, but who are referred to in the text in their role as the former, are listed in the general index, e.g., Rousseau, Mattheson.* Crucifixus *settings that have received more detailed treatment (case studies), are listed under a composite heading of composer/work, rather than composer (heading), work (subheading).*

Abos, G., *Messa a 4 Voci* (1), *73, 103, 104, 225, 239*

Albrechtsberger, J. G., *Missa Annuntiationis* (2), *73, 79, 79, 80–81, 103, 130, 141n, 225, 239*

Bach, J. C., *Credo in C* (3), *73, 79, 96, 106, 225, 236*

Bach, J. S., 68, 73, 220

Bach, J. S., *Crucifixus* from *Mass in B Minor* BWV 232 (4), xx, xi, 64, 72, *73, 96, 97*, 121–42, 145, 198, 204, 213, *225, 239, 241–53*; *a cappella* conclusion, 129, 195; adaptation, processes of, 124–30, 136–38, *139, 241–53*; *Christ lag in Todes Banden*, Cantata no. 4, BWV 4, 122, *123*; *Credo (Symbolum Nicenum)* BWV 232, 72, 122–24, *123*; *Crucifixus* traditions, awareness of, 137–38; *Et incarnatus* BWV 232, 122, *123*, 125; *Et in unum* BWV 232, 122, *123*; *Et resurrexit*

BWV 232, 122, *123*; *Herr, gehe nicht ins Gericht*, Cantata no. 105, BWV 105, 125; *lamento*, use of, 124–25, 128; musical rhetorical figures, 127–29, 138, *241–53*; texts to BWV 232 and BWV 12, comparison of use of, 129, 130, 136–37; *Weinen, Klagen, Sorgen, Zagen* BWV 12, 121–22, *122*, 124–30, 136, 220, *241–52*

Beethoven, L. van, 82, 201, *202*

Benevoli, O., 66

Bertoni, F. G., *Crucifixus con Organo a 4 Voci* (5), *73*, 89, 100, *100*, 141n, 152–60, *225, 234, 273–77*; contrapuntal nature of music, issues for analysis of, 153; paradigmatic analysis 152–58, *154–56*; sequence of text, 159; syntagmatic analysis, 157–59

Biber, H. I. von, *Missa St. Henrici* (6), *73*, 81, 83, *83, 225, 234*; *Mystery Sonatas*, 58

Biffi, A., *Credo in D Minor* (7), *73, 87, 87*, 89, 99, 100, *100, 225, 234*

367

About the Author

Jasmin Melissa Cameron is a lecturer at the University of Aberdeen in Scotland, United Kingdom. She initially studied music at the University College of Wales, Aberystwyth. She continued as a postgraduate at the University of Liverpool, where she completed her doctoral thesis under the supervision of Professor Michael Talbot in December 2001.

Her research interests, as demonstrated by this book, lie with sacred Italian and German music of the late baroque and classical periods, analysis (particularly of texted music and the issues that arise thereof), rhetoric and music, development and transmission of musical conventions, and editing. Other research projects have included the editing and study of the sacred music (settings of the *Gloria*) of Giovanni Maria Ruggieri.

She is the author of various articles (such as "Vivaldi's *Crucifixus* in Its Descriptive and Rhetorical Context," *Studi Vivaldiani* 3 [2003]), has produced the recent edition of Vivaldi's *Gloria* RV 589 for the New Novello Choral Series (2002), and is preparing an edition of Giovanni Maria Ruggieri's two *Gloria* settings for A-R Editions.

LaVergne, TN USA
02 April 2010
178036LV00005B/105/P